EDUCATION TODAY: LANGUAGE TEACHING

Teaching English to Immigrants

EDUCATION TODAY

Other titles in this series
An Introduction to the Child Care Service *John Stroud*
Social Science and Social Studies in Secondary Schools
W. Philip and R. Priest
Communication in Speech *Arthur Wise*
Student Guidance *F. Claude Palmer*
Programmed Learning in the Schools *John Leedham and Derek Unwin*
A Basic Science Course for Secondary Schools *Edited by Michael Robinson*
Development through Drama *Brian Way*
Introducing Social Studies *W. J. Hanson*
An Approach to Literature *R. T. H. Stevens*
Social Learning and its Measurement *M. L. Kellmer Pringle*
Living Speech in the Primary School *Diana L. Morgan*
Investment in Children: A Symposium *Edited by M. L. Kellmer Pringle*
An Introduction to the Philosophy of Religion *J. L. Goodall*
Literature and the Young Child *J. Cass*

EDUCATION TODAY: LANGUAGE TEACHING

The Visual Element in Language Teaching *S. Pit Corder*
The New Pattern of Language Teaching *David H. Harding*

Teaching English to Immigrants

JUNE DERRICK
Research Fellow, Institute of Education
University of Leeds

93576

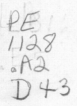

LONGMANS

LONGMANS, GREEN AND CO LTD
48 Grosvenor Street, London W1
*Associated companies, branches and representatives
throughout the world*

© June Derrick 1966
*First published 1966
Second impression 1967*

*Printed in Great Britain by
The Camelot Press Ltd.,
London and Southampton*

Preface

This book has been written in an attempt to give some guidance to those who for one reason or another find themselves teaching English to immigrants in Britain. In many schools this work has been under way for some time and advice about methods and materials is becoming available locally as a body of experience is built up. But in many places teachers and others suddenly find themselves embarking on it for the first time with little or no guidance. They have unexpectedly to teach English to pupils for whom it is not the mother tongue; they have in fact to become language teachers.

There is no short cut to learning how to teach English as a second language effectively, but it helps very much if the teacher can begin to be aware of the language from the point of view of his pupils. He needs to become aware of English – and above all to hear it – in an entirely new way. The main part of this book tries to help him do this.

This language awareness is the basis of all the teacher's work. To give full advice as to how he should proceed with infants, junior or secondary school pupils, or with adults, and how he should deal with pupils of different nationalities with their many different mother tongues, would need a whole set of different books; and so it has been necessary to make many generalizations about these practical matters. In order to simplify and to give more details of particular cases, many of the sections on procedures and methods of teaching deal only with the teaching of pupils of school age – mostly in primary school at that. This has been a necessary limitation; it will be found that with slight modifications and allowing for differences of age and outlook, many of the same techniques and procedures can be used with older pupils.

In particular, teachers of English to immigrants want information and advice about materials and books available for themselves and their pupils to use. Very little has so far been prepared that is designed for their particular purpose; much of the mass of literature about second-language teaching and about language will be found interesting but relevant only in part. I have therefore been sparing in my lists of books and have tried to indicate those that are of real use. Should teachers wish to explore further, the bibliographies in these books will be found to contain the necessary references. Booklists are therefore kept down to a minimum.

Similarly, the list of materials usable – or adaptable for use – in class is also minimal. Teachers can turn to catalogues and other sources of information indicated for more comprehensive lists, but their first need is to know which reading and writing materials they can take into the classroom with them.

The only experts on the teaching of English to immigrants are to be found among those who are already involved in this work. It is not quite the same as any other language-teaching situation, and many of our existing ideas, both about language and about teaching, have to be modified by experience. As this is enlarged, and as information is shared, we can hope to meet the particular problems that arise more and more efficiently. In the meantime, all who have already put effort and thought into this work, particularly the teachers practising in the local authority schools, are owed a debt of gratitude. They are the real authors of much of what follows, although responsibility for the final formulation of it, and for any distortions and impracticalities, rests with the writer.

I should especially like to thank the teachers of Huddersfield and Leeds who have been generous with their information and advice, and as patient with the visitors to their classes as they are with their immigrant pupils. Of the many others who have given help and encouragement I should like in particular to mention the staff of the Contemporary English Department of Leeds University and Mr Allen Jones of the University of the West Indies.

JUNE DERRICK

Contents

PREFACE   V

1 PROBLEMS AND PRINCIPLES   1

2 A SCHEME OF WORK   22

3 PRONUNCIATION   106

4 TECHNIQUES AND PROCEDURES IN ORAL TEACHING   136

5 READING AND WRITING   180

6 'REMEDIAL' LANGUAGE TEACHING—WEST INDIAN AND OTHER PUPILS   210

7 AIDS AND APPARATUS   218

BIBLIOGRAPHY   236

Acknowledgements

We are grateful to the following for permission to reproduce copyright material:

A. & C. Black Ltd for 'Guess what is making . . .' and 'What does the Cat say?' by Clive Sansom from *Speech Rhymes*, and 'Pitter, Patter' by Winifred Kingdon-Ward from *Rhymes and Jingles*; Bureau of Public Schools, Manila (Department of Education) for 'One, Two, tie your Shoe', 'I've got Ten Little Fingers', 'Hush, Children, hush' and 'What does the Crow say', and adaptations of 'Game about the Postman', 'Game of Twiddle Thumbs', 'Game with Ball', 'Game up the Stairs', 'Game of Hands on Heads' and 'Game of Snakes and Bees' from *Teacher's Guide for English in Grade I*; Longmans, Green & Co. Ltd for 'The Old Kettle' from *Reading with Rhythm*, Set 2 by Jenny Taylor and Terry Ingleby; Macmillan & Co. Ltd for 'Silly Billy' and 'My Motor is Humming' from *Trippingly on the Tongue* by Mona Swann; Oxford University Press for 'One, Two, this is My Shoe' and '1, 2, 3, 4, Come in, Please, and shut the Door' from *New Peak Course Standard 1*, Book 1, and material from *New Peak Course Standard 2*, Book 1; Sir Isaac Pitman & Sons Ltd for 'Skipping is Fun' by Paul Edmonds from *Songs and Marching Tunes for Children*; and University of London Press Ltd for 'What's the Time, Mr Wolf?' and 'Hunting the Tiger' adapted from *Modern English for Malayans*, Teachers' Book II by John Parry in collaboration with James Dunhill.

I

Problems and principles

The language problem

In many parts of Britain the presence of large numbers of foreigners, adults and children, has long been taken for granted and no one looks twice if the bus conductor or postman or nurse or waiter has a brown or yellow skin or speaks with a foreign accent. In some towns this has been the situation for several generations. In other places the arrival and settling of immigrants is a fairly recent feature; everyone must now be aware of how rapidly their numbers have grown in certain areas in the fifties and especially the early sixties. The children of immigrants, some of whom come to this country with their parents, some of whom are sent for after the parents have settled down in their new homes, and some of whom are born here, take their places in local schools alongside British[1] pupils. In schools and classes where their numbers are small, teachers feel there is no great problem: some of these immigrant pupils speak good English, some speak 'a kind of' English; others, who speak none at first, manage to get along either by learning it fairly quickly with help from teachers and play-fellows, or by learning enough for them to be fairly easily assimilated into the school and to cause no acute social problems. But where single schools or single classes have had an influx of non-English-speaking pupils in more significant numbers, certain problems have inevitably been brought into sharp focus.

These problems are many and varied. Some are essentially of a social nature, originating in the fact that immigrant pupils come from different societies where the pattern of living and of what is socially acceptable differs in very many respects from the British

---

[1] The term *British* is for convenience applied in this book to the *native* (usually long resident) English-speaking people of the British Isles.

pattern. It takes a great jump of sympathy to realize all the implications of this, as also to understand the immediate psychological shock many children must suffer at their sudden almost overnight transplantation. Adjustment to the new milieu is made the more difficult by the language problem. The immigrant child's difficulties can be contrasted with those of a British pupil who moves from one area to another and has then to settle into a new school and learn its ways and make friends. The British child may in fact be disturbed for a time but in the long run he adjusts fairly easily; he knows the general pattern of behaviour that is expected of him, he can always have things explained, and he can ask for help when necessary. But the non-English-speaking immigrant pupil not only has a far greater adjustment to make, but in all probability cannot communicate directly with the teachers or with British pupils. One hears of some pupils who after even a year or more at school in Britain have hardly opened their mouths or uttered one word in English.

Many teachers have made great efforts to help such children, to establish communication with them and to begin to make their stay at school profitable. Many admit that they have simply not had the time to do so; they may well feel that they have little choice if they have a large class of children to cope with, of which the immigrant element forms but a small proportion. But this means that the non-English-speaking pupils are often carried as passengers through lesson after lesson without their being able to participate in any way. The language problem in this case remains untackled, and it remains so – or part of it remains so – even if these same pupils begin to pick up a little English. For they will still lag behind the rest of the class, and many of them will be unable to follow a normal lesson fully in any subject. Their intelligence can never be fairly tested. As often as not, as they proceed up the school, they will be relegated to backward streams. Social problems and behaviour problems – growing more acute at adolescence – will complicate matters. The pupils may fail to comply with school rules and codes of behaviour because they cannot be made to understand them, or because at some stage they may seek to protect themselves by pretending not to understand them. Thus the language problem has untold ramifications, and these are identified and discussed wherever teachers have non-English-speaking pupils in their classes. But the concomitant of the language problem, the special language-*teaching* problem, is often only very dimly recognized for what it is.

There are various reasons for this. One, that seems almost too obvious to require stating, is that when an immigrant of the type considered here learns English, he learns it as a second language; the teacher therefore has to teach him English as a second language, and *teaching English as a second language is not the same as teaching English as a first (native) language*. The Indian or Italian or Chinese immigrant pupil who has to learn English, albeit in Britain, faces learning problems more akin to those of the British child learning French or German than to those of the British child learning English. The materials and methods used in the normal English lesson in school are not a great deal of use; text-books, even the most elementary primers, designed for pupils whose mother tongue is English, are usually unsuitable for pupils learn-ing English as a second language. Often immigrant pupils are blamed for making no progress in English when in fact they have not been given a true opportunity of learning it. Teachers who try and fail, or find their pupils making no progress, can hardly be blamed either: we are often the worst teachers of our own mother tongue simply because it is our mother tongue. We learnt it and we do not know how we learnt it, and certainly we find it very hard to teach it successfully.

This is chiefly because in this country we have not until fairly recent years thought about language or language teaching very realistically. Many of us, for instance, have learnt to describe English in the terms that are used for dealing with Latin, dis-regarding the fact that the two languages work in different ways and the terminology applicable to the one is not always suitable to the other. It is only fairly recently that efforts have been made to suggest new approaches to English in our schools. And while our attitude to English has thus been largely 'non-linguistic' (i.e. not taking account of it as a complete and independent system of communication), this is also true of our attitude to foreign languages and to the way many of us have tried to teach them. It is a commonplace that the majority of school-leavers who have had five or so years of French or German cannot speak either language when they come into contact with French or German speakers; this points to a weakness in the teaching system which is again related to a view of language that can also be described as non-linguistic – or to no view at all.

A linguistic view of language stresses the primacy of the spoken language and defines the aim in teaching language as training the learner for communication in it. Language is first and foremost sound. The written language, or 'writing' as some linguists[1] prefer to call it, is merely the symbolization of the spoken language. We become so book-minded through our education that we tend to forget this and to think of the written word as having a greater 'validity' than the spoken word. We even forget that a child learns to speak his own language years before he learns to read it. There are various reasons why the foreign learner should tackle the language skills in this order too and be thoroughly taught the spoken language first. Moreover, the immigrant pupil, if we now return to him, is in exactly the situation of needing language for the purpose of oral communication. The solution to all the immediate and urgent problems that face him – learning to live in a new society, to play with new friends, to take part in school life – lies in his understanding and speaking English. There can be no other approach for the teacher but the oral one; and like walking before running, speaking must come before reading and writing. These other skills must of course be mastered in time if the immigrant is to become a fully literate member of society, and if, as an adult especially, he is to cope with the reading of written instructions, the filling in of official forms, and so on. But to begin with the emphasis has to be on understanding and speaking – the aural-oral skills.

The word *skills* is important. For language should not be confused with content subjects in the curriculum such as geography or history. It is essentially a skill subject. Language, if you like, is not a subject at all. It is best thought of as an activity in which there are the four basic skills of understanding, speaking,

---

[1] 'Linguist' is here used in the technical sense of one versed in linguistics, not in the popular sense of one who speaks many languages (for which the technical term is 'polyglot').

reading and writing. Teaching language therefore is not teaching pupils about things, but teaching them to develop these skills, giving them the chance to practise and practise until they make perfect. One cannot learn to swim or to ride a bicycle by simply being told about it; one has to do it oneself. Getting one's feet off the ground, learning the first simple co-ordination of movements, balance, and so on, and progressing later to more complicated manœuvres is the normal method. The pupil has to *perform* throughout his learning. So with the language learner.

A method of teaching a subject will depend on what the teacher believes the nature of that subject to be; similarly a method of teaching language will depend on what you believe about the nature of language. If you believe that teaching language is teaching a skill, then you will try to organize your teaching to fit that idea. For instance, frequent short practices will be aimed at, rather than infrequent longer sessions. If all pupils are to practise and use language as much as possible, then small groups are better than very large ones, so that each pupil has as many opportunities as possible to speak and hear and, where necessary, to be corrected by the teacher. These, and general organizational problems, arise from the overall consideration of how best to tackle second-language teaching and will be discussed in more detail with other practical matters below.

The structural-situational approach

Obviously this general view of the nature of language and of language teaching is not enough for the teacher to act upon. If he accepts these basic principles, he will still need to know how he is going to set about his language teaching, how to plan his work and present it to his pupils in such a way that the principles are put into practice.

The approach to language teaching that is found most satis-factory on this score can be called the structural and situational approach. This takes into account the form and content of what the teacher tries to teach.

To deal with form first: there is a danger that, because lan-guage is apparently made up of words, the learner or teacher will confuse *words* with *language*. Teaching language does not consist simply of teaching words, any more than learning language consists of learning just words. Many people will have had the experience of spending a holiday in a foreign country where they did not know anything of the language to start with but where, within a day or two, they had learnt a lot of the necessary vocabulary for the recurrent items of food on menus, could ask for stamps or fruit or chocolate, go to the cinema or get their hair cut. And yet how much they were prisoners of these words. How hard it was to explain that they wanted just a little bit more or less, or perhaps something a little dearer or a little cheaper. Words alone were not enough. Something was very obviously lacking, as indeed it is lacking in the kind of English that many immigrants, school pupils and adults, can be heard speaking and which is often loosely described as a kind of 'pidgin'. In fact it consists of a lot of words – verbs, nouns, adjectives – that are used to convey meaning in the broad sense but without any fine shades of meaning. This is the kind of English that must not be accepted (or spoken) by the teacher; it is both inadequate as a means of communication and socially unacceptable. It is really 'words' without grammar, and without grammar we cannot go far. But there is the danger that teachers will teach grammar in the wrong way, or in a way that is not suitable to the present purpose. The teacher of English as a second language has to teach *grammar-in-action*. This is a very different thing from teaching *about* grammar or from teaching grammar as a kind of independent subject unrelated to the pupil's actual use of the language he is learning. The teacher will in fact find it most useful to think of grammar in terms of structure – the way words and forms of words are used together to convey meaning.

One aspect of structure is simply the arrangement of words; the fact, for instance, that the usual order of the parts of a statement is Subject followed by Verb followed by Object (if there is one):

The man is hitting the horse

and that to make this into a simple question we reverse the Subject-Verb order and say:

Is the man hitting the horse?

Or the original statement can be made negative by saying *not* or *n't* immediately after *is*:

The man *isn't* hitting the horse.

If the original sentence had used the past tense,

The man *hit* the horse

it would not have been quite so simple to form the interrogative, for instead of simple inversion,

Hit the man the horse?

an entirely new verb would have been required as an addition:

Did the man hit the horse?

The same verb, *did*, would also have been needed to make the sentence negative:

The man *did not* hit the horse.

Other questions of arrangement arise if we extend parts of the original sentence. For instance, we might qualify the nouns by adding a few adjectives:

The *cruel old* man is hitting the *big white* horse.

We could say *cruel old man* and *big white horse*, but not *old cruel man* or *white big horse*. Further, if we wanted to qualify the verb by adding *always*, or *often*, or *brutally* or *naturally*, we would again be involved in questions of arrangements of words, some of which are permissible and some of which are not. Problems such as these hardly ever arise for the native speaker of English and are therefore rarely mentioned in traditional grammars; but for the foreign learner they are features of structure that have to be learnt.

But there is also another aspect of structure to consider, one which concerns not so much the actual arrangements of words, but the choice and form of word chosen at different points in the structure. First of all, let us be clear where these points are. Thus if we take our first example again,

The man is hitting the horse

we find we can substitute any one of a hundred or more different items for the words *man, hit* and *horse*:

> The *boy* is hitting the horse
> The *soldier* is hitting the horse
> The man is hitting the *boy*
> The man is hitting the *table*
> The man is *selling* the horse
> The man is *saddling* the horse
>   etc.

But if we try to do the same thing at one of the other places in the sentence, we find we can only substitute a limited set of words, a dozen or so perhaps, certainly not a hundred:

> *A* man *is* hitting *the* horse
> *That* man *was* hitting *his* horse
> *Neither* man *has been* hitting *my* horse
> *Your* man *has* hit *a* horse

The words in these places, where the choice is limited, are what writers have called the structural or grammatical words of the language, while the other words have been called content words or lexical items, and *it is the structural or grammatical words that need to have most attention paid to them by the teacher*. There are perhaps about 200 of them in our total vocabulary, but they occur so often that they make up about a third of the words in any English conversation. They could well be called the most important part of the total vocabulary, but on their own – and this is why it is dangerous to think of them simply as 'words' – they are practically meaningless. How fully, for instance, can *the* or *a* or *this*, or *in* and *on*, *is* and *are*, be said to have meaning on their own? Their meaning lies in their combination with the content words like *horse, man, hit*, etc., and with each other in the total utterance. Content words are fairly easily learnt: the language teacher has to look beyond them to the grammatical words and to the structural features in which they operate.

In some respects, of course, this part of grammar has been dangerously overemphasized in the past; at the expense of meaning and usability, pupils have been taught too many of the grammatical words and their variations all at once, and made to memorize them in undigested lumps. Too often all that is remembered of a foreign language learnt at school is a collection of tables and paradigms, 'the future of the third conjugation', 'the present subjunctive of *avoir*', 'the principle parts of strong verbs'. We ignore this part of grammar at our peril, but obviously it has to be seen in perspective and dealt with cautiously and sensibly.

The structural approach to language teaching does this for us. In it, we break down the structure of the language into the features of arrangement and choice of which it consists, and we try to teach these features as separate items, one by one and bit by bit. But when we say 'we teach them', let us again emphasize that this means teaching our pupils to *use* them. We do not teach facts about them. We do not spend time explaining grammar, but training learners to speak grammatically – a vastly different thing.

The grammatical 'features' taught in this way – or 'structural items' as we most often call them – should, if they are selected carefully enough, build up into an interlocking system of usable meaningful language. At this point, then, we can return to our original question, which concerned not only the form but the content of what the teacher is trying to teach. The language he is trying to teach in class should, it is suggested, always be meaningful. This means that it must be taught *situationally*, i.e. in and through situations that actually occur or are talked about in the classroom. Language that is presented as meaningfully as possible will be learnt the more readily and effortlessly by the learner. This point will be discussed at greater length later in this book (see Chapter 4 on 'Techniques and Procedures in Oral Teaching'), but a very obvious example will serve to illustrate it here. The teacher who touches a hot radiator or who drops a book on his toe and then uses an expletive, mild or otherwise, to give vent to his pain and annoyance, may be sure that that particular language item will be remembered and repeated, and, when opportune, used by any pupils who witnessed the happening; they will learn this far more accurately and quickly than other items the teacher may have tried to teach them in more conventional circumstances. But obviously no school day is ever going to consist of a set of situations through which the structural items of English can be neatly and realistically presented to the learner. If a teacher tried to teach language entirely by this method, i.e. by allowing the situations to control his choice of structural items entirely, he would in fact be unable to follow a structural approach for very long. The structural approach presupposes a grammatical grading; the situations of everyday life do not usually contain one.

The teacher therefore has to compromise or, rather, has to see that situations, apparently spontaneous but very often contrived by him for the purpose, are provided through which he can teach whatever structural items he wants to teach.

The immediately usable situation is that of the pupil in the classroom, consisting of himself, the things he can see and hear and feel around him, the actions he can perform, and the code of behaviour he has to follow in order to fit into the school society. In the classroom too he can enact the situations of his home, and then of his environment – the shop, the post office, the bus station, etc. Actions performed by the teacher and by pupils, gestures, objects, models, pictures, the contents of a dressing-up box, and a hundred and one other things, can also be used to create situations, and to ensure that no single item of language is produced by the teacher or taught as an isolated 'example' (like the unconnected sentences in a grammar book), but is always part of a situation, however brief or make-believe or occasionally even improbable that situation may be.

This again relates to what was said earlier in this chapter about teaching 'just words'. Teaching situationally means that both grammar and content words (lexical items) will be taught and used as parts of whole utterances or sentences used in meaningful situations. Even when, as can happen, the teacher wishes his class to master some new vocabulary (such as the rooms of the house or the parts of the body) for use in developing a centre of interest, it should still be possible to present and practise this vocabulary situationally. The teacher might, for instance, point to the different rooms in a model or a picture of a house, and name them by talking about them in language the class was already familiar with, such as:

> This is the bathroom
> The bathroom is next to the bedroom
> The kitchen is next to the living-room
>   etc.

The same vocabulary might be used later in order to practise a new structural item:

> We cook in the kitchen
> We eat in the living-room
> We wash in the bathroom
>   etc.

Discussing what one does from day to day in the different rooms of the house would then be seen as a situation in which this 'habitual' use of the simple present tense could be practised.

Obviously, a teacher new to the teaching of English as a second language has first to think about the different items that he wants to teach, and then has to decide which situations, like the one in the above example, allow him to present and practise these in the way most suited to his particular class.

These then are some of the different aspects of the structural-situational approach to language teaching. An awareness of the structural items of English is necessary as the foundation on which all the teacher's efforts must rest. The teacher of immigrants has in fact a very special language-learning situation to deal with, for in a way he has to try to control – or organize – a learning process that is going on not only in his own lessons, but at many other times of the day. For the immigrant pupil may be exposed to the language he is learning almost all through the day; in this way his position is very different from the one referred to earlier, that of the British child learning French or German. Although many immigrants, children and adults, live here and yet apparently manage to do without English to a remarkable extent, others, perhaps the majority, must inevitably learn something of the English they hear in out-of-school situations, in the playground, the shop, the clinic, or on the television. It is hard to evaluate this process, and to say how much English actually is learnt by them at these times; often, as suggested earlier in this chapter, it may simply be that they acquire more and more content words rather than accurate use of structural items. All the same, the teacher has to be aware of these possibilities. It is necessary for him to look out for and accept into his teaching this out-of-school language; it is, above all, necessary for him to see that it gets used correctly and does not lead his pupils into the use of more and more pidgin English.

Ideally, the teacher of immigrants will follow a course of work in language that is to some extent influenced by these external language factors. Pupils' motivation will be highest if work at school seems to follow rather than direct their needs and interests. But however much the teacher allows these factors to influence his work, in outline at least he will need to have a clear idea about the deliberate language teaching he should be doing. At the back of his mind there must be some sort of inventory of language items, a minimum list of structural items and content words to be mastered by pupils if they are to become competent in English. He may not be able to follow a hard and fast sequence in his teaching of these items, but he has to have a clear idea of what areas of language he is going to try to cover; in other words, he has to work according to – but not be bound by – a language syllabus.

There can be no single best way of working out such a syllabus. There is considerable agreement as to the amount of language that should be covered in the first year or two, but not about the order in which separate items should be presented. One must consider the relative simplicity or difficulty of each item, the way it interlocks with or leads to other items, its usefulness to the pupil and teacher, and whether it is usable both in the classroom and elsewhere, its teachability, its frequency, etc. Any of these criteria necessarily varies from one teaching situation to another, according to the age of the pupils, the facilities of the school they are in, their attitude to the teacher, to the school and to the language they are supposed to be learning, and – a major point – the nature of their own first language. Things that are difficult for children who speak one language may not be equally difficult for children who speak another. Obviously the immigrant teaching situation presents a multiplicity of problems on this score.

These considerations must be borne in mind when reading the language syllabus or scheme of work offered in the next chapter. The intention in including this scheme in the present volume is twofold. First, it is to show what a syllabus can be like; in this sense it is illustrative and not prescriptive at all. It presents one way of analysing and grading English, and it is a scheme of work that might be followed in the first year of teaching. A teacher following it with his class would no doubt find that he had to alter the order in which certain items are presented because the needs of his particular class, the type of children in it, the interest that developed in one particular lesson, all diverted him from the given order. This is as it should be. It is hoped at the same time that by reading through this scheme, teachers who have never thought about the structure of English in this way before will be helped to see more clearly how the language has to be broken up for teaching purposes, how, in fact, they could make their own itemization. They might also compare it with the itemization and arrangement of any language courses that may come into their hands.

Although no two syllabuses or schemes of work are exactly alike, it will be found that very many begin, for instance, with *This is a —*, proceed to *That is a —*, and fairly shortly afterwards stipulate that the *an* form of the indefinite article should be introduced by varying the content word in the first two items (e.g. by using *an apple*, *an egg*, etc., instead of *a book*, *a pencil*, *a bag*). A teacher who set about teaching immigrant children with no professional knowledge of *how* to set about it, no books, no syllabus, no equipment – only good intentions – in fact found himself teaching the above items because, as he saw it, this was the best way to introduce his pupils to the names of things they could see about them. On the other hand, a syllabus published to guide teachers of adult immigrants in Australia, begins with *I am Mr Scott*, *You are Mary Brown*, *He is Tom Brown*, etc., and then goes on to *I'm here*, *You're here*, *He's here*, and does not introduce *this* and *that* until the fifth lesson unit, some considerable time later.

But whatever the order followed, the method is one of progression, ideally of introducing structural items one by one so that each new one builds on and extends what has gone before, so that the learning of the new consolidates the old. To achieve this, progress must be steady and slow. For instance, verbs are not thought of as wholes, to be swallowed all in one dose. In approaching the verb *have*, at a fairly early stage in the course, one would not think of presenting it in a kind of table with all its parts in a row – *I have, you have, he/she/it has*, etc. One would not even necessarily introduce more than one of its forms in a first lesson. Thus, if the personal pronouns have already been dealt with, *has* alone might be introduced first through some such procedure as:

> Look at the table. This is a leg, and this is a leg. . . . It has four legs. The table has four legs . . .

and so on through other examples, coming then to persons:

> Iqbal has two legs

and possibly to possessions:

> Iqbal has a red book. . . . Maria has a brown bag . . .

so that by the end of the first presentation of this single item, the teacher in one lesson might aim at having taught *has* used with pronoun subjects, proper names, and nouns, with the intention of reserving *have* for some other time. This analysis of the separate teaching items within larger ones, is what is known as *grading* and is the key to successful language teaching.

Language teaching that follows this pattern may seem to the observer to cover the ground too slowly. Wouldn't pupils learn more, and learn it more quickly, by translation, by learning larger comprehensive stretches of grammar at a time? The answer to this objection lies of course in what one means by 'learning ; if learning a language is learning a skill, it can rightly only proceed in a way which gives the learner the chance to try out what he learns, to learn by doing and thus to master the skill. This the slowly graded structural approach enables him to do.

Ultimately the teacher is concerned with teaching the language as efficiently and economically as possible. The approach suggested here is the most economical because, however small a bit of language is taught at a time, it is taught in such a way that it is usable as language. This principle holds true not only for the teacher of beginners, of pupils whose English has to be built up from nothing, but also for the teacher who has pupils who already speak some English. All too often immigrant pupils may have a deceptively fluent flow of language, language by which they can fairly effectively get what they want, but in which, as suggested earlier in this chapter, the accurate use of the grammar of English is lacking and the fluency is really only in their use of content words. The teacher should not be deceived by this, but should base his work firmly on a structural approach, following a revision and consolidation course worked out by himself or taken from a suitable textbook.[1]

Organizational problems

Arrangements for special instruction of immigrant pupils fall into two main patterns, which, roughly speaking, are either full-time or part-time.

(1) *Full-time instruction.* This may be given in a *special centre* to which all new immigrant pupils in one area are sent; or it may take place in *special classes* set up within existing schools in areas where there are large numbers of such pupils. Teachers of classes under either system usually have their pupils for the larger part of every school day, and have to decide on a scheme of work; into this they have to fit a large amount of formal language teaching, together with suitable subjects from the normal school curriculum, such as number, physical education, movement, art or handwork. Arrangements may also be made – especially at special centres – to give the pupils social training and to help them make their first adjustment to British life.

The teacher in this situation can well look on his work as 'education *through* English'; the language needed for everything he teaches must itself first be taught, and at first he will not be able to go very far in any subject. He will need to include in his programme of language work the special items of language needed for other subjects. His plan of work will probably be to set aside each day one or two short periods in which he consciously works

[1] See Chapter 6 below, and Section III of the Bibliography.

on structures with his pupils, practising those already learnt, presenting new ones, demanding as far as possible accuracy of pronunciation and intonation, as well as of grammar and use of vocabulary in general. In teaching other subjects he will inevitably be teaching English too, but with a less deliberate concentration on structural items.

He will need to collect a great deal of apparatus for both verbal and non-verbal work since his pupils have to be kept busy for the whole of the school day. Until they are at the reading stage, this apparatus will be based very largely on the material found in the typical primary-school store cupboard: materials for drawing, painting, crayoning and tracing, picture-card and number games, weaving, cutting and sticking paper, etc. (See Chapter 7.)

Older pupils of secondary school age are of course more of a problem in this respect and cannot be expected to occupy themselves too long with apparatus suited only to young children. One would hope that they could join in as many normal practical classes as possible, especially handwork classes. But any arrangements made for them to attend this kind of class must not be allowed to interfere with the smooth and methodical running of their language classes. These language periods can obviously be longer than those arranged for junior pupils, and the work done in them can be more intensive and formal.

The aim of all this teaching, whether carried out in a special centre or in special classes within a school, is to make the pupils proficient enough in English for them to pass into 'mixed' classes of their own age-group (or a little below) and so to integrate as fully as possible into 'normal' school life. This process is obviously facilitated if all along the immigrant pupil has been attached to an English school (i.e. in a special class *within* a school), and for this reason the establishment of full-time special centres independent of schools is perhaps not a completely satisfactory arrangement.

(2) *Part-time instruction.* In schools where numbers of immigrant pupils are not great enough to warrant the employment of full-time class teachers, small groups of immigrants may be withdrawn from classes for special English lessons with a language teacher (employed within the school, or, in some cases, peri-

patetic). In these classes obviously the concentration will have to be entirely on English language; inevitably in many cases they meet too infrequently to give the pupils the opportunity for the intensive work in English that is needed if they are to make progress.

In these circumstances the English-language teacher should co-operate as fully as possible with the class teacher, letting him know what structural items and vocabulary have been introduced and practised, so that where possible this can be gone over by him, or even by other pupils in the same class, who can take it in turns to help the immigrant pupils.

On the whole, this second type of arrangement is bound to be less satisfactory than the first, since the language teacher may not see his pupils often enough for him to give them the close personal attention that goes with effective language teaching. There is no doubt that intensive language teaching is the most effective, and that the biggest gains are made when the teacher sees his pupils often.

In many areas special centres have been set up to which children from several schools are sent for part of the school day, during which they can receive fairly intensive language instruction. It is again difficult to make this arrangement as effective as the full-time centre or language class, and again there are problems of co-ordination, linking the work done at the centre with that done in the separate schools. Unless this kind of co-operation is achieved in some measure, there is bound to be some waste of effort. Moreover, it seems that pressure on places in some areas means that pupils are passed out of these part-time centres without their English being really adequate for them to join fully in classes in their own schools. But where co-ordination between work done in the part-time centre and in the pupils' schools is possible, this arrangement may in fact offer something of the best of both worlds. The pupils may obtain adequate and intensive instruction in their halfday attendance at the centre, and may also feel that they really belong to, and can thus be fully integrated into, their own schools.

A few other points relating to language-teaching arrangements should be made.

It has been indicated earlier in this account that ideally numbers in special English classes should be kept down so that as much individual practice as possible may be given. Twelve or fifteen is the ideal number, but classes of twenty are manageable if they are homogeneous. Above that it is extremely difficult to organize work so that all pupils get adequate attention.

One of the major difficulties that teachers have found in this work is the constant fluctuation in numbers of immigrant children entering a school. A class of twelve or more pupils at the beginning of term will perhaps gain a new member or two in several consecutive weeks, and the teacher is faced with the problem of having to allow for a beginner when the rest of the class have already made some progress. This is frustrating for many reasons, and causes new organizational problems most of which can only be solved by dividing classes into groups, as is done in much junior school work anyway. Group work has much to recommend it to the teacher of language, to allow for different rates of progress within a class and also for the variety of activity that is necessary with any prolonged stretch of language teaching. The span of attention of even the mature learner of language is very short, fifteen to twenty minutes or so, and with young pupils ten minutes may be the maximum time they can concentrate on one form of language activity. The teacher has thus to have a variety of activities and techniques to fall back on, and group work will often facilitate quick changes.

Teaching language in the way suggested here will involve the class in movement and activity, and will also involve the collecting and use of a great deal of apparatus by the teacher and pupils. This means that a classroom for the use of the immigrant class alone is essential, ideally a room which is large enough for the necessary mobility and activity of individuals and groups, and a room in which equipment may be kept and displayed. This is asking much in these days of limited space and over.ull classes: but again, for the sake of effectiveness and economy, it is something teachers should aim at having for their classes.

It need hardly be repeated that the aim of special English teaching for immigrants is to teach them English and to help them, through English, to integrate more fully into the life of the school and of society as a whole; special classes should obviously therefore be run within schools rather than apart from them, so that pupils can feel they belong, and every opportunity should be taken to see that they learn about and, when able, join in the normal life of the school. It is to be hoped that a year to eighteen months of special English classes would bring the average intelligent immigrant pupil up to the standard where he could merge into the normal teaching pattern of the junior or secondary school. With pupils who know some English when they arrive, and with European immigrant pupils especially, this period may be considerably shortened. But in all cases the placing of immigrant pupils in special classes should be seen as an educational necessity, as a means of giving them the special training demanded by their lack of ability in English. It should have no political or racial overtones, except in the positive sense of making towards a better understanding and integration of the pupils at a later stage.

Other educational problems remain to be solved once the machinery of English-language classes has been set in motion. The teachers have at some point to make decisions as to when their pupils' English can be considered adequate for them to pass out of the special class. Most teachers in practice will do this subjectively, but it should in time be possible to establish certain tests of language ability, tests which take the different skills into account and which make a fair and objective assessment of the pupils' attainment. It can be assumed, too, that once pupils have passed out into the main stream of the school, their English will still lag behind that of most of their British contemporaries. They will probably need extra help with writing and reading, and teachers who have such pupils in their classes should be aware of some of the special texts and techniques that will help them to continue to improve their English, which it should be remembered will always be their *second* language.

BOOKLIST TO CHAPTER I

Full details of each entry are given in the Bibliography at the end of the book, to which the Roman numerals (the section numbers) and the Arabic numerals (the entry numbers) in brackets after each title, refer.

HALL, *Linguistics and Your Language* (X)
Probably the most readable introduction to linguistics that can be found. It is a popular but scholarly presentation of a linguistic view of language and would be the best place to begin for anyone who wanted to know more about the subject as a whole. Paperback edition available (American).

HALLIDAY, MCINTOSH AND STREVENS, *The Linguistic Sciences and Language Teaching* (X)
The most recent British survey of this wide field. More heavy-weight than Hall, it serves as an introduction to linguistics, and shows how the teaching of all languages may benefit from the teacher's fuller understanding of the nature of language in general and of the particular properties of the language being taught.

KELLERMANN, *Two Experiments on Language Teaching in Primary Schools in Leeds* (X)
A description of some successful language teaching to young children, based on the linguistic principles outlined in this chapter. The language taught is French, but the account is highly relevant to teachers of English as a second language.

MINISTRY OF EDUCATION PAMPHLET NO. 43, *English for Immigrants* (X)
Useful introductory survey, containing an interesting biblio-graphy of works the teacher should read in order to understand the immigrants' cultural background and social problems that arise in and out of school.

PALMER, *The Principles of Language Study* (X)
A brief and outstandingly clear outline of the nature of language and language learning; originally written in 1921 and only just available to the general public again in a paperback edition.

QUIRK and SMITH (Eds), *The Teaching of English* (X)
Chapter II on 'The structural approach', and Chapter VII on 'The teaching of English as a foreign language' should be read by all teachers of English.

ROBERTS, *Patterns of English* (X)

One of the most useful introductions to modern English grammar. Especially helpful on the nature of the structure of English.

STREVENS, *Spoken Language* (X)

A short crystal-clear outline of the problems of teaching oral English. Originally intended for West African teachers, but highly relevant to other situations.

2

A scheme of work

Introduction

The language teacher is first and foremost a teacher, not a technician; if in the rest of this book we go on to discuss what might be called the technology of language teaching, it should not be thought that expertise alone is what makes a good language teacher. The best teacher of language to young immigrants in, for instance, the primary school will be the trained primary school teacher who, to the teaching skill that he already has, now adds a language teaching skill and develops an awareness of the problems that face the learner of English as a second language. In the next two chapters we try to help him towards this awareness. (In passing we might add that for many reasons, such as the need to allow for different rates of progress in different pupils, to organize group work, to involve the pupils in different activities, and also in many cases the need to teach the basic skills, it may well be that even in the secondary school a knowledge of primary school teaching techniques will be one of the language teacher's greatest assets. Teachers who are not trained in these techniques will benefit from learning as much as they can about them.)

The previous chapter will already have suggested some of the aspects of language that present problems to the foreign learner. It is proposed now to give a scheme of work which is in effect an inventory of the first forty or so structural items of English that might be taught to new learners of the language. This in a way is the core of the book; it is of course hoped that the advice contained in the later chapters on techniques and procedures, reading and writing, aids, etc., will be of use to the teacher, but it is not felt that any of it can be of really effective use to him unless he has a firm grasp of the essentials of the structural approach, has actually studied a structural syllabus and seen the need to work according to one. So it is hoped that the reader will at least examine part of this scheme of work in detail before passing on to the later chapters, and that he will return to it and study it more closely still as he realizes the need to come to grips with the facts of language that it contains albeit in an oblique form. For these are the most essential piece of equipment of the teacher of English as a second language.

It should be stressed that the scheme of work given below is meant only as an example, and there is no intention of prescribing it to teachers as the one they should follow. They may well want to work out their own schemes, or to follow those in some of the printed courses available. It will be found that most first-year courses for English language in the primary school (printed for use overseas) do in fact show broadly the same content of structural items. In the present scheme, the content words are left very much to the teacher's discretion – obviously certain structural items demand certain kinds of content words (e.g. verbs of action for use with the present continuous tense; words for containers or for surfaces with prepositions *in* and *on*). What it is hoped will be clear from the scheme is that the teacher should be aware of what language he is *formally* teaching, in terms of both grammar and content; he should for his own benefit, and for a guide to other teachers he may be co-operating with, keep a record of the items he is teaching. (The summaries at the end of each stage of the scheme of work suggest one way of doing this. The ideal record of work done would be even more comprehensive, and should include the situations used for teaching language items, details of centres of interest, projects, speech rhymes used, etc.)

In order to produce a comprehensive scheme it has been necessary to oversimplify. Teaching English to five-year-old Indian children is obviously different from teaching it to seven-year-old Italians or thirteen-year-old mixed groups. Activities that can be used with one group will not necessarily be suitable for another. Most of the procedures suggested here would in fact be suitable in the junior school and to a large extent in the lower ranges of the secondary school too. The selection and choice of the structural items and the general approach could be used even with adults, allowing for the fact that a different range of content words and of social formulas would be included to meet their particular needs. The hints on method are not in any case meant to be comprehensive. They illustrate how items can be presented and practised. To supplement them, and to see how they would fit into a wider teaching pattern, the reader should turn to Chapter 4.

As a general principle it may be said that the more activity and informal language work there is, the better will be the learning at practically any stage. There will obviously be the widest scope for activity of all sorts in the junior school, and the least in classes of fairly mature pupils. Teaching in the latter case may have to be almost entirely formal language teaching, whereas in the junior classes 'formal' will hardly be applicable as a description. The teacher there will in fact be teaching English almost every moment of the day, in everything he says and does with his pupils. The language involved in P.E., movement, number, etc., will all be part of the language-teaching process, and the teacher will need to be constantly aware of the interrelation of the language of his 'special' English teaching times and the language used at other times, taking every opportunity to make the latter contribute to his pupils' mastery of the former. 'Formal', applied to teaching in this pattern, may hardly seem the right word to use; all the same, we insist that the teacher should be working according to a scheme and should, at least for some short periods each day, deliberately practise new structural items and vocabulary and revise the old. 'Formal', in the pages that follow, should perhaps then be thought of as referring to the teacher's intention about the structural items he is concentrating on at each step rather than to a method of presentation and practice.

Briefly to recapitulate the major points and principles of language teaching to be borne in mind when working through this scheme:

1 The immigrant child needs to learn English for the purpose of communication.

2 He needs to be able to understand and to speak the English he hears about him every day.

3 He needs intensive oral teaching to train him to understand what he hears and to say what he needs to say.

4 He should not be led on to reading and writing until he has made some progress in understanding and speaking.

5 All that he does in language work should be as realistic as possible; i.e. utterances should relate to real situations, though the situations themselves may be contrived.

The pre-speaking stage

Just as there is a pre-reading stage in teaching British children in the junior school, so in language teaching to overseas children there should be a pre-speaking stage .The normal British child comes to school already equipped with the skills of understanding and speaking, however limited his range. But the non-English-speaking immigrant child has neither, and it should not be assumed that progress in both these skills will occur simultaneously.

All around him the new immigrant will hear English being used. This must be a confusing meaningless jumble of sound at first (similar to the impression one gets when tuning in by accident to an unknown language on a foreign radio station). Gradually with the immigrant the significance of certain small groups of sounds becomes clear, because they recur in the same situation and are associated with some definite pattern of action: 'Sit down', 'Stand up', 'Look', 'Out you go'. . . . The gestures of the speaker and the behaviour of other people around him make him understand what is required of him at first, until he identifies the pattern of sound in each utterance and interprets it without necessarily being helped or prompted by the non-verbal features of the situation. The immigrant's first real response to the language, therefore, may well be simply within the kind of formulas suggested here. The teacher who receives newcomers should realise that this phase, in which the pupil is gradually sorting out sounds that mean something from the vast babble of sounds that as yet mean nothing, is the all-important first step in the teaching of English to immigrants. It might be better called a learning rather than a teaching phase, for it is a time of incubation, in

B

which the real work goes on unseen and unmeasured in the pupil: his ears are accustoming themselves to the sounds of a language that fall into patterns – patterns of speech sounds, including pitch and rhythmical features – that he has never heard before. He is beginning to recognize these patterns and to respond to them as they emerge from the 'confusion'.

At this stage of language learning the teacher's manner, his attitude to the pupils, the tone of his voice, all have continually to reassure them, to make them feel accepted, so that they can begin to get over their sense of strangeness and start responding to things outside them, responding above all to language.

By his awareness of the language he is using at this stage, the teacher will help the pupils in this process of responding; the teacher's awareness must be towards *what* he says and *how* he says it. This means that in some measure the teacher has to limit himself; where for instance there are several ways of giving the same instruction, he has to try to confine himself to one – the clearest and simplest – only later adding variations. He will always speak as clearly as possible, but also naturally, so that sounds and rhythm are not distorted.

He will need too a range of gestures to accompany his instructions, and even the more varied resources of mime for some purposes. (This is true not only in the first few weeks of teaching but even later, and gestures that 'go with' some items of language, e.g.: *you/I, your/my, we/he*, etc., may well have to be decided upon and used with consistency for months until the pupils have a sure command of the items in question.)

It is useful for the teacher to make a list of what expressions he needs and uses, as this will help him in his conscious control of classroom language: first, for example, to conduct the class:

> Good morning, *or* Good afternoon
> Sit down
> Listen to me
> Be quiet
> Look
>   etc.

Other formulas for maintaining general discipline and for getting things done will be added to this list as necessary, expressions such as:

Open the door
Come in
Give out the milk
One at a time
Stay in your places
Line up
Wait
    etc.

It is not that the teacher is necessarily limited to these, but the effort at control of language used with beginners pays off in the later stages in their swifter recognition of, and familiarity with, the items used, and in their greater confidence and therefore the learning-readiness that follows.

There is also very soon a place at this stage for commands that involve the pupils in actions and, within a while, in repeating the teacher's words themselves. This may be thought of as a transition to 'formal teaching' and it can only come when the pupils are ready to pass from being simply hearers to being speakers, when language is something which they begin to use actively themselves, whereas before they were not expected to do more than respond to it with certain actions or kinds of behaviour. The teacher alone can gauge when this moment has been reached – it may be in less than a week, or with very young or nervous pupils it may be after several weeks, and it will not be the same for all pupils in any one group – the surest sign being that they are beginning spontaneously to try to repeat what he himself is saying. When the teacher actually expects them to give commands to one another, we can say that we are at Step 1 of the language scheme that follows here.

Finally, we might point out that the process described above, in which pupils begin to respond to language and obviously understand it before they are ready or able to use it themselves, is one that has a wider reference through all the stages of second-language learning. For in this respect, the second-language learner is like the native speaker of a language who, at any age, has a passive vocabulary which is wider than his active vocabulary. In the immigrant situation in particular, it will be found that pupils other than pure beginners respond to far more language than they themselves can produce (though there is the danger of crediting them with understanding when they may often only be appearing to do so). With essential items of structure and vocabulary the teacher's task will often be to activate the pupils' passive knowledge and make it productive; but on many other occasions, and notably in story telling, the teacher may actually rely on the pupils' passive understanding without expecting them to be able to reproduce all the language that they have heard.

The scheme of work that follows is divided into stages, the division being intended to help the teacher to revise and consolidate material at the end of each stage before proceeding to the next. Rather more details about procedure and the language items themselves are given towards the beginning, the object being to sharpen the teacher's insight into grading and to give him a sense of the difficulties involved for the foreign learner of English. As he proceeds through the syllabus, presumably the teacher will begin to make the application himself, and may also then begin to exercise his own discretion in selecting items to teach and the order of their presentation. The scheme as it stands covers all the major items which might be presented in a first year of English, leaving the later choice of tenses to the teacher's discretion.

The teacher must also decide for himself how quickly to proceed through the work offered here, as also at what stage he will introduce reading and writing (see Chapter 5). Roughly speaking, it seems in practice that one or two steps per week is all that can be expected at first, but there can be some acceleration as work proceeds. The great danger is that the teacher will try to hurry in the early stages. Admittedly immigrant pupils need to learn English as quickly as possible if they are to fit into the school society; but learning a language, as we said before, is not like learning facts, and nothing is to be gained by speeding on too quickly from one item to another. Let the pace be decided by the pupils' mastery, and as a faster and a slower group develop within one class, they may have to be dealt with separately. Boredom must be avoided, of course, but not at a cost of uncertain control of basic items of language.

The summaries of work covered in the different stages may be found useful for reference and for revision. In the scheme itself, items taught at each step are printed in bold; those in brackets are optional. Additional vocabulary that is useful at each step is also included here and there throughout the scheme, and is printed in italic.

Scheme of work

STAGE I

STEP I
IMPERATIVES

Stand up.   **Sit down.**   **Come here.**   **Touch . . .**
Point to . . .   **Put . . .**

As they gain in confidence, the least shy children should be asked to give commands themselves, beginning with the few easiest, *Stand up, Sit down, Come here,* but then progressing to more elaborate ones which will involve the use of new vocabulary as it is learnt: *Bring me a book, Touch the table,* etc. Children should take it in turns to give commands to the whole class or to individuals, or to groups if these are already established.

These will be the first English words the children are *expected* to use, i.e. within their English period, and from these very first weeks the teacher must see this as an opportunity to encourage correct speech habits. His own pronunciation will be the model, and he should see that while it is clear it is also natural, keeping the normal rhythm and intonation of everyday English. (For an explanation of these features of pronunciation, see p. 110.) The procedure in this step, 'imperative drill' as it is often called, can go on being used as the term proceeds, and can of course be combined with new items as they are formally taught at each stage, becoming more and more complicated to maintain interest:

Give me your book.
Bring me Ali's book.
Draw a big red house.
Put your left hand on your right elbow . . .

STEP 2
INTRODUCING NAMES OF THINGS
a book   a box   a desk . . .   .

If the teacher has begun with the step suggested above, his aim and method will simply be to get the pupils, individually and in groups, to repeat what he says *when they are ready for it*. Gestures and encouraging expressions must be used to give the children confidence and to get them to try to imitate the teacher's voice. Often, if the 'incubation period' has been thoughtfully carried out, they will be beginning to try out their 'English' voices of their own accord. The teacher should ideally look for 'speaking-readiness', just as the ordinary infant teacher looks for reading-readiness. The pupils should be encouraged to handle objects as they name them, just as the teacher does.

In this first introduction of 'the names of things' *always* use the indefinite article *a*. There may in fact be no such article in the child's mother tongue, and unless great care is taken to introduce it from the beginning – and to insist on it – it will disappear from the child's English or be misused later. Preferably choose items of vocabulary of which there are several in the room (e.g. not the blackboard or the door if there is only one of each, for you would then need to say '*the* blackboard' and '*the* door', and this is a separate item which must be learnt later). Avoid objects beginning with vowel sounds, so that you do not have to use *an* at this stage. Avoid plurals too for the moment, because they cannot be used without introducing several other complications both in pronunciation and in grammar.

Pronounce *a* naturally with a 'weak' neutral vowel sound [ə] (like the first syllable in *about*);[1] it should not be pronounced so that it rhymes with *day*. At all times speak clearly but with natural pronunciation and rhythm.

This is a book.

Some teachers (and most course books) prefer to start with this 'whole sentence' from the very beginning, and certainly once the children have got their tongues round a few nouns they should begin to use this complete utterance; the aim should always be to get the children to use complete utterances, for if they are allowed to get into the habit of shouting out single words this will encourage them later in the use of the ungrammatical form of English which many adult immigrants use. (There will of course be many occasions when it is perfectly right and natural for the answer to a question to consist of one word only.) Let the children say *This is a* . . . while actually holding or touching the object in question. This structure is the natural one to use when naming things without having been asked what they are.

(That is a —)[2]

Do not move on to *That is a* . . . here, unless you feel it is really helpful or necessary to do so; it can in fact be left out altogether at this first stage, although many textbooks introduce it side by side with *this*. If you decide to introduce *that*, always get the children to point to things that are some distance away for it, so that the contrast between the use of *this* and *that* is kept clear.) In getting the children to use *This is* . . . it is essential to see that the situation always demands *this* and not *that*. It would be wrong to indicate an object on your own desk, a yard or so away from the child, and request him to say *This is a* . . . when *that* would be the appropriate form.

---

[1] See Chapter 3 for meaning of phonetic symbols (page 118) and for explanation of terms such as 'weak', 'strong forms', etc.

[2] Bracketed items are optional.

and

> A variety of procedures can be used to practise this structure; the early introduction of *and* will be found convenient, e.g.

> 1ST PUPIL: This is a book (*picking up object on own desk*) and this is a pen (*going to next desk and touching object*).
>
> 2ND CHILD: This is a pen (*touching object on own desk*) and this is a . . . (*going to next desk*).

This is an aeroplane.

> It is obvious that the introduction of nouns beginning with vowels cannot be left too long, and the teacher must decide for himself when to let them in. The children themselves, by their questions, by their interest in certain pictures or objects, may make it necessary earlier rather than later. It is placed separately from *a* here to impress upon the teacher that it is a separate difficulty, not just a difficulty of spelling as it often is for British children, but a difficulty in basic pronunciation in these early stages of oral English. The teacher should not be tempted to stress *an* unnaturally (as is often done in teaching British children) so that it rhymes with *pan*; but it should, like *a*, be given its normal weak unstressed form, so that the children learn from the very beginning to pronounce sentences like *This is an aeroplane* with the rhythm of natural speech.

This is Ali.   This is Farida.

> When the teacher has learnt some of his pupils' names, he can begin to practise them with the preceding structure. Pupils can go round the class naming one another, or presenting their neighbours to the teacher.

That is Yusuf.

> When *this* is firmly established, the teacher may at last introduce *that*, always using it with an appropriate pointing gesture to indicate objects or people at a distance from the speaker. In most of the items that follow, variety can be added by changing from situations demanding *this* to others demanding *that*.

STEP 3

POSSESSION

This is my . . . This is your . . . (That is your . . .)
head nose leg hand . . . . . .

Gestures must convey the meaning of *my* and *your* at their first introduction. It is often a good idea to use them at first with parts of the body (e.g. *head, nose, leg, hand* – if you are still trying to avoid initial vowel sounds) and only after that to move on to personal possessions. If *that* has already been introduced, you should take care here not to associate *this* always with *my* and *that* always with *your*, otherwise the pupils may connect the original pairs too closely together. Moreover, they should not be confused at this stage by introducing *mine* and *yours*; these must be kept till later.

This is his . . . This is her . . .

Do not underestimate the difficulty when moving on to introduce *his* and *her*. (In some languages there is only one word for both *his* and *her*, and in others quite a different system operates, depending on the grammatical gender of the following noun, etc.) Imperative drill (see Step 1) and plenty of other activities should be introduced here and the new points brought in only slowly. It takes a long time before *his* and *her* can be used freely and accurately.

Again, in presenting these items, gestures have to be most carefully and consistently used. When teaching *his* and *her*, point to the boy or girl in question, but look at the class. Maintain a clear distinction – especially by way of gesture – between *your* and *his/her*. Of course, if the class is not a mixed one, it may be difficult to demonstrate both of these 3rd-person adjectives; it may be possible to leave one out for a little while, but it cannot be neglected for too long. A doll, picture or flannelgraph figure can be used at first to introduce the missing person.

His name is . . . Her name is . . .

His, her, your and *my* can soon be usefully practised in a new pattern with pupils' names, as a variation on the procedure suggested at the end of Step 2: *His name is . . . Her name is . . .*, etc.

STEP 4
POSSESSIVE OF NAMES

This is Ali's box.

This form can be arrived at through the preceding steps: *This is Ali. This is his book. This is Ali's book. This is Farida. This is her book. This is Farida's book,* etc.

Great care and a lot of patience will be needed to get all the children to hear and then to produce the final sibilant sounds on the end of names in the possessive: *Ali's, Ahmad's, Yusuf's, Mr Black's.* Notice how some of these final sounds are [s] sounds, while some of them are [z]. Moreover, if the name ends in a sibilant itself, a whole syllable is added: *Lopez's* [iz]. The pupils' pronunciation of these endings will vary, and some will substitute [s] for [z], or omit the sounds altogether. It may be necessary for the teacher to exaggerate his own pronunciation of them at first, simply to draw the pupils' attention to the differences. At this stage especially the teacher has to be very careful not to over-correct, or pupils will lose their confidence, or, what is equally bad, become bored. (When a similar problem of pronunciation arises later in teaching plurals of nouns – Step 15 – the teacher may take up this point with rather more insistence.)

(Whose book is this?)

For question work involving these items the teacher will find it natural to try to use *Whose?* though he need not expect the pupils to use it themselves until later (Step 23, for instance). If he chooses to use *Whose?* here, he should try to use it in one pattern only (e.g. *Whose book is this?* rather than *Whose is this book?*). Notice, though, that at this stage the only really natural answer to this question, out of the language work so far covered, would be 'Ali's', or 'Farida's'; but once Step 5 has been covered and *it is* has been introduced, the teacher can expect the replies *It is Ali's*, and *It is my book*, etc.

There is great scope for games[1] and activities once these four first steps have been mastered. More and more vocabulary can be introduced – parts of the body, personal possessions, relations (*brother, sister*, etc.), class-room and outside objects. The aim should always be to practise these content words in structures and in situations which are as interesting as possible to the pupils. The activities used in the junior school will sometimes be suitable in the secondary school, but it must be remembered that the pupils' attention span, the need for variety and diversity, are the variables which ultimately shape the working out of lessons and the division of the day's activities.

STEP 5

QUESTIONS FOR IDENTIFYING OBJECTS

What is this? What is that? It is a . . . (It's a . . .)

It is suggested that at this step the teacher makes a formal approach to training the pupils to use questions themselves. Although it is possible to conduct oral work for a considerable length of time without actually *asking* questions – e.g. by the use of gesture, pointing to differ-ent pupils, using the formula *Your turn . . .*, etc. – it is obvious that many questions will have found their way into lessons and some have in fact been suggested in the preceding steps. Questions will also have been used in other school situations, e.g. at reception: *What is your name? Where do you live?* (It is often found that this type of standard question is one to which practically all new pupils respond.)

When training pupils to use questions it is often sug-gested that one pupil at a time should come out to the front of the class and take the teacher's place; but most new immigrants will be too shy to do this and will

[1] See Chapter 4 for use of 'structural games' in language teaching.

respond better if questions and answers are used around the class, e.g. a pupil in one row holding up an object or pointing to a picture and asking someone in the next row to identify it by asking *What is this?* or *What is that?* The teacher should be aware of the new language problems that he introduces at this stage. He should encourage pupils to imitate his voice exactly, and notice if they are making the same pitch changes as he does – for questions introduce several new intonation patterns and these are as important as their structural patterns. It will be helpful if the teacher guards against varying his intonation too much at first, though if he has had no phonetic training he may find this difficult. (Again, for intonation, see below, pp. 114 ff.)

Here, as elsewhere, the teacher has also to take a firm line about elisions and the use of 'strong' or 'weak forms' of certain structural words (see below, p. 112). It is suggested that up till now he should use the unelided forms only (i.e. *that is* and not *that's*), as this seems to make for less confusion in the pupil's mind at first. Some teachers also find that *What is* . . . rather than *What's* . . . and *It is* . . . rather than *It's* . . . are easier for children to learn at first. (Some Asian pupils in particular find the combination of consonants in *It's* difficult to pronounce.) There is no need for utterances which use the full *is* form to sound stilted; it is often heard in normal English conversation, and as long as it is unstressed, the sentence rhythm will not sound distorted (i.e. *It is a 'book*, — three unstressed syllables followed by a stressed one in the noun). Many pupils transfer to the elided forms quite naturally from this, but the teacher will also have to see that they all do so at some stage. Or, of course, the teacher can choose to teach the elided forms from the beginning, on the grounds that these are eventually what the pupils have to use and respond to in everyday English conversation.

The vowel sounds in *it* and *is* present another pronunciation problem both for European and for many Asian pupils, and they must be trained not to say 'eet eez' [iːt iːz] or 'eet ees' [iːt iːs].

This is a ball. It is Ali's ball. That is a box. It is my box.

Other opportunities of practising *it is* should be taken by the teacher so that the pupils become more and more familiar with it. Care has to be taken to make sure that it is used naturally. *It*, in the simple use taught here, has to refer to something that has already been identified, for instance, by way of a question; or it introduces a new piece of information about something, e.g. *This is a pencil. It is my pencil.*

It, of course, will already have been heard and possibly used as an object pronoun in many of the instructions given by the teacher to the class and repeated perhaps by pupils themselves in imperative drill: *Give it to me, Put it down*, etc. At a later stage (Step 19), it is suggested that the teacher pauses to see that *it* is being used correctly as object.

STEP 6

NEGATIVE

It isn't Ali's box. That isn't her book. This isn't my book, etc.

Although it is useful to introduce the negative forms of *be* fairly early, the teacher should be careful that he does not cause confusion by doing so. He should also see that, for the sake of doing so, he does not produce an artificial kind of classroom English. Once a range of expressions for possession and introductory *it* have been taught, negative forms can in fact be introduced very naturally. It is suggested that although the unelided forms of words have mostly been used up till now, the elided form *It isn't* seems best here. It saves the pupils learning the long answer *it is not*, which generally has a strong emphatic meaning not required here at all.

The teacher can contrive simple situations such as the distribution of pupils' possessions, in the course of which he makes deliberate mistakes about their owner-ship:

This is Yusuf's book. This is Ali's book.
Oh no – It isn't Ali's book. It is Antonio's book, etc.

He can then make similar statements to individuals and get them to contradict or correct him:

TEACHER: This is your book. This is his book.
PUPIL: That isn't his book. It is Farida's book.

Other simple situations in which the negative occurs naturally can be practised.

This item relates to the next teaching step (and in some courses would follow rather than precede it). *No*, which is formally taught in the next step, will probably have to be used in Step 6 for the sake of naturalness, and in any case is one of the expressions that most pupils will have picked up already.

STEP 7
'YES/NO' QUESTIONS
Is this Yusuf? Is this a book? Is that a pencil? Is it your pencil?

This form of question expects the answer *Yes* or *No*, and the voice usually rises on the important part of the question: *Is this ⌐ Yusuf?*[1] The teacher again needs to watch his intonation when presenting these forms, and although in the give and take of the classroom he will find that this type of question often occurs with a falling and not a rising intonation (e.g. when a question is repeated, with a brusquer, more urgent effect), it will be helpful if he regularly gives examples of the simple rising pattern to start with.

---

[1] Many different notations can be employed to indicate pitch change, but the one used here, an arrow placed immediately before the word that bears the main part of a rise or fall, seems the simplest for the present purpose. It is the notation used (and explained in detail) by Hornby in *The Teaching of Structural Words and Sentence Patterns* (see Bibliography, Section X).

Yes, it is.   No, it isn't.

Yes and *No* must now be presented with the short-answer forms, *Yes, it is* and *No, it isn't*. It is enough to expect pupils to give short answers only at first, but later on, if it can be done naturally, they may be required to practise 'full' answers:

Is this a book? – No, it isn't.
                      No, it isn't a book. It is a ruler.
Is this Yusuf? – No, it isn't Yusuf. It is Ali.

But there is always a danger that because the teacher demands long answers, he may reject short answers which are in fact correct, good English and frequently used in all conversation. Here, as elsewhere, it is easy to baffle and frustrate the pupils, who are usually not sophisticated enough to see why a teacher wants something else when they have apparently given him a correct answer. It would be better for the sake of interest, and for the sake of English as it is really used, not to insist too strongly on the other forms.

STEP 8
ADJECTIVES

This is a red pencil.   Is that a big book?   Draw a fat man.

red   blue   yellow   white   black . . . . . . *fat   thin   big small* . . . .

Adjectives, especially of colour, and of clearly perceived and contrasted qualities, need to be introduced early, especially in the primary school where so much work centres on sensory perception. When introducing new items to fill this need, the teacher should beware of trying to introduce too many at once: only a few colours at a time should be taught, and only adjectives that can be clearly illustrated by reference to the children themselves or to things they can see.

Notice, too, when introducing adjectives, that it should not be presumed that the children can manipulate them in more than one position in the structure all at once. First, they are only learning to say *This is a red pencil*; once this is learnt, and some practice given in identifying colours of different objects, the teacher can introduce the question *What colour is this?* and train pupils to give short answers *It is red, It is black*, etc., later providing practice too for negative answers, *It isn't blue, It isn't yellow*, etc.

What colour is this?

One of the most difficult things for a native teacher of English as a second language to realize is that he himself uses simple words in a wide variety of patterns, and that although these patterns seem simple to him, they are not necessarily so for the pupils; they present difficulties simply because they are different from one another and often because they are only slightly different. Thus while at this stage the pupils have learnt to say *This is a red pencil* and *It is red*, they have not yet come to *This pencil is red*. This is a separate pattern in the use of adjectives, and it will not necessarily 'come naturally' to most of the pupils. At Step 16 below it is suggested that the teacher actually goes on to practise this particular pattern formally, together with other adjectival usages. While referring to colours, it is worth mentioning that teaching the names of colours is not as simple as it sounds. Teachers may find that they have to teach actual identification of colours to pupils of some nationalities who have learnt to divide up the spectrum in a different way from us. Thus some African pupils may not see orange as orange but as red.

STEP 9
PREPOSITIONS: ON, IN

My pencil is on your desk. Ali's book is in Yusuf's desk.[1]

[1] If the teacher wishes to anticipate the introduction of prepositions, he will teach vocabulary that will help provide situations in which they can be used; e.g. for use with *in*: *pocket, cup, bag, box*, etc.

It is a good idea to introduce *a few* prepositions fairly early, as they immediately add interest to what can be demonstrated and said about objects and people in the classroom. Objects can now be placed *in* desks, pockets, bags, etc., or *on* surfaces provided by window-sills, desks, tables, and so on. Many games and activities suggest themselves, and when later on more prepositions are introduced (*behind, in front of, between, near, with,* etc.) these can become more exciting.

Many guessing games can be played which involve the pupils in using prepositions, e.g. hiding different objects about the room inside things and letting someone who is 'it' guess where each item is (*Is it in my desk? Is it in Ali's pocket?* etc.). At this stage it will be found increasingly difficult to do without the definite article, and teachers will need to exert great care if they are to avoid it. The safest practice for preposition work is with questions using possessive forms and possessive adjectives; and until the definite article has been taught, it is best to keep to very few prepositions.

Where is . . . ?

The teacher may now introduce questions with *Where?* first of all allowing pupils to get used to hearing it in his own speech and then coming to use it themselves. He should be clear about what type of answer he expects. This in fact is another good opportunity for practising *it is*:

Where is my pencil? – It is on your desk.
It is in your pocket.

Opportunities for practising the negative should also be taken:

It isn't in my pocket. It is on your desk.
etc.

Gradually, throughout the succeeding steps, more prepositions should be included. The teacher should introduce a few at each stage, preferably as they are needed for giving instructions in P.E., or in handwork:

Throw the ball *over* your head.
Stand *in front of* the class.
Run *between* the rows.

There should always be a carry-over from one type of lesson to another.

Sometimes, too, a preposition will need to be taught in preparation for a teaching item to be presented soon after, e.g. *between* is useful, if not necessary, when presenting later stages of telling the time (Step 26 below); *at* with time expressions is useful when introducing the Simple Present tense (Step 34).

SUMMARY OF STAGE I (Steps 1 – 9)

Structure

Note. Most teachers will be familiar with the form of the tables used here to summarize the sentence patterns introduced in each stage. The general rule is that in reading across the table a vertical line may be crossed at any point but a horizontal line cannot be crossed.

Stand up Sit down etc.

This That	isn't is	a my your his her Ali's	book coat
		an aeroplane	
		Ali Antonio	

(Whose book is this?)

What is	this? that?

It	is isn't	a(n) my Ali's etc.	book aeroplane

Is	this that	Yusuf?	
		a my your etc.	book? coat?

Yes, it is
No, it isn't

This That It	is	a	red small etc.	house

What colour is this?

It	is isn't	red etc.

Where is	my Ali's	pencil? coat?

My Ali's It	pencil	is isn't	on in	your his	desk pocket

Vocabulary

The teacher should keep a record of all items taught, grammatical and lexical, in relation to the above structural items; e.g.

a, an
this, that, it
my, your, his, her
is, isn't
and
yes, no
where, (whose), what
in, on

aeroplane, book, ball, car, chair, crayon, cupboard, desk, lorry, pencil, shelf, table, wall, box, pen, cup, pocket, bag, head, nose, leg, hand . . .

big, small, fat, thin; blue, black, red, green, yellow, white . . .

STAGE II

STEP 10

ALTERNATIVE QUESTIONS

Is this Ali or Yusuf?   Is that a blue pen or a red pen? Is this my bag or your bag?

It may be found that some of the steps suggested in the first Stage take longer to learn than others. There may, for example, be very many occasions on which the pupils claim their own belongings, and consequently gain practice in *my* and *your*, whereas they may not need to use *his* and *her* nearly so often and hence may take much longer to learn them thoroughly. Some items may simply have a greater intrinsic difficulty for them than others.

The vocabulary taught may extend much more rapidly than is suggested here, as the children or teacher bring different objects into the classroom. To go over these items, and to recapitulate the structures so far taught, it is useful to introduce *or* and to try out alternative questions. An alternative question puts the answer into the mouth of the pupil and is a very good way of re-treading familiar ground. The more often he hears the nouns and adjectives he has been introduced to, the more automatic will his own use of them become and the better his pronunciation.

When asking questions with *or*, pay attention to the way the voice rises and falls. Try to keep the intonation regular, for instance, with a rise on the first part of the question and a fall at the end:

Is this a ↗ pen or a ↘ pencil?

The pupils will quickly imitate this.

left   right ... ...
> The introduction of *left* and *right* can add interest to many games at this stage, and also fit in well after the introduction of *or*:

Is this my left hand or my right hand?
Is his pencil in his left hand or in his right hand? etc.

(Muddles over *left* and *right* in pupils' responses can often be avoided if the teacher, when asking a question and demonstrating with one hand or the other, stands momentarily with his back to the class.)

STEP II
THE DEFINITE ARTICLE

the floor   the blackboard   the door   the clock ...
> By now, probably in the giving of instructions, the teacher will have found himself using the definite article, and the pupils may have imitated his use of it without being told to do so. For general purposes they may misuse and confuse the definite and indefinite articles, *a* and *the*, and in the interests of encouraging them to speak the teacher may refrain at first from correcting them too often. But at the same time he must be aware of the difference in correct usage, and may, at this stage, begin deliberately to draw attention (e.g. by the repetition of the correct form) to *the* blackboard, *the* clock, *the* teacher, because in fact there is usually only one of each in the classroom. These can be deliberately practised, through questions and imperatives:

Clean the blackboard.
Open the window.
Look at the clock.
Where is the clock?

and also with prepositions:

The blackboard is near the door.
The clock is on the wall.

the sun   the sky   the moon ... ...

At the same time, new vocabulary items which always occur with the definite article may now be introduced: *the sun*, *the sky*, etc.:

This is a star, and this is a star. This is the moon. The moon is in the sky. What is this? It is the sun.

But in trying to get the pupils to use the correct article, the teacher must again beware of wrongly stressing it in his speech and of giving it an unnatural 'strong' form. Before words with initial consonants *the* is pronounced with the neutral vowel sound [ə].

As with the indefinite article, the teacher may at first try to avoid using the definite article with words with an initial vowel sound; when, however, they occur – and they must sooner or later – he must again see that *the* gets pronounced correctly, not, however, with the long [iː] sound that occurs in *bee*, but with [i] as in *bit*. (Practise: *the aeroplane*, *the apple*, *the orange*, etc.)

STEP 12

TELLING THE TIME (1)

It is one o'clock.   1 – 12.

There is no definite moment at which it is best to introduce the first steps in telling the time. Much depends on the age of the pupils and their readiness for dealing with this, together with their need to know it. In a secondary school it may seem to have relatively more importance and may also be more easily digested by older immigrant children.

However, the language dealt with up till now leads conveniently to an introduction to telling the time at this point, since we can now talk about *the clock* and *the small hand* and *the big hand*. Numerals *one* to *twelve* can be practised, and the following procedure can be used:

The big hand is on twelve.
The small hand is on one.
It is one o'clock.
   etc.

What is the time?

The question *What is the time?* is preferable to *What time is it?* as it repeats a pattern the pupils have already heard.

In the early stages one should be content with hours only and not try to go into more complicated divisions of time. Later on, *It is half past . . .*, etc., can be dealt with (Step 26).

STEP 13
PRONOUNS 'HE'/'SHE' AND THE VERB 'BE'

He is . . . She is . . .

Is has already been used quite often, and personal pronouns may now be introduced, although it is quite likely that *he/she* will cause difficulty, and be confused with one another, like *his/her* earlier. They can, however, be used continually and very naturally in many classroom situations throughout the day, e.g. at roll-call or after playtime, when the teacher can even pretend to look for certain children in order to provide the occasion for the necessary practice:

Where is Ali? Oh, he is here.
But where is Farida? Where is she?
(*Class answers*) She is here.
   etc.

(everyone) here there ... ...

At this point the teacher may also find that he needs and can himself use the pronoun *everyone*, though not yet expecting the pupils to use it:

Is everyone here?
Everyone stand up.

Here and *there* will have been used quite often in commands – *Come here*, *Put it there* – and will be found increasingly useful, indeed necessary, at this stage.

He is and *she is* can also now be practised with adjectives in the predicative position: *He is big*, *She is small*; and, in multi-national classes, with adjectives denoting nationality. Pupils can, for instance, pretend to introduce one another to visitors:

Indian   Italian ... ...

This is Antonio. He is Italian.
This is Kanda. She is Indian.

man   woman   boy   girl   father   brother   postman   bus-driver
teacher   pupil   soldier ... ...

This sentence pattern can be extended to *He is a big boy*, *She is an Indian girl*, and can go on to include relationships (practised with real-life relationships in the classroom where these exist, or through pictures and other aids), jobs, etc.:

This is Farida. She is my sister. She is an Indian girl.
This is a man. He is my father. He is a postman.

STEP 14
PRONOUNS 'I'/'YOU' AND THE VERB 'BE'; INTERROGATIVES; AFFIRMATIVE AND NEGATIVE ANSWERS

I am ...   You (singular) are ...
short   tall   good etc.

These pronouns, again, will have crept in earlier. The forms of the verb will need special care, especially if they are not to be stressed in a distorted and unnatural way.

At this stage *I am* and *you are* can be practised with the content words and in the patterns suggested in Step 13, but this may also be a good opportunity to introduce some new prepositions and adjectives, and to practise telling some more personal details, e.g. what class one is in, one's age, etc.:

I am Rashid. I am short. I am seven.

Ali is my brother. He is tall. He is ten. He is in Class III.

You are in Miss Brown's class.

Is he . . .? Is she . . .? Is Ali . . .? Am I . . .? Are you . . .? etc.

Questions with *I, you, he, she, it* must now be practised, but the teacher should first be aware of the difficulties these involve him in, and should grade this work very gently. He should also be clear in his own mind about what responses he expects to questions used.

The best order would be to revise questions with *is*, as this has already been practised, and to aim at short answers similar to those in Step 7:

Is this a pencil? – Yes, it is.

No, it isn't.

Is Ali Indian? – Yes, he is.

Is Maria Indian? – No, she isn't.

Is she tall? – No, she isn't.

Questions with *I* and *you* should then be practised, but it should be realized that these involve the pupils in considerably more difficulties, as they have to produce the opposite pronoun and verb form for the answer:

Are you a soldier? – No, I am not.

Are you a pupil? – Yes, I am.

Are you tall?, etc.

Are you Indian?

Am I a teacher? – Yes, you are.

Am I a postman? – No, you are not. (No, you aren't.)

Note on elided forms of 'be': It is at this stage that the teacher will have to give special thought to the use of elided and unelided forms of the verb *be*. In the short affirmative answers to the type of question used immediately above, only unelided forms can be used:

Yes, I am.

Yes, you are.

Yes, he is.

In the negative short answers, however, the unelided forms can very easily sound artificial or over-emphatic. As *isn't* is already known, it seems fairly easy to move quickly from *are not* to *aren't* in the 2nd person; *No, he isn't* and *No, you aren't* should be practised close to one another for the analogy to be clear. But the teacher is still left with the 1st person form, *No, I am not* (*am* to be pronounced with the weak vowel [ə]), where elision can only take place between the *I* and *am* (=*No, I'm not*) and not between the verb and *not* as in the other two persons. It will in fact be found that many pupils make this particular elision quite automatically.

If these procedures are followed, the teacher will then have to practise as his range of negative short answers:

No, I'm not.
No, you aren't.
No, he isn't.

and should of course be consistent and careful not to fluctuate between different forms (e.g. between *No, you're not* and *No, you aren't*).

This would be a good moment for him to pass to other elisions, e.g. in the affirmative form, and to give the class opportunities to repeat what they have previously learnt, substituting

I'm   for *I am*
You're ,, *you are*
He's   ,, *he is*
She's ,, *she is*

and not forgetting

It's for *it is*.

From here on the teacher must obviously use his discretion, and while continually aiming at establishing a natural use of 'weak' forms (see below, p. 112) should make sure that the pupils are not confused or baffled. The main argument for using elided forms such as *it's* and *that's* from the very beginning is of course that the transference to these forms does not then have to be made at a later step such as the present. However, there are many arguments for following the order given here. One should insist that if long forms are used at the beginning, they should never be given undue stress or made to sound over-emphatic: this would be really damaging to the pupils' ability to use English naturally later on.

For the rest of this scheme of work, unelided forms will be printed wherever it seems likely that they could be used naturally. Where it seems that the elided form is preferable to the unelided form, it has been printed as such. Teachers of course may choose to teach elided forms throughout.

To return to the present step: concentrated revision and practice of questions and answers using prepositions, adjectives, etc., will be useful for establishing the new forms. Alternative questions should also be practised:

Is Ali eight or nine? – He's . . .
Is he in the corner or under the table? – He's . . .
Are you tall or short? – I'm . . .

Finally, the negative has also to be mastered in long answers:

It isn't my pencil. It's Ali's.
Ali isn't here.
Farida isn't tall; she's short.
You aren't short; you're tall.
I'm not a soldier.

The more all these question and answer patterns and uses of the negative can be practised, and the more secure the pupils become in using them (i.e. both in answering and in asking questions, etc.), the easier will later stages of language work be when, for instance, tenses of verbs are taught in more detail.

very

Other adjectives, where appropriate, can be introduced here to add plenty of variety to the work. It should also be possible to use *very* from here on:

Ali is very small.
That is very good.
etc.

SUMMARY OF STAGE II (Steps 10–14)

Structure

Is	this	Ali or Rashid?
		a pen or a pencil?
	it	in my bag or my box? etc.

This	is	the	floor
That			sun
			sky

The	moon	is	in the sky
	blackboard		near the door

What is the time?

It is	one	o'clock
	ten	

He	is	my brother
She	's	his father
	isn't	Indian
I	am	Italian
	'm	a postman
	am not	a teacher
You	are	here
	're	there
	aren't	in class three
		near the door
		etc.

Is	he she	tall? a good boy?
Am	I	an Italian girl?
Are	you	a postman? in the corner? etc.

Vocabulary
or, the
he, she, I, you
is, am, are
here, there
1 –12 o'clock
under, near, on (the wall)
very
everyone
floor, blackboard, door, clock, corner (of the room), window,
hand (of the clock), sun, sky, star, moon, man, woman, boy, girl,
father, mother, brother, sister, postman, bus-driver, teacher,
pupil, soldier . . . left, right, Indian, Italian . . .

STAGE III

STEP 15
PLURALS

These are books.   Those are aeroplanes.

When he comes on to teaching plurals, the teacher is
faced with a whole complex of new problems. With
immigrant children at this stage it is not – as in teaching
British children – simply a case of the pupils learning
new spellings, remembering to change 'y' to '-ies', etc.;
but it is primarily a problem of teaching pupils to add
one of three different sounds to the singular forms they
already know: the sounds [s], [z] or [iz]. We do this
automatically in our own speech; the foreign child has
to learn to select the correct sound. Sometimes of course
with words like *man, woman, sheep*, he has to learn to

leave the word unchanged, or to change one or more of the vowel sounds (*man* → *men*, *woman* → *women* [wimin], etc.); these 'irregular' forms are best learnt a few at a time.

Words like *book*, or *coat*, ending in voiceless[1] consonants, add a voiceless [s] sound to form the plural: *books, coats, desks, hats.*

Words like *aeroplane*, that end with a voiced[1] sound, or like *door*, ending with a vowel sound, add a voiced 'buzzing' sound [z]: *aeroplanes, doors, chairs, cars, balls.*

Words like *box*, or *bus*, which end with sibilant sounds, add a whole new syllable, [iz]: *boxes, buses, dishes, coaches.*

Teachers should be aware of these differences. They should never attempt to teach these plural forms by way of rules or explanations, only by imitation; but they must keep their ears open all the time to the difficulties their pupils have in trying to imitate them, and they should devise games and drills which introduce plurals in as controlled a way as possible at first, so that the pupils are helped to learn to produce them automatically and correctly.

The teaching of plurals of nouns of course involves the teaching of other new items: *these* has to be substituted for *this* when identifying plurals, *those* for *that*, and *they* for *it*; the indefinite article has to be omitted ('zero' plural) – i.e.

This is a book.
These are books.

– and the pupils have to learn to use *are* for *is*. This, again, should all be achieved by imitation, not by explanation.

Plurals can be practised first in imperative drills, while numerals are revised at the same time. The teacher can ask individual children to bring things:

[1] See Chapter 3, p. 119 ff.

Give me three crayons.
Bring me two books.

Children can then take the place of the teacher, who must make sure all the time that they use the correct forms. (At this stage numerals and colours or numerals and adjectives can be combined with the plural forms of nouns, e.g. *Bring me four red balls, Give me three blue counters,* etc. (See below, next step.)

Similar procedures, based on those used for teaching Steps 1 to 9, can be gone through to practise the plural versions of those introductory structures. For instance, to practise Step 1, each child can be given some pencils or crayons. Holding up one pencil at a time, the teacher can say: *This is a pencil, and this is a pencil. These are pencils. They are my pencils* . . . Children repeat these sequences working in *my, your, his, Ali's,* etc., so that plural forms are eventually used in all the patterns so far dealt with; i.e.

(1) These are pencils. Those are crayons.
(2) These are my books.
(3) These are Ali's books.
(4) What are those? They are lorries. (They're . . .)
(5) Are these lorries? Yes, they are. No, they aren't.
(6) These are red pencils. Those are blue crayons.
(7) My books are on my desk. My shoes are on the floor. (Where are . . .?)
(8) Are these pencils or crayons? Are they blue crayons or red crayons?
(9) The boys are here. The books are on the desk. (Plural definite article.)
(10) Ali and Rashid are here. (Where are . . .?)

('Compound subjects' like that in (10) do not properly come in this unit of grammar. They are mentioned here in case teachers take it for granted that their pupils will make the necessary transference themselves and use the plural verb *are* automatically with a compound subject such as *Ali and Rashid*. They will not necessarily see the relation of this compound subject to forms like '*They* are here', or '*My books* are here', and this item will have to be carefully practised and manœuvred into the lesson by the teacher.)

Within the above examples the possibilities for error are very great; but it cannot be over-emphasized that too much correction, too much insistence on getting everything right all at once, can easily do more harm than good. Mastering plural forms of nouns and verbs is a big step and will have to go on being worked at throughout the term.

Once pupils are confident in their use of the above forms, the negatives should of course be practised, again using the elided form *aren't*, e.g.

These aren't my pencils.
The books aren't in the cupboard.
Ali and Rashid aren't here.

STEP 16
MORE ADJECTIVAL USES
This house is red . . .
a pretty little house . . . a big black cat
pretty   heavy   full   empty   straight   grey   brown   orange . . .

While the teacher concentrates on the above area of language in his formal teaching, he should also think about enlivening his work while he does so, and should consider, as always, the natural needs of the pupils. Interest, fresh stimulus, and the enlargement of experience are always necessary. One thing that it is important to pay attention to is the constant need children have to find words for expressing their awareness of their surroundings, and especially for developing their sensory perception at the same time. For this reason it is a good idea to introduce more adjectives and colours, not of course indiscriminately but related always to things and people at hand, to the pupils' activities in school and at home, and to the language they will hear in the playground. Teachers will best be able to select these new words themselves as they get to know their pupils.

It should be noticed that in this scheme of work adjectives were first introduced in one pattern only, *This is a red house*, and after that in the final position after *be* (predicatively). This present stage would be the moment to provide occasion for other predicative uses:

This house is red.
Rashid's coat is small.

and the teacher should see that he gradually introduces other adjective patterns, such as those combined with numerals (suggested in the Step above), and then combinations of adjectives used together, such as, *pretty little*, *big black*, etc:

This is a pretty little house.
Draw a big black cat.

The teacher should be aware of the new complications that this may involve him in, namely, the order of adjectives when used in series. Pupils will best learn to use them in the right order if they are not taught too many adjectives at a time and not encouraged to use too many together at a time.

SUMMARY OF STAGE III (Steps 15–16)

Structure

These Those They	aren't are	pencils my books red crayons Ali's books
Ali and Rashid		boys

What are	these? those?

c

Are	these those	lorries?

Yes, they are
No, they aren't

The pens My books	are aren't	on the table in my desk
Ali and Rashid		here

Where are	the books? Ali and Rashid?

Are	these they	pencils or crayons? blue crayons or red crayons? etc.

Vocabulary
these, those, they
are (pl.)
house, cat . . .
pretty, heavy, full, empty, straight, grey, brown, orange . . .
Note. While consolidating plural forms of nouns, pronouns, etc., it
would be advisable not to introduce many new nouns as
vocabulary items.

STAGE IV

STEP 17
PLURAL PRONOUNS
We are . . . They are . . . You are . . .
These plural subject pronouns will have been used by
the teacher often enough before now, unavoidably, and
he should at this point begin to encourage the class to
use them. If the class is arranged in groups, this will
make practice of the plural pronouns easier: e.g.

We are group one.
They are group two.
You are group three.
Are you group one or group three?

Again, it is easy to introduce the elided forms here; when unelided forms are used, *are* should be pronounced lightly with the weak vowel [ə]; the transition from *we are* to *we're*, etc., is made almost automatically.

all both

All and *both* will be found useful here, the latter especially to emphasize the plural of *you*. It is best to use *all* in one position only at first (*you all*, not *all of you*):

You are both in this group
They are all in that group.

open shut

They can be easily practised with the opening and shutting of eyes, hands, books, windows, etc.

Open your eyes. Are they open or shut?
They are open.

Are we . . .? etc. No, we aren't. We aren't boys.

In practising the interrogative and negative of these forms of the plural, it is obviously best to take the 3rd-person form first:

Are they Italian girls? Yes, they are.
Are those boys from India? No, they aren't.

and then to move on to the 1st and 2nd persons:

Are we in the classroom. Yes, we are.
Are you in group one? No, we aren't.

Again, the negative short answers need special care, and the teacher should not switch from one form to another (i.e. from *No, we aren't* to *No, we are not*). Negative long forms must also be practised as in Step 15 (*They aren't here, We aren't in group one*, etc.).

STEP 18

PRESENT CONTINUOUS TENSE[1]

I'm drawing. He is tracing. You are talking. We are playing. They are working. Farida is crying.

jumping   running   skipping   walking   reading   fighting

If many verbs have been introduced in imperative drills, work in P.E., etc., these together with the forms of the verb *be* which have already been practised, lead naturally to the teaching of the present continuous tense of verbs.

Apart from the fact that it presents fewer learning problems than the simple present tense (the tense used in many first readers: *I run, he jumps*, etc.), the present continuous is a 'better' tense to teach first since it can be combined very easily with action words, and with activities that the children can perform in the classroom and find interesting to talk about. Physical action makes the work interesting to the participants, and with the additional possibilities of mime and acting games, this section of language teaching can be made thoroughly enjoyable.

Some teachers prefer to practise this tense at first with intransitive verbs only, since this makes for a shorter utterance (there being no direct object) and full attention can then be given to getting the pronoun-verb agreement and the -ing form of the verb correctly pronounced. Other teachers have found that children seem to manage transitive verbs with direct objects more easily, and as many of these (e.g. *Clean the board*) will have been heard in imperatives, the teacher may prefer to base his first work on these:

Clean the board. – I'm cleaning the board.
Touch your toes. – I'm touching my toes.

One popular procedure is for the teacher, once he has

---

[1] Also known as 'present progressive'. It often denotes an action which is going on at the time of speaking, an activity in progress, and so is most useful in classes where there is plenty of activity and movement.

given plenty of examples himself, to give a series of instructions to pupils while they say what they are doing, e.g.

TEACHER: Go to the cupboard.
PUPIL: I'm going to the cupboard.
TEACHER: Open the door.
PUPIL: I'm opening the door.
TEACHER: Take a book.
PUPIL: I'm taking a book . . .

Variations on this 'action chain' can be played, for instance with the class giving a kind of commentary so that 3rd person forms are practised:

TEACHER: Go to the cupboard.
PUPIL: I'm going to the cupboard.
CLASS: He's going to the cupboard, etc.

and later with groups of twos and threes performing the actions (to introduce *we*, etc.), with other groups then commenting on them (to introduce *they*).
All and *both* can again be used with plural forms of the verb (*We are all sitting, You are both talking*), and compound subjects with plural verbs should also be practised (*Ali and Rashid are talking*). It will be useful to introduce the adverb *now* at this point too:

now

Now I'm opening the book. Now I'm reading the book.

QUESTIONS
What are you doing? etc.

The teacher will soon find he needs to use the question *What are you doing?* (*What is he doing?*, etc.), and by imitation the pupils can learn to ask this of one another. *Yes/No* and alternative questions can follow, and, at a later stage again, the negative forms. These can all be practised through guessing games, e.g. by letting the class guess what the man in a picture is doing, or what actions are being mimed by one or more of their number. The accurate use of questions

Is he writing?
Is she drawing?
Are you singing?

depends on accuracy in the question forms of the verb
be, as also do the negative forms

He isn't writing.
They aren't drawing.
   etc.

and this is why thorough practice of these is necessary
before pupils come on to this step.

Other questions can be practised using the present
continuous in guessing games, or in straightforward
questioning about pictures, blackboard drawings, etc.

What is the boy reading?
Where is the girl sitting?

Who?

It will also be found useful to introduce and teach *who?*
at this stage; it can be used in many of the structures so
far taught, and is particularly helpful in questioning
about pictures and cutouts:

Who is sitting near the door?
Who is riding a bicycle?
Who is reading a book?
Who are marching along the road?

Although it is fairly easy to devise procedures for
practising this tense with various verbs, the teacher
should also ensure that there is constant natural
individual practice of it all through the day. Thus, when
the children are engaged in free activities, he can question them as he goes round the room – *What are you
doing? What is Ali doing?* – and prompt the right answers
until they are given easily and correctly; in similar
work with pictures or blackboard drawings, he can
increase the range of verbs used in this way; mime and
acting games can follow.

In all of this work, alternative questions will be found useful to 'prompt' the right answer:

Look at this boy. What is he doing? – He is smiling.
Now look at this girl. What is she doing? Is she smiling or crying? – She is crying.

The teacher should not underestimate the learning load that all this represents to the average pupil, and it will pay him to consider carefully which verbs he is going to use at this stage. Often – as with nouns and other vocabulary items – the choice will be imposed upon him by the spontaneous questions of his pupils, or by the practical demands of school life. At this stage, for instance, it will begin to be possible to talk about the weather:

It is raining.
The sun is shining.

and pupils can make and use a weatherboard.
Amongst the first verbs used will be those that are closely linked with 'adverb particles': *sit down, stand up, put . . . on, take . . . off.* Some of these when used with direct objects present difficulties of word order (e.g. *Put on your coat, Put your coat on, Put it on,* but not *Put on it*); but teachers often create difficulties for themselves by thinking of these verbs as *verb root + particle,* as if these were two vocabulary items instead of one *compound* item. Such verbs here, and certainly later when many more will be met with (*give in, give up, change over*), should be presented always as single items and learnt as single new units, not as variations on the one basic unit represented by the verb root.

STEP 19
OBJECT PRONOUNS: 'IT', 'ONE', 'MINE'.
    Take it.   Look at it.   Touch it.
    As mentioned earlier (Step 5), *it* as object pronoun will

have been heard and probably picked up automatically by the quicker pupils and used in their own speech.

Once the present continuous tense has been introduced, the teacher may devote a little extra attention to this pronoun (i.e. well in advance of other object pronouns *him*, *her*, etc.) and see that there are plenty of opportunities for practising it.

Look at the picture, Ali. Is he looking at it or is he touching it?

What are you doing? – I'm looking at it.

this one . . . that one . . . the small one (. . . the green ones)

This is also an opportune moment for paying attention to other pronouns which cannot be long avoided in day-to-day English. The pronoun *one* will be found to be almost indispensable:

Yes, this one. That's right . . .

Take that one.

Give him the green ones.

Which is Ali's? The small one or the big one?

The teacher may be content at this stage with the pupils' passive knowledge of these – and should of course even avoid them if at any time they seem to cause confusion (the pronoun *one* being confused with the numeral *one*, for instance, or the plural *ones* causing confusion elsewhere) – but there will be opportune moments for practising them, e.g. in giving out equipment, in letting children choose free activities and games (counters, ludo, etc.), talking about cutouts and drawings done by the children in other periods:

Which one is Ali's?

Ali's is the green one.

Rashid's is the second one.

 etc.

(It's mine.)

It is suggested that the personal possessive pronouns

(*mine, yours, his, hers,* etc.) should not be taught formally too early. One of the major faults in language teaching lies in teachers' practising similar constructions because they seem 'to go together' ('It is *your* book – 'It is *yours*') and because this seems to be the natural thing to do. Natural as it may be for the teacher, it often results in the pupils' having an imperfect grasp of both items, the similarity between them leading to confusion and interference. It would often be better to establish one form at a time, soundly and firmly, and to go on to the other after a reasonable interval. Thus here we suggest that the possessive pronouns should *not* be formally taught and practised at this stage, so soon after the possessive adjectives (in this scheme of work they are not dealt with till Step 31). Of these pronouns, however, in practice *mine* will often be found to be in use in the give and take of the classroom. In which case the teacher should see in passing that it is correctly used (e.g. that it does not get used in 'It is mine book'), and he may choose to give opportunities for it to occur in individual conversations with pupils.

STEP 20
NEGATIVE IMPERATIVES (PROHIBITIONS)
Don't go.   Don't run.

Finally, probably long before this stage is reached, the pupils will have become familiar with the negative imperative form: *Don't go, Don't do that,* etc. They should be made to practise these forms themselves in the course of imperative drills (extensions of Step 1), and at this stage this can be usefully combined with practice of object pronouns, especially *it*:

Go to the door. Don't touch it.
Run to the window. Don't go by the cupboard.
Get out the balls. Give me one. Don't throw it.

Note on Negative Questions: It will be found that many language courses which introduce the affirmative and negative verb forms in statements

He is a tall boy.
He isn't a tall boy.

also introduce them both in questions:

Is he a tall boy?
Isn't he a tall boy?

If teachers observe their own conversation, they will notice that in fact they use negative questions very idiomatically throughout the day:

Isn't it cold?
Haven't you done your homework?
Didn't you know you had to . . .?

It is suggested here that these negative question forms should not be deliberately taught in an elementary English course as they are very likely to lead to considerable difficulty and confusion for most pupils. If pupils naturally assimilate and copy some correct usages, they can be encouraged, but teachers should not feel that they should make a formal teaching point of them simply for the sake of grammatical completeness. In more advanced work much practice in this area of grammar will be necessary and exercises in some of the books listed in the bibliography (Section III, p. 244) should be consulted.

SUMMARY OF STAGE IV (Steps 17–20)

Structure

We You They	are 're aren't	(all) (both)	girls group one Italian

Are	we you they	group one? etc.

Yes, No,	we you they	are aren't

I	am 'm am not	walking
We You They	are 're aren't	walking to the door
He She Ali The man	is 's isn't	writing a letter

What	am	I	reading? doing?
	are	we you they	
Where	is	he she	sitting?

Who	is are	marching?

Am	I	
Are	we you they	listening? listening or talking?
Is	he she Ali the man	

Take Touch Look at	it the small one this one
Don't touch Don't throw	the green ones

Vocabulary

we, you (pl.), they

all, both

one, (ones), it (obj. pronoun), (mine)

who

to, from, near

now

(Vbs.) draw, trace, talk, play, work, write, jump, run, skip, walk, fight, take, clean, sit, cry, smile, shine, rain, open, shut, sing, touch . . .

bicycle, road . . .

open, shut (adj.) . . .

STAGE V

STEP 21

INTRODUCTORY 'THERE'

There is . . .   There are . . .

When working within a limited range of structure and vocabulary it is often easy to slip into unnatural English. In the effort to practise all the possible uses of the structural items so far taught, pupils may in fact be called upon to make statements such as 'A lorry is in the street', 'A pen and a pencil are on my desk', which, though grammatically correct English and likely to occur within a certain context, would not in fact be used in the simple descriptive style of English we are at this stage expecting the pupils to reproduce. In these examples, which merely state what can be observed, it would be much more natural to use the introductory phrase *there is* or *there are* (*There is a lorry in the street*, etc.).

It is impossible to say at what stage precisely *there is/are* should be introduced, but certainly it cannot be left too long, because as the pupils get a wider range of words for dealing with their environment, they will in fact need to make more and more simple descriptive statements.

Whenever the teacher chooses to teach this item, he will probably come up against confusion with *they* and *they are*, as the expressions sound fairly similar. Only patience and careful pronunciation will get the pupils over this hurdle. Again, it is essential that the teacher should not exaggerate his pronunciation of *there* in his efforts to make his pupils hear it more clearly.

It can be introduced through simple statements of what can be seen in the classroom:

There are three books on my desk.
There is a cat by Ali's chair.
There are three girls in group one.
There are a box, a book, and a pen . . . on the tray.

Numerals should be used with plurals at first, to avoid difficulties over *some/any/no*, etc., and the teacher may find it best to introduce the question *How many . . . are there?* but to postpone questions beginning with *Is there . . .?* and *Are there . . .?* for a while, together with the negatives *There isn't . . .* and *There aren't . . .*

How many . . . are there?   . . . only   . . . altogether

The word *altogether* will come in naturally here, possibly contrasted with *only*:

There are two counters in this box and three counters in this box. How many are there altogether?
. . . No, there are only five.
There is only one counter in my hand.

(*Altogether* and *only* will also be practised with *have* and *has* in Step 24 below.)
inch   foot   penny   shilling . . . Sunday   Monday etc. . . .
half   quarter . . .

Obviously number work gives most scope for practice of this kind, and work with rulers and measuring equipment, and with simple money (*How many pennies are there in a shilling?*, etc.) will fit in well here. *Half* and *a quarter* will soon be needed in later stages of telling the time, and could be introduced about now, especially in conjunction with numbers (e.g. *5 is half of 10, 2 is a quarter of 8*).

The days of the week might also be conveniently practised here (*There are seven days in a week . . .*).

What is/are there . . .?

Questions with *What* (*What is there . . .? What are there . . .?*) will be found most useful for work with pictures.

STEP 22

COUNTABLE AND UNCOUNTABLE NOUNS; 'SOME'/'ANY'

(a) some

It will soon be found necessary to deal with a problem avoided so far, the use of *some*, and the way it 'changes' to *any* in certain positions.

The transition from *There are three . . .* to *There are some . . .* is not difficult. It can best be practised by the teacher indicating collections of articles (e.g. milk bottles in a crate, pencils in a tin, beads, etc.), where it is obvious that the exact number of each kind of article cannot be stated off-hand but would have to be obtained by counting. In this situation, *some* is the natural word to use and can then be extended to include more and varied situations, such as what is seen through the classroom window or in a picture: *There are some clouds in the sky . . . boys in the playground . . . boxes on that lorry*, etc.

Some will probably have been used quite often by the teacher – *Give out some paper, Who wants some paint?* – and it is likely that in certain formulas (i.e. structures operated without an awareness of the grammatical patterns contained in them) the pupils will already have learnt to use it with certain words (*Can I have some paper, please? . . . some crayons, please? . . . some plasticine, please?*).

It will be as well for the teacher to consider at this stage the ways in which *some* and *any* are used with nouns. In learning English as a second language, the classification of nouns into the categories given in old grammar books – 'abstract', 'proper', 'common', etc. – is of comparatively little importance. What is much more important is whether the noun names something 'countable' or not. We can count pens, pencils, boys, bats, etc., and the nouns which name them – 'countable' nouns – can be used with numerals and usually have a plural form ending in *-s*. But in the general sense we cannot count substances like wood, iron, rice, or milk (or, if we do, we are implying some additional concept like 'kinds of', 'different species of'), and the nouns naming them are not ordinarily used with the indefinite article, with numerals, in a plural form or with a plural verb. Foreign learners may misuse these 'uncountable' nouns by analogy with 'countable' ones and say such things as 'I want two milks', 'This is a rice', 'These are moneys', 'This is an ink', etc.

Special attention must be paid to these uncountable nouns by the teacher of immigrants, because sooner or later mistakes will arise in their use of them. The teacher should always be on the watch for the occurrence of errors here and may take opportunities to drill in correct habits by the implicit contrast in pairs of countables and uncountables: e.g.

This is a glass. This is water.
These are glasses. This is water.
These are pens. This is ink.
There are some glasses on the table.
There is some ink in the glasses.
There are some pens on the desk.
There is some ink near the pens.

a lot of a little a few a pound half a pound a pint a packet of a piece of a cup of . . . . . . empty full . . .

It will be useful here to introduce *a lot of*, *a little*, and *a few*, and also some expressions of quantity with which to measure uncountables, such as *a pound*, *a half a pound*, *a pint*, *a piece of . . .*, *a cup of . . .*, *a packet of . . .*, etc. *Full* and *empty* will also be found useful at this stage:

Is the cup full or empty? – It's full.
What is there in the glass? – There is some rice in the glass. There is a lot of rice in the glass.
The glass is full, (but) the packet is empty.

It is obvious that activities based on shopping, involving money, make-believe substances such as butter, tea, rice, etc., and weights, give good opportunities for practice of these items, as well as fitting in with the general need to do work on weights, measures, money, etc.

(b) any

Obviously the rate of progress of a class in mastering the above material – as distinct from merely using parts of it ('Some paper, please') in routine classroom formulas – can only be estimated by the teacher, and confusion will result from trying to pile too many things on at one stage. Harm can often be done by introducing contrastive forms even though they seem to 'go together', as suggested above. With the use of *some*, the teacher will be on safe ground as long as he does not use interrogative and negative sentence patterns and for this reason it was suggested earlier that they should be postponed for a while. But sooner or later he will be obliged to introduce them, and will then need to establish the correct use of *any*:

Is there any ink?
Are there any pencils in the box?
There isn't any ink in the bottle.
There aren't any pencils in the box.

These patterns should all be thoroughly drilled. The other statement of the negative form, using *no* – *There is no ink in the bottle, There are no pencils in the box* – is better reserved for a later stage still.

Again, examples like the above will be used incidentally throughout the day (e.g. the teacher asking for chalk, the children demanding paper or water for painting, and so on), and by patient correction of misused forms and repetition of correct ones, the teacher must try to establish the right usage.

(c) . . . made of . . .

iron   wood   cotton   steel   . . .

The age of the pupils and the rate at which they progress will determine the order of the presentation of material. With older children it might be as well to go on here to other uncountable nouns such as *iron*, *wood*, *cotton*, etc., and to introduce the question and answer:

What is this made of?
It's made of ——

Collections of objects grouped according to the substance they are made of can be organized and put on display in the classroom, and there is obvious scope for guessing games.

STEP 23
PLURAL POSSESSIVE ADJECTIVES
your   their   our

Your will have been heard very often in the classroom, used probably with the singular meaning by the children themselves, and with the plural meaning by the teacher:

Put up your hands,
Touch your heads.
Put your things away now.

If children have taken part in giving commands in imperative drills, they have probably fallen into the way of using *your* with the plural meaning themselves. The teacher can now check that this is so, and teach *our* and *their*, e.g. by calling out groups of children with their possessions, collecting some of them in and demonstrating to the group:

These are your pens

to the class:

These are their pens

and, adding his own possessions to the collection:

These are our pens.

Gestures are of course, as ever, important for this kind of work, and the pupils should be led to copy the teacher's gestures when first using the possessive adjectives themselves.

Our can be used very often – *This is our school . . . our classroom . . .*, etc. – but it will be necessary to contrive situations and to use pictures to practise *their* naturally.

Whose . . . ?

The pupils should now get used to using the question *Whose —— is this?* or *Whose is this ——?* if this has not been taught earlier (e.g. as in Step 4). Answers can be encouraged to practise the possessive of proper names – *It is Farida's, It is Ali's* – since the final [s] or [z] is often forgotten and needs constant attention. 'Full' answers using the plural possessive adjectives should also be practised, but the teacher should not confuse them with the pronominal forms (*mine, yours, hers*, etc.) which have not yet been taught formally (but see Step 19 above).

The possessive adjective *its*, which has not yet been dealt with, will also have to be taught at some time, but not at the cost of confusion with *it's*, nor simply for the sake of completeness at this still elementary stage.

STEP 24

THE VERB 'HAVE'

**I have ten fingers.   He has two books on his desk.
Ali has a book in his bag.**

Many teachers believe it necessary to introduce the verb *have* early, perhaps because they themselves learnt it early in French or German. It is in fact quite easy to do without it for a time, and many other verbs may seem more vital (e.g. *can, want, must*). However, it is placed here in this scheme since it follows very naturally on the possessive adjectives which have now (all except *its*) been dealt with, and can also be used to consolidate *some* and *any*.

This is another point at which the teacher should stop and consider his own usage, the usage of the local children, and the kind of English he wants his immigrant pupils to speak. Is it best to teach his pupils:

Ali has a bicycle.
My sisters have new dresses.

when in fact it would be more natural to say *Ali's got a bicycle*, etc.? *Got* is still thought of as vulgar though in fact it is used unselfconsciously by most speakers in nine cases out of ten. On the other hand, in written English, which our pupils also have to use, it is for the most part avoided; and furthermore, there are occasions in informal spoken English when *has* and *have* without *got* are more acceptable:

The classroom has four walls.
A bird has two legs.

The teacher may choose to compromise and keep to *has/have* only at first, trying to use them as naturally as possible and not placing undue stress on them. They are, after all, much easier to master than the colloquial forms. But if the children introduce the *got* forms of their own accord, they should be left uncorrected unless they are completely out of place. The teacher must of course try to keep his own usage consistent in the classroom.

A fairly natural way in which *has* and *have* can first be presented is by some such procedure as:

This is a box. I have a box in my hand. What have I in my hand?
(You have a box in your hand . . .)

This kind of question and answer can easily be used as the basis for a set of guessing games, and can later be extended to introduce the third person singular form *has*:

What has he in his pocket?
(He has a . . .)
What has Farida in her bag?
(She has a . . .)

Has and *have* should also be practised with *some*:

Ali has some rice on his plate.
I have some chalk in my hand.
    etc.

Have you . . . ?   Has he . . . ?
Questions can be practised, again by way of guessing games:

Have you a pin in your hand?
Has he a penny?

and especially of course in shopping procedures, which can then be made to include the use of *any*:

Have you any rice?
Have you any eggs?

No, I haven't.   No, he hasn't.
The negative forms can be practised in similar situations:

I haven't any rice (but) I have some eggs.

and in short answers, *No, I haven't, No, he hasn't.*
Guessing games in groups or with the whole class (e.g. sending one pupil out to be 'it' while several objects are concealed around the class) can also be played to give practice in short answers.

SUMMARY OF STAGE V (Steps 21–24)

Structure

There	is isn't	a	lorry in the street
	are	some two	boys in the playground
	aren't	any	

Is	there	a pen	in the box?
Are		five pens any	

What	is are	there	in the box? on the table?

How many	pens books	are there . . .?

The desk My pen It	is	made of	wood steel
They	are		

These (They)	are	our your (pl.) their	pens
This (It)	is		school

Whose	book	is	this? it?
	pens	are	these? those? they?

I You We They	have	a	pen
		some	money
He She Ali	has	some two	eggs

Have	I you we they	a	pen?
		any	money?
Has	he she Ali	two	eggs?

Yes	I you we they	have
	he she	has
No	I, etc.	haven't
	he, etc.	hasn't

Vocabulary
there (introd.)
some, any
how many?
only, altogether
a lot of, a little, a few
your (pl.), their, our

whose
have, has (got)
(but)
inch, foot, penny, shilling, pound, pint, piece (of), packet (of),
half, quarter . . .
Sunday, Monday, etc. . . .
money, ink, rice, butter, tea, water, wood, steel, iron, cotton . .
(a) glass, bottle, egg, bird, dress, dog . . .
full, empty, made of . . .

STAGE VI

STEP 25
ORDINALS
First, second, third, etc.

By this time numerals beyond 12 will have been used
to a greater or smaller extent, depending very much on
how much number work is done with the immigrants.
Immigrant pupils often prove to be excellent at arith-
metic and may in consequence master numerals very
quickly.

In normal classroom routine, some of the ordinals will
have been used – *Who's first? You are second. This group
is third*, etc. – and these and others, up to about *twelfth*
can be practised here.

Next   last   before   after . . . . . .
January   February, etc.

Days of the week, months, and any other series so far
learnt can be used to practise ordinals, e.g. *What is the
fourth day of the week? Is Thursday the third or the fifth day of
the week?* etc. (But in passing it should be pointed out
that not all immigrant pupils will naturally understand
the concept of days – weeks – months – seasons, etc.,
and may need to be helped over more than just the
learning of their names.) *Next* and *last* can also be introduced here, and the words *before* and *after*:

Monday is after Sunday. Tuesday is before Wednesday.

today   tomorrow

It is also time to introduce telling the date, and the words *today* and *tomorrow* can be used in conjunction with this. Ordinals up to *thirty-first* will then have to be practised to deal with all dates:

Tomorrow is the thirtieth of April.
Today is the twenty-ninth of April.

STEP 26
TELLING THE TIME (2)

It's half past . . .   It's a quarter to . . .   It's a quarter past . . .

With many classes it will also be opportune now to go into more details of telling the time. It will help if *at* and *between* have been introduced earlier, so that the teacher can ask questions about the position of the hands of the clock:

Where is the long hand now?
It's at three.
Where is the short hand now?
It's between six and seven.
Then it's a quarter past six. What is the time?
It's a quarter past six.

This material should be kept in use by the teacher asking the time on occasions throughout the day and asking casual questions such as

Are you thirsty? Perhaps[1] it's time for milk.
What is the time, Ali? . . . Then it's time for milk.

(Also 'time for play', 'time for dinner', 'time to go home', etc.)

---

[1] The class will not be expected to learn usages such as *then* and *perhaps* here but the teacher should use such words naturally where the context and the intonation make the meaning perfectly clear to the pupils.

STEP 27
CAN/CAN'T

Can you see the board? I can't. He can. I can see Ali.

Can and *can't* will need to be used from early days. Note: *cannot* is rarely used in spoken English and could be omitted here at first.

Can and *can't* are relatively easy and plenty of situations occur throughout the day in which they can be naturally practised in context. It is probably best if, to start with, the pupils are encouraged to give responses in which the short forms are used, since in this way the two forms are clearly contrasted. Insist on the final [t] being clearly heard in the negative. The teacher can ask questions which involve possible or impossible tasks, such as

Can you lift the cupboard? (No, I can't.)
Can you write your name?
Can you drive a bus?

The long form, *I can see . . .*, can be practised in descriptions of pictures. Here the teacher should be careful to get the pupils to use the natural rhythm of English speech and to produce the unstressed form of *can* [kn] or [kən].

too

The introduction of *too* at this stage is also useful to allow further elaboration in the procedure suggested above:

Can you lift the cupboard?
No, I can't.
Why not?
It's too big/heavy/etc.

(why?) (why not?)

It may be too early to expect children to use *because* clauses, but there is no harm in introducing *why?* and *why not?* in simple situations such as this, where, again, the context makes the meaning clear.

If *too* is introduced here, it will be found that many pupils are likely to confuse it with *very*. To avoid this, the situations in which *too* is used must be ones in which there is a very obvious notion of excess. This can be expressed quite clearly within the range of the structural patterns so far taught (without, for instance, going as far as to teach 'It's *too* heavy *for me to* lift'), e.g.

The table is very heavy, but Ali can lift it.
Ali is very strong.
The bookcase is too heavy. Ali can't lift it because it's too heavy. And *I* can't lift it; it's too heavy.

At this stage the teacher might also consider what his own (and local) usage is in respect of *Can I have . . .?* as a form of request. We often insist on teaching British children to say *May I . . .?* while they are at school, whereas in fact natural usage out of school is nearly all on the side of *can*. The pupils should by now be able to approach their teacher with requests (e.g. for books, for paper, etc.), and he must be clear in his own mind as to how they are to do this. The same point of usage occurs in formulas like *Please may (can) I leave the room?* which will also be used from the very first stages.

STEP 28
COMPARISON

Ali is bigger than Rashid.

The growing use of adjectives in the language practised up to now, and the introduction of *too* in the above step, should have paved the way for the introduction of the idea of comparison. The exact point at which this can usefully be introduced may well depend on the age of the pupils: to many it is an interesting concept, and they will take great delight in the manipulation of objects and language which involve it. Very young children may not yet be ready for it, while older ones may learn and then dismiss it rather easily and quickly.

If the teacher decides to introduce it here, he should

have a clear idea of these limitations, and also of the limitations he should impose on himself. It is easy, for instance, to fall into the old textbook routine of 'good – better – best', and think that comparatives should be accompanied by superlatives, though this would mean the as yet unnecessary addition to the learning load of new forms of words with the accompanying new concepts. Superlatives in fact are best dealt with in separate stages. It is also necessary to think out which adjectives are best used at first. Although *good* and *better* will probably have been used as separate items when commending pupils for doing different things well, it would probably be as well to leave them out here, together with other 'irregular' comparisons, and to take only adjectives which follow a simple pattern like *big/bigger*, *small/smaller*, *heavy/heavier*, etc.

One of the difficulties in teaching comparatives is in the terms of reference: if the teacher holds objects in his hands or points to pictures and says 'This house is bigger than this house' he will find that the use of *this* causes a certain amount of linguistic or even physical confusion: pupils either have to point and substitute *that* for *this*, or must come out individually and reproduce the situation from the teacher's point of view. Certain vaguenesses can creep into these procedures and it would be better, for instance, to make comparisons about pupils, or people, mentioning them by name in referring to what should be clearly discernible differences between them in the comparison, e.g.

Ali is tall. He is very tall. Ali is taller than Rashid.

If objects are then used to demonstrate other comparisons, they too should be clearly differentiated, e.g. by different colours or by different owners:

Here are two balls. The blue ball is very big. It's bigger than the white ball.
Look at Antonio's lorry. It's bigger than Ali's car.

(Sequences like these can be adjusted to the procedures in Step 27: *I can't lift the cupboard. It's too big. I can lift the chair. The chair is smaller than the cupboard.*)

a lot   a little

Adverbial expressions can also be combined in this type of sentence: *It's a lot smaller than . . . Ali is a little bigger than . . .*

Practice on comparatives, using a limited range of adjectives, should be kept up through different activities, and should also be introduced in interrogative and negative forms:

Is Ali bigger than Rashid?
Is Rashid bigger or smaller than Ali?
Is the box bigger than the cupboard?
It isn't bigger; it's smaller.
    etc.

STEP 29
COMPARISON OF EQUALITY

as . . . as

Grammatically there is no reason why this form should come before or after the introduction of the comparative form of adjectives, though in practice it will be found useful to introduce it near it, in situations which develop those used in the previous step, e.g.

PUPIL: Ali is bigger than Yusuf.
TEACHER: No, Ali isn't bigger than Yusuf; and he isn't smaller than Yusuf. He is as big as Yusuf. (*They are the same size.*)

Or in reverse:

Antonio isn't as tall as Ali. He is shorter than Ali.

Similarly, these forms can be introduced in sequences with *can* and *can't,* and should be used incidentally as opportunities arise.

STEP 30

OBJECT PRONOUNS

it me/you him/her us/them

It was suggested at Step 19 that the pronoun *it*, in object position, should be formally practised. Other pronouns, such as *me*, and to a smaller extent *him*, *her* and *them*, will also have been heard in object positions (*Give me your drawings, Put them down, Tell them again, Give her the box . . .*). By association and through context there should have been little or no difficulty over meaning here (*Put your pencils down → Put them down*), and the pupils may have adopted some of these uses correctly into their own speech. They will thus have been building up a recognition of object pronoun forms *while not being expected to use them*: nouns and not pronouns will mostly have occurred as direct objects of verbs.

This situation, in which there is a passive response to certain forms as distinct from active use of the same forms, is of course a feature of all language work, in the mother tongue as well as in second-language learning. But it is a specially significant feature of the language-learning situation discussed in this book; the teachers' deepest sensitivity is called on to respond to it and to use it to the best advantage in the course of his teaching.

Pronouns become increasingly useful from now on, and not only useful but necessary if the English used in the classroom is to sound spontaneous and natural. The teacher should take every opportunity to see that they are practised and used correctly. By listing them all together in this Step, it is not implied that the teacher should try to teach them all formally at one and the same time. This is merely pointing to a teaching opportunity which the teacher must interpret for himself according to the needs of his pupils. His awareness of the different pronouns and their uses must combine with his response to the pupils' needs.

The teacher should see that there are opportunities for

practising these pronouns using material with which pupils are familiar, e.g. in imperative drills:

Look at me. Give me two pens. Tell me your name.

Go to Anil. Tell him your name. Give him this book.

Take these pens to the cupboard. Put them in the black box. Now take them out again.

Note. You, as it is unchanged in subject and object form, causes little difficulty and needs less attention than the other pronouns. *Us* can hardly be practised by individuals and there are few verbs (e.g. *look at, point at, smile at, wave to*) with which it is appropriate to use it at this stage. It would be best to let the class use it in chorus or in groups at intervals in between the other types of drill:

Stop a minute, Anil. Look at us.

What is he doing, children? – He is looking at us.

STEP 31

POSSESSIVE PRONOUNS

mine/yours his/hers ours/theirs

It will be found that, as with object pronouns in the step above, some learning of personal possessive pronouns will already have taken place, although the teacher may never have actually taught them (see above, Step 19). Possession is a strong instinct, even over temporary possessions which are in the child's hands only for the length of a lesson, and *It's mine* comes early into use without much prompting.

The other possessive pronouns should now be taught. They can be practised in close connection with the possessive form of proper names – *Malik's, Ali's, Farooz's* – where the teacher will always have to be on the lookout for the tendency to drop the final sound [s], [z] or [iz]:

Is this my pen or Ali's pen? – It's Ali's pen.

leading to

It's Ali's. It's his.

etc.

Whose . . . ?

Questions with *Whose?* can again be used when giving out books, looking at drawings, etc. The collecting of possessions and then their redistribution by one pupil, can also be the occasion for practising these pronouns. Use of groups can involve practice of *theirs, ours* and *yours* (pl.), but again, these words will all be best learnt by being used carefully whenever real situations allow. The teacher, by pretending forgetfulness – *This is yours. No, it isn't; it's theirs* – can help to ensure that plenty of such situations arise.

Just as earlier (Step 19) the teacher was advised to guard against pupils' saying 'It is mine book', so now he must see that they do not confuse any of the other personal pronouns with possessive adjectives, producing forms such as 'It's hers dress', 'It's yours bag', etc.

This one   that one   the next one

One, introduced earlier as an object pronoun, can also be utilized here, the teacher pointing, for instance, to each drawing in turn along a row hung on the wall:

This drawing is Ali's. This one is his and that one is yours. Whose is the next one?

STEP 32

INTRODUCTION TO SIMPLE PRESENT TENSE[1]

I want   you want

By now the pupils should have considerable control of the present continuous tense of a wide range of everyday verbs. New verbs that fit into the known patterns should be introduced as necessary through work in English and in activities, especially P.E. and handwork.

There are some English verbs which are not normally used in a present continuous tense, and some of these are among the most common in the early speech of children,

[1] Also known as the present habitual tense; see Step 34 below.

especially the verbs *want* and *like*. Although through sheer necessity these may already have been heard in the classroom, the teacher could now base some formal teaching on them so that the basic patterns of usage sink in before other verbs are introduced that follow similar patterns. This is a good moment for the teacher to consider the commonly used simple present tense, so that he sees what a learning load this represents for foreign children.

The main considerations are:

(1) The [s], [z] or [iz] sound in the third person singular: *he wants, he watches*, etc.

(2) The negative, which is formed by using a completely different verb as an 'auxiliary': *I don't want, he doesn't want*, etc. (Contrast with this the simple addition of *not* (or *n't*) that performs the same function in the present continuous tense: *I am not running*, etc.)

(3) The interrogative, like the negative, enlists the use of *do, does*: *Do I want? Does he want?*

(4) Short answers to questions in this tense again take up the *do/does* forms: *Does he want . . .? Yes, he does/ No, he doesn't.*

The first three of these points certainly cause difficulty for the learner, and it is because of this, amongst other reasons, that the present simple tense is not used as the introductory tense in most English language teaching today. Its presence on the first pages of many reading primers used in infant classes in English schools is also one of the reasons why such books are often unsuitable as early reading matter for foreign learners.

These difficulties in the simple present tense also mean that the teacher must proceed slowly when teaching it. In the first term or so, he need not go beyond the two verbs *want* and *like*, and need not even try to teach all the uses of each verb at first.

It is simple, for instance, to avoid the third person

singular form (*he wants*) altogether for a time, and to use these verbs only in the first and second singular forms: *What do you want? – I want some plasticine*, etc. A little later, situations may be devised in which the 3rd person forms are practised:

TEACHER: What do you want, Farida?
PUPIL: Some paper. I want some paper, please.
TEACHER: Listen, Ali. What does Farida want?
She wants . . .

The teacher should prompt pupils in their answers at first, so that they learn to imitate the final [s] sound and then begin to use it automatically themselves.

It should be noticed that questions in the third person are quite likely to evoke wrong answers – *What does he want? – He want to go out –* because pupils often echo the form of the verb heard in the question, and this of course lacks the final [s]. The teacher must proceed slowly and patiently, and again has good reason for confining questions to 1st and 2nd person forms only at first. The negative, and different interrogative patterns, should only be introduced very gradually.

I like   he likes

Like can be practised with foods and fruits, etc., and this is again a good place to practise adverbials such as *very much, a little*:

I like potatoes very much. Do you? – No, I don't/Yes, I do.
What does Ahmad like? Does he like rice or potatoes?

Both *like* and *want* can be used with infinitive patterns:

I want to draw. I want to play with plasticine.
I like to play. I like to eat rice.

It would be best to avoid the other use of *like* + gerund at this stage (*I like singing*) to avoid confusion of forms.

D

STEP 33

SUPERLATIVES

Both *want* and *like* provide verbal contexts in which superlatives can naturally be used, and this would be a good moment to introduce some of them such as *smallest, biggest, heaviest, thinnest*, etc.

It is still best not to introduce the three-fold pattern *small–smaller–smallest* and the concept of relativity of size that this involves (*This box is small, this box is smaller*, etc.); a better procedure would be to have collections of objects again (e.g. a bundle of pencils, a bunch of sticks) and to get children to select the smallest, the biggest, etc. This can be arrived at through such procedures as

Look at these pencils. I want the smallest one,

which can be said quietly by teacher or group leader to a pupil who has then to select the right object and say *This is the smallest pencil, This is the biggest one*, etc.

SUMMARY OF STAGE VI (Steps 25–33)

Structure

It's	half past six a quarter to four a quarter past five	
	time	for milk to go home

I You, etc.	can can't	lift this cupboard(?) see the blackboard(?)
Can	you he	

Yes, I can
No, I can't

Why? Why not?

It's He is	too	heavy short

Ali	is isn't	bigger than Rashid(?) as big as Rashid(?)
Is	Ali	

I You We They	like (don't like) want (don't want)	a red pencil to play
He She Ali	likes (doesn't like) wants (doesn't want)	

Do	you they I we	like want	potatoes? to play?
Does	he she Ali		

This is	the	biggest smallest longest	pencil

Vocabulary
first, second, etc.
today, tomorrow; next, last
before, after

past (a quarter past)
too
why? why not?
than
a lot, a little (adv.), very much
as . . . as
me, him, her, us, them, you (obj.)
mine, yours, his, hers, ours, theirs
one (subj. pronoun)
January, February, etc.
can, want, like . . .
see, lift, reach, look at, stop . . .
plasticine, paper . . .

This is a suitable point at which to perform a major revision of the work done so far; in a good class the teacher might aim at reaching this stage by the end of the first term. (This is roughly speaking parallel to two terms' work in *The Peak Course*[1] and covers structures that appear in the first thirty pages of *Peak Reader I*; many teachers of immigrant children have found that they can proceed at approximately double the pace of *The Peak*.) It cannot be said too often that nothing is gained by trying to build too fast and leaving the foundations in this basic language work insecure and shaky. Although the children's natural curiosity will encourage the teacher to push onwards, and although – as with young British children – some 'mistakes' will right themselves (particularly in irregular plurals of nouns, irregular comparisons of adjectives, and later in past tenses of irregular verbs), this self-correcting process should not be trusted too far. Let the children's confidence and enthusiasm speed the build-up of vocabulary while all along structures are carefully worked at and consolidated.

LATER STAGES

The presentation of certain tenses is discussed in this section. This does not imply that these are the only items to be taught next –

[1] See booklist at end of this chapter, and entry 10 in Bibliography, page 241.

though it is true that a mastery of English can often be assessed through the student's mastery of the verb. The teacher must see to it that while he is constantly revising and revitalizing areas of language already 'learnt', he is steadily adding more grammatical and lexical items to the pupil's repertoire as these arise spontaneously or as he judges it suitable to fit them in.

STEP 34
SIMPLE PRESENT TENSE

As implied in the step dealing with *want* and *like* above, it is difficult to avoid the simple present tense for long, in spite of its difficulties, since many verbs are not in fact often used in the *-ing* form and occur largely in the simple present (e.g. *want, like, know, think, wish; feel, taste, smell*). These are needed more and more to deal with everyday occurrences and concepts, and the simple present tense also recommends itself for entry here because it admits the discussion of the day's routine at home and in school, a topic of interest with wide possibilities for activity in the classroom. The simple present is also the tense used in the expression of generalizations, general truths, etc. – *Birds fly, fishes swim; The sun rises in the east* – and although these will also be found useful and interesting, they are likely to be of less practical value in the early stages of work on this tense.

It is suggested that the first practice of it be based on the children's everyday life:

I live at 10 Bridge Street
I get up at 7 o'clock
I wash my face. Then I clean my teeth
        etc.[1]

---

[1] In this series it might be best to omit '*have* breakfast', etc., at this stage; if it is used, the teacher should realize that *have* in this and certain similar combinations (*have a lesson, have tea*) behaves differently in some ways from the *have* that simply denotes possession. Cf. *Have you (got) any matches?* and *Do you have an English lesson now?*

every day often sometimes generally Fridays Mondays

The use of expressions of time which point to the habitual nature of these activities – *every day*, *often*, *sometimes*, *generally*, etc. – will be found helpful. School routine can also be described:

We drink milk at half past ten every day.
We swim on Fridays (every Friday).

At first **avoid** 3rd-person singular usages, but once these are introduced the tense can be practised in a wider range of situations, e.g. in discussing jobs, other people's routines, etc.:

My father gets up at 6 o'clock.
He goes to work at 8 o'clock.
The postman comes at 9 o'clock.

Question practice, in which pupils ask questions, will be most effective at first if the 2nd-person form is kept to:

Do you get up at 6 o'clock every day?
Do you like football?
Do you wash your hair every day?

and if short answers only are expected:

Yes, I do. No, I don't.

Plenty of practice should be given in this form before deliberate drill involving the third person is introduced. Long negative forms must also be drilled eventually (*I don't play football*, etc.).

nasty bitter sweet ugly old rough smooth soft hard ...
Later, the simple present may be used in expressions dealing with sensory experiences, and suitable vocabulary can be included:

It tastes nasty/bitter/sweet.
It looks pretty/ugly/old.
It feels rough/smooth/soft/hard.

This will link up with work in other lessons, and with mime, acting games, and so on. Work in lessons such as nature study will eventually necessitate the use of this tense in the general and habitual types of statement referred to above, e.g. *Birds fly, frogs hop, ducks swim; birds build nests, frogs live in a pond;* etc.

STEP 35

FUTURE EXPRESSED BY 'GOING TO'

I'm going to tell you a story.

Some teachers like to introduce the future (using *going to*) earlier in the course than this. It will of course have been used incidentally from quite near the beginning:

Now I'm going to show you . . .
Listen. Ali is going to be the teacher.

Teachers may find this tense easier to teach, or more interesting to demonstrate, than the simple present, because it can be used to apply to things that are actually going to happen in the classroom:

Yusuf, come here. Clean the board. He is going to clean the board. (What is he going to do? He is going to clean the board.) Go on, then.

This procedure is the one most often adopted for introducing and drilling this item, i.e. telling someone to perform a certain action, then interrupting him for a moment, just before he begins to do it, while asking a question about the action he is about to perform. It is fairly easy to halt an action for a moment or two – by not giving the boy the duster, for instance, or by arresting his hand – so that the intention about what is going to take place can clearly be seen, 'described', and then witnessed when it is finally performed. The contrast with the present continuous tense can be made use of: *He is going to . . ., Now he is doing it.*

Going to + the base form of the verb expresses what is often called a future of intention, i.e. it points to something the speaker intends to do; it is also used to indicate probability (*It is going to rain*). As the pupils already know *am going/is going*, etc., and are familiar with the base form of the verb from the imperative, there is no great learning problem here; moreover school routine gives many opportunities for this form to be practised in real situations:

Who is going to fetch the milk?
What are you going to do?
Tomorrow we are going to see a film/visit a railway station, etc.
Are you going to help, Rashid?

The interrogative and affirmative forms should be used as much as possible at first, reserving the negative till later.

If the teacher feels that it is more natural sometimes to use the simple future tense (*shall/will*), it would be best to keep strictly to the elided forms of it at first (*'ll*) – *I'll help you, We'll all do that* – avoiding both interrogative and negative.

STEP 36
PAST TIME (SIMPLE PAST)
was/were ...

The need will also be felt to introduce the notion of past time in speech, and it is found useful in practice to begin this with the past tense of *be*, which involves the two forms *was/were* and problems of concord. *Was* and *were* should be used for the simple expression of past time at first, and not as auxiliary verbs in the continuous tense *I was walking*.

yesterday   last week ...

Yesterday was Monday.
Aminah was absent last week. She was ill.
Yesterday was Farida's birthday. She was eight.
Where is my bag? It was on the floor. It isn't on the floor now.

In action chains, this sort of work can be combined with procedures suggested in the preceding step:

This is my hat. Here it is, on the table.
Ali, put it in the cupboard. He's going to put my hat in the cupboard.
My hat was on the table. Now it is in the cupboard.
Where was my hat? Where is it now?

ago

Plural objects in similar sequences give the opportunity for practising *were*.

The books *were* in the cupboard. *Now* they are . . .

Time expressions with *ago* can be incorporated into this work:

A minute ago my hat was on my head.
Ten minutes ago you were in the playground; now you are in the classroom.

Negative forms *wasn't* and *weren't* should be practised, and forms with introductory *there* (*there was/there were*, etc.) can also be used, but should not be pressed if they seem to cause confusion:

First there were five boys in that group. Now there are two.
Was there a girl in the picture?

Games involving observation (e.g. of details in a picture, objects on a tray) can be engineered to provide plenty of practice with *was* and *were*, before a move is made to introduce a wider range of verbs in the past.

had

The introduction of the past tense of *have* can also follow here; there is only one form to learn, namely *had*, and the negative is simple. The interrogative, however, to sound natural, makes use of *did* (*How many pencils did I have on my desk?* rather than *How many pencils had I?*).

If this question form is introduced at this point, it could be considered a good step towards preparing the pupils for the difficulties of the interrogative form of the past tense of verbs in general, which will soon be needed. Similarly, the negative form with *didn't* (*I didn't have a pencil*) is probably more acceptable than the use of *hadn't* (*I hadn't a pencil*) though the teacher might prefer *I hadn't got a pencil* for the sake of the colloquial expression.

STEP 37

SIMPLE PAST TENSE: REGULAR AND IRREGULAR VERBS

Although a certain amount of story-telling can be done using the present tenses, many teachers feel the need of the simple past tense (he *came*, they *went*, we *said*, etc.) for this purpose if for no other.

The use of this tense in English is fairly straightforward, but the forms it takes are a large learning load. It is salutary for the teacher of immigrants to consider how British children themselves have difficulties with this tense and will, till quite a late age, misuse not only *was* and *were*, but also the past form of irregular verbs, using forms like *digged*, *buyed*, *boughted*, *catched*, *throwed*, etc. One should not expect immigrant children to maintain a higher standard of 'correctness' than British children; consequently teachers need to exercise both patience and tact in dealing with this and other items. The past tense will be especially used in work allied to free expression – news, descriptions, story-telling – and it is precisely in this area, in encouraging children to express themselves freely, that correction can be most out of place.

There are several possible approaches to this tense, and in choosing which he will follow the teacher may like to consider the major difficulty which lies in the two main ways in which verbs form their past tense in English: there is the apparently easy, regular pattern which some verbs follow:

kick   kicked
jump   jumped
like   liked
cry   cried
stop   stopped

(a pattern which is easier to hear than to see, because it consists of the adding of [t], [d] or [id] as sounds to the base form of the verb), and there is the more difficult assortment of patterns, most but not all of which involve a vowel change within the base form of the verb itself:

buy   bought
say   said
read   read (*change in vowel sound*)
hurt   hurt (*no change at all*)

Many of the verbs of highest frequency in the classroom (e.g. *say, go, sit, stand, give, put, take*) belong to the second category, that of irregular or 'strong' verbs. There is no easy way of teaching these forms to children; they will learn them only by imitation, and they will only imitate them spontaneously through hearing them used correctly time and time again.

The teacher could quite well let his choice of verbs be controlled by those he needs in stories, and then work from the story outwards to wider practice of the same – and later other – verbs around the class. But he cannot expect his pupils to master and use themselves more than a very few new forms at a time. Stories, whether introduced for this or other purposes, have always to be narrated with a firm sense of vocabulary control on the part of the teacher. Most stories will contain far more material than the pupils are expected to reproduce themselves (i.e. relying on and helping to build up their 'passive' or recognition vocabulary), but the structural items contained in them that are intended for the pupils' active use – such as the simple past tense as described here – must obviously be chosen with care.

But the teacher may also introduce the notion of past time through situations, spontaneous or contrived, in which the children take part. This may be an easier way of controlling the forms used at first. For instance, it is perfectly possible in this way for the teacher to use only 'regular' verbs such as *touch, kick, ask, clean, rub, push, pull.* If he does this, the verbs chosen should be presented in statements about actions performed by the pupils and now finished, and the use of adverbials such as *on Sunday, yesterday, last week, five minutes ago* (as in Step 36) should be firm and frequent, to help keep clear the notion of *time past – action completed.* It is obvious that common irregular verbs cannot and should not be kept out for very long, and they too should be introduced gradually.

If actions in the classroom are used, procedures with imperatives can be followed (as in Step 35 with *going to*), but there should be a clear indication that the actions are completed so that the past tense, rather than the present perfect, is appropriately used in commenting on them. That is, if you say *Ali, clean the board* and he does so, the natural immediate comment is *Ali has cleaned the board.* To make the past tense usable and appropriate here, it would be better to get Ali to perform a series of actions, and then to sit down in his place, before commenting *First, Ali walked to the cupboard; next he took the duster; then he cleaned the blackboard . . .*

INTERROGATIVE AND NEGATIVE

The interrogative and negative forms of this tense necessitate the use of *did* (cf. simple present) and therefore present an additional problem. Teachers may at first use questions without expecting the pupils to use them themselves, e.g. by asking for the details of a story:

What did the old man say?
What did the boys do next?
What did they see?

but notice how this type of question may in fact hamper the pupil. *What did they see?* leaves the infinitive form *see* echoing in his mind and he is quite likely to reproduce it in his answer: *They see the king*.

On the other hand, the *did/didn't* forms in short answers to *yes/no* questions are easily practised, since the question 'helps' the pupil:

Did they see the king? Yes, they did./No, they didn't.

STEP 38

PRESENT PERFECT TENSE

Many up-to-date courses in oral English prefer to introduce this tense earlier than we indicate here. This, as with the future with *going to*, is mainly on the grounds of its suitability for demonstration work and for the convenient way it fits into sequences which pupils can carry out in class and which they seem to find interesting: *Tom is going to open the door. Now he is opening the door. Now he HAS OPENED the door.*

The tense is also in many respects easy for pupils to operate once they have mastered *has* and *have*, since its negative and interrogative forms are simply those of *have* followed by the past participle. The past participles of irregular verbs, are of course extremely difficult for pupils.

The teacher will have to decide for himself whether these considerations should lead him to place the present perfect earlier than the simple past tense in his scheme of work.

The point about the use of the present perfect in the example suggested above is its 'present-ness': the tense indicates the importance of the action to the speaker here and now, *in the present* as its name indicates, an action, however, which is completed and the result of which, in this case, can be seen or is uppermost in the consciousness of the listener:

We've finished the story.
Yusuf has forgotten his books.
Ali has brought a new toy to school today.

(There are of course other uses of the tense, but the ones indicated here are some of the easiest, and the teacher should confine himself to them at first.)

As suggested, sequences such as those used for demonstrating *going to* can be used in the classroom with the present perfect, and these can be accompanied quite early by questions:

Have I shut the door?
Has he opened the window or opened his desk?

and by negative forms. The teacher should consider the difficulties in the past-participial forms, as with the simple past, and may try limiting himself to verbs that follow regular patterns – *walked, opened, closed,* etc.; but, again, the irregular forms of frequently used verbs – *sat, gone, written,* etc. – cannot and should not be avoided for too long.

As for other uses of the present perfect tense, at this stage it should suffice for the teacher to be aware of them – and indeed it is vital to recognize that they *are* different usages – and to be content with the class hearing them from time to time naturally in context:

How long have you been here?
Has anyone seen my pen?
I haven't told you to go yet, have I?

No summary of Steps 34 – 38 is provided. But in dealing with these as with the earlier ones, the teacher should thoroughly examine the complexities of the separate items before embarking on them. In the case of verb forms, for instance, he should decide exactly which question or answer patterns he is going to teach, whether he is going to use the negative as well as the affirmative forms, and which verbs he is actually going to use and in which sentence patterns. Above all he should be aware of underestimating the difficulties of any item and its parts. Preparation before-hand will save waste of valuable time in class.

The books listed below will be found to offer information about the structural approach to language and ways of teaching it which will be useful to the teacher of English to immigrants. The list contains several titles of handbooks designed originally to accompany complete reading courses in English as a second or foreign language. They are quoted here because they are useful in their own right – apart, that is, from their use in conjunction with the courses to which they belong. These teacher's handbooks will often be found to be of more use to teachers than the general run of books on method and grammar. For language work which goes beyond the Stages given here, the teacher should turn to printed courses such as those suggested in the Bibliography (Sections I, II and III).

BOOKLIST TO CHAPTER 2

HEMMING and GATENBY, *Absorbing English*, Teacher's Book (I, 1)
The handbook to this English course for primary school child-ren gives details on the presentation and teaching of an elemen-tary language syllabus which is a very useful general guide to teachers whether they are using the accompanying texts or not. The scheme of work is based on 'the activity group work method' and is relevant to the situation of immigrant classes in English schools. The language is gently graded (e.g. the only tense covered in Part I of the course is the present continuous). The lesson notes are illuminating and provide help in drill and revision of language items.

HORNBY, *The Teaching of Structural Words and Sentence Patterns*, Stages One, Two and Three (X)
Presents a syllabus of teaching items for an introductory English course, with detailed notes on a method of presenting each one, together with helpful explanations on points of grammar and pronunciation. Intended to cover the language work con-sidered suitable for the first stages of a course for children 10 – 11 years old, but adaptable for younger children and for adults. The three volumes which comprise this text are generally felt

to be the most useful and comprehensive guide to graded structural language teaching on the English market.

PARRY, *Modern English for Malayans*, Teacher's Books 1 and 2 (I, 6)
Teacher's handbooks which would again prove useful to teachers of immigrants whether used with the reading course they accompany or not. Book 1 provides the first stages of oral teaching (for use in primary school) intended to be covered before reading is started. (A set of pictures is published for use at this pre-reading stage, and much of the language used is based on the colourful scenes in them.) A very clear scheme of work is outlined, with carefully timed revisions, detailed notes on presentation, lesson enrichment, etc. The handbooks also contain very helpful discussion of general principles and language-teaching procedures.

PATTISON, *Key to New Nation English* (I, 7)
The introductory teacher's guide to a course designed to teach English language throughout a 6-years' primary school course in Africa. The *Key* explains how to use the course as a whole and in particular contains the first term's oral lessons, with notes for teachers on the method of presenting and teaching each language item, carefully explained and illustrated.

The Peak Course. Teacher's Notes (Standard I, Volumes 1, 2, 3; Standard II, Volumes 1, 2, 3, etc.) (I, 10)
The teacher's notes accompanying this course designed for Asian children attending English-medium schools in Kenya will be found to offer a comprehensive primary-school syllabus in terms of elementary English language. Details of grammar and vocabulary to be presented at different stages are given, the vocabulary being not only that of the formal English period, but of P.E., handwork, nature study, etc. Notes on method and the special problems of this kind of education are given, and much of this material is of obvious relevance to the immigrant-teaching situation in the English primary school. The detailed schemes of work and of language revision are of special value.

Situational English, Part One, of Teacher's Book (II, 15)
The teacher's book to this course, originally designed for

immigrants newly arrived in Australia, is not only an excellent introduction to second-language teaching (with very useful sections on pronunciation, teaching aids, etc.), but also gives detailed lesson plans and notes on teaching procedures. This would be a very comprehensive guide for new teachers (especially of adults or of secondary-school pupils) whether or not they used the accompanying pupils' books.

3
Pronunciation

One often meets foreigners – children, students, adult workers – who have some considerable mastery of the way English functions and in addition have the confidence to use it, but who when they do so are practically incomprehensible. Many immigrant children, for instance, when they speak English are comprehensible only to the class teacher who has been teaching them; a visitor is baffled and dismayed by the flow of what passes for English. Teachers themselves constantly say that they do not know what to do about their pupils' poor pronunciation; it 'sounds funny' but they cannot put their finger on what is wrong with it. Is there any way to help?

To be able to help, a teacher needs first to learn something about the way English is pronounced. This is a vast subject and can only be treated in outline here, but teachers who are seriously concerned should consult some of the books listed at the end of this chapter. 'Learning something about the way English is pronounced' is in fact a parallel process to learning about the way English is patterned and structured which was dealt with in the preceding sections; it is in fact a process of *becoming aware* of yet another aspect of the language. For as with the structure of English, so with its pronunciation: we are so familiar with it that we do not know its intricacies in the analytical way that is necessary for someone who approaches it from the outside as the learner or teacher of English as a second language has to do.

Becoming aware of what we say and how we say it is a process full of surprises, and in the question of pronunciation there is often a barrier to our full acceptance of the actual facts. This is because of the way English is spelt and because of our own surprising subjection to the written form of language. As soon as people are

106

asked to think about pronunciation, they confuse 'eye-language' and 'ear-language':

'. . . because we have been conditioned to the written word by long tradition and by the processes of our education, we find it difficult to separate the two and are apt to think what is written in the black and white of the printed page is by some alchemy transformed exactly into the noises we make and recognize as the spoken language, and that *vice versa*, the ephemeral thing called speech is capable of accurate and standardized presentation on paper. This confusion of sounds and letters is a frequent cause of the attitude of many to 'standard' and 'correct' pronunciation, viz. that it should conform in some way to the printed word.'[1]

In speaking naturally, at normal speed, the word *of* in a phrase (i.e. not in isolation) is pronounced in a way that hardly 'reflects' the spelling at all: it may simply be heard as [v] or, a little stronger, as [əv] with the vowel a weak sound like the first syllable of the word *about*. And yet teachers, when this fact is pointed out to them, have been known to deny that this is so in their own pronunciation. It is salutary, and indeed a very good way of learning about one's pronunciation of the language, to record and listen to a passage of conversational English at normal speed on a tape recorder; if one then tries reading and recording it again at a slower speed, one discovers some revealing facts about the pronunciation of English and about what one *thinks* the pronunciation of certain words and phrases should be. Thought can often seriously distort our impression of pronunciation.

What in fact is the pronunciation of English, and how are we to expect our pupils to pronounce it?

Perhaps the first thing that needs to be said, as in the discussion of grammar above, is that we can only teach our pupils the English that we use, not that we think we use, i.e. it must be natural everyday English, and in many parts of Britain this will

[1] Ida Ward, *The Phonetics of English* (1958), p. 13 (X).

mean English pronounced with a regional accent. To all intents and purposes the teacher's pronunciation will be the pupil's model, and the teacher should never be tempted to speak other than naturally to him.

It is timely to repeat here what has been said earlier: that the teacher, remembering his pronunciation is the pupil's model, will *not* be helping him if he speaks with an exaggeratedly slow or distorted diction. Obviously he should not speak too quickly at first, and should always be ready to repeat things not just once but many times, and should at all times speak clearly; but if, for instance, he drags out and separates the syllables of words, places strange emphasis on what he thinks are awkward sounds, stresses inflected endings long and loud with unnatural pitch, he will only be encouraging bad habits. If pupils are to begin to make sense of the English they hear outside the classroom, then the English they hear inside the classroom must lead to an understanding of it.

If we now go on to attempt to analyse English pronunciation, we are faced with a marathon task. The English spoken by many people in London, for instance, sounds different from that spoken in Birmingham or Bedford, Ipswich or Bradford. There may be a commonly accepted level of correctness in grammar and vocabulary ('Standard English') with just a few local variants, especially of the latter (e.g. *poorly* for *ill* in parts of the north of England); but there will certainly be several features of pronunciation which are quite different. (We should perhaps not overemphasize these. Admittedly they exist, but they rarely cause difficulties in understanding, and teachers should not feel that their existence raises many problems in practice.) For convenience it is proposed simply to outline here the pronunciation of that accent of English which we do not associate with any particular geographical region but which can be heard all over Britain, and indeed all over the world, and which has therefore the widest received intelligibility. This 'accentless accent' is known as 'Received Pronunciation', 'R.P.' for short, and is thought by many to be the 'best' kind of spoken English accent, though for the purposes of teaching English to foreigners it is not necessarily the 'best' accent at all and presents more difficulties to the learner than do some other English accents.[1] However, it is the kind of English that has been most thoroughly described and analysed by phoneticians, and which many textbook-writers, when they give help with pronunciation, expect their readers to aim at. There is a lot to be said for teaching it to foreign learners of English overseas, if not to learners in England.

'Phonetics' and 'phoneticians' have been referred to several times, and it is a fact that many teachers become defensive at the mere mention of either. This resistance to the whole subject is often due to the misuse of phonetics in their own experience of language-learning or speech training, and to what often amounts to the identification of phonetics with phonetic transcription or with 'elocution'. Phonetic transcription has something to do with the teaching of pronunciation, but not everything; while what sometimes goes by the name of elocution – the teaching of fine speaking, which is often equated with a self-conscious acquisition of R.P. and frequently even with distorted speech sounds – has very little.

The ability to use phonetic transcription is in fact a very useful thing for the teacher of language, as also for the learner, who thus equipped can, for instance, find out for himself by consulting a pronouncing dictionary how a word is to be pronounced. Phonetic transcription, which makes use of a set of unambiguous symbols, each representing a separate sound of the language, provides a way of referring to the sounds of the language for which the normal alphabet and conventional English spelling are inadequate. Such symbols need not be used in the classroom at all: they are primarily a part of the teacher's equipment, not the pupils'; the teacher who has mastered them will find them invaluable. He can, for instance, make quick notes in passing on individual pupils' difficulties, specific sounds that need attention, etc. (Many different systems of notation of the sounds of speech are in use, as will be seen from some of the textbooks that are available to the teacher, but most books for foreign learners keep fairly near to the system given below.)

[1] For a valuable discussion of this question, and indeed of general English language-teaching problems, see Abercrombie, *Problems and Principles in Language Study* (X).

Here it is not intended to give a detailed account of the phonetics of English, nor is it suggested that the teacher of immigrants should become a phonetician before he can teach his language efficiently. But in fact he cannot help becoming one: as has been said, 'All language teachers willy nilly *are* phoneticians',[1] only they do not recognize themselves as such nor do they realize how, with a little more understanding of what speech consists of, they can become more efficient, and by a systematic approach to certain problems can be more economical of time and effort.

Rhythm and intonation

One of the biggest difficulties of the immigrant pupil, both in understanding what he hears and in being understood when he himself speaks English, is not in the individual sounds of English at all, but in the way these sounds are fitted together in utterances. This 'fitting together' of speech sounds involves correct rhythm and intonation; if these are wrong, the speaker may well be misunderstood or not understood at all, even if the vowels and consonants that make up his speech are more or less correct. Because of this, and because many teachers feel baffled by the subject, this section is placed first in the present outline of English pronunciation whereas in most descriptions it comes after the treatment of individual sounds.

Speech sounds are made by breath being expelled from the lungs and passing out of the body through the mouth and to a lesser extent through the nose. On its outward passage it is modified by movements in the position of the tongue, the lips and the soft palate (the back part of the roof of the mouth which can be raised or lowered, and which when raised cuts off the passage of air from the throat to the nose), and by the vibration of the vocal cords, the membranes which are stretched across the larynx behind the Adam's apple. The tongue, lips, soft palate and vocal cords are known as the movable organs of speech. Their movements can be combined in many different ways, articulating in conjunction with the immovable organs of speech such as the teeth, gums and hard palate (the hard part of the roof of mouth)

[1] Abercrombie, *op cit.*, p. 28.

to make the different sounds of speech. (See diagram below. Many of the possible sounds made in these various ways are not used in English at all but may occur in other languages.

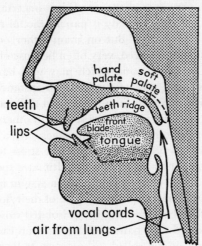

The actual force with which the air is expelled can be varied, and this fluctuation causes us to ascribe to some words or syllables of words a certain extra force known as *stress*. In any word of more than one syllable, one of the syllables 'stands out' and carries what we call the primary stress:

po**lite po**litics po**lit**ical poli**ti**cian.[1]

In polysyllabic words there may be a secondary stress, a syllable uttered with a breath force clearly not as strong as that of the primary-stressed syllable but not as weak as that of the others:

*po*li**ti**cian.

This distribution of stress in the individual word, 'word stress' as it is called, is a basic difficulty for the foreign learner. If he is a good learner and a quick imitator he will simply follow the teacher and may not deviate from the correct form, as this is all he has heard. But older pupils especially, both when speaking and

[1] Primary stress is most often indicated by the mark ' placed before the stressed syllable, thus: *po'lite*.

even more so when reading and when speaking with any excitement, will not automatically place the stress correctly. In words like *'politics/po'litical, 'photograph/pho'tography*, where there is a shift in stress in the very root of the word, this uncertainty is understandable and the only remedy is patient tactful repetition and correction by the teacher. But on many other occasions word stress may be wrongly placed, very often because of the influence of the pupil's mother tongue which may well have a different system of stress from that of English. For instance, whereas in English the stress tends to 'jump' about in different words, and be on the first syllable in some, the second in others, the penultimate or the final in others, many languages have a simpler, more regularly patterned system. In French the stress tends to be on the final syllable, in Italian on the penultimate; speakers of such languages will try to carry over their own system into English, a major contributory factor to the creation of their 'foreign' accent.

This will affect the pronunciation of isolated words and also of longer utterances; for the pattern of stresses in an English sentence – 'sentence stress' as it is called – also proves to be a difficulty for foreign learners. Its most important characteristic is its regularity, the steady periodicity of the stresses as they occur on the stressed syllables of the 'important' words of the sentence. Listening to an English sentence, we are aware of what one writer has called a regular series of peaks and troughs, i.e. stresses occurring at regular intervals, almost like beats in music, with unstressed syllables, many or few, between them, spaced out or crowded in, whichever is necessary to preserve the regular drumbeat of the utterance. The following sentences, for example, all have the same number of stressed syllables, but the number of unstressed ones in between them differs widely:

It **used** to be an **old** **school**.
It **could** have been a medi**ev**al uni**ver**sity.
But it **could**n't have been a satis**fac**tory ar**range**ment.

One feature of English pronunciation which is very important for the teacher to understand at this stage is the presence of what are known as 'strong' and 'weak' forms of certain very common words. These have been mentioned in the previous section (e.g.

pages 36, 50), and consist of forty or so structural words of very high frequency which, when pronounced in isolation or in a stressed position, have a 'strong' form (near to what we would call the 'spelling pronunciation'), but which most often, in the regular structures and usages in which they occur, take a 'weak' form. These weak forms, in which the vowel sounds disappear or are reduced to vowel sounds which have considerably less sonority, are essential to the rhythm of the English sentence and to maintaining the regular series of heavy stresses we have described above. Compare, for instance, the pronunciation of the italicized words in the following pairs of sentences read at normal speed:

I'm going *to* town today. (weak – [tə])
Where can he have got *to*? (strong – [tuː])
Is he the King *of* France? (weak – [əv])
What are you thinking *of*! (strong – [ɔv])
Have *some* more tea. (weak – [sm] or [səm])
Is there *some*? (strong – [sʌm])

The most important words that occur in both strong and weak forms are:

1 the many verbs which either elide (*'ll*, *'s*, *'ve*, *'d*, etc.) or are pronounced unelided (i.e. as separate syllables) but weakened:
   be [bi], *been* [bin], *are* [ə], *was* [wəz], *were* [wə], *do* [du, də], *does* [dəz, dz], *can* [kən], *could* [kəd], *must* [məst, mst, ms]:
2 many pronouns:
   you [ju, jə], *he* [hi,] *she* [ʃi], *we* [wi], *me* [mi], *him* [im], *her* [hə], *us* [əs], *them* [ðm], *who* [hu];
3 some prepositions:
   at [ət], *for* [fə], *from* [frm], *of* [əv], *to* [tu, tə], *upon* [əpən];
4 some conjunctions, and other very common words:
   as [əz], *but* [bət], *and* [ənd, ən, n], *that* (conjunction and relative pronoun) [ðt], *there* (introductory) [ðə], *than* [ðən], *some* [sm].

Some of these words, such as *than*, so rarely occur with strong pronunciation that it would perhaps be better not to think of them as having two forms. The same could be said of the articles *a*, *an* and *the*, which, except perhaps in the schoolroom in this country, are only heard in so-called strong forms in very emphatic or distorted speech.

It should be emphasized, of course, that the opposition of strong and weak forms should not be used to make a formal teaching item in an English lesson; it is the teacher's awareness of their existence that matters, so that he does not allow himself to misuse them or inadvertently encourage his pupils – especially at the reading stage – to do so. Attention should be paid to the correct use of weak forms from the very beginning if pupils are to develop any feeling for the rhythm of English.

Going back, then, to the pattern of heavy stresses within the utterance as a whole, we can say that if the heavy stresses are misplaced, or if there is no alternation of light and heavy stresses but instead a series of more or less regular stresses (for instance, on practically every syllable), this strange staccato-like speech will sound essentially un-English and will be difficult to understand.

But it is not only stress that is important. We also have to consider *intonation*, the effect produced by the rise or fall or steadiness of pitch of the voice. No one normally speaks on a monotone. Regular patterns of pitch-change at the heavily stressed syllables in an utterance make up the intonation of English, and intonation itself is as important in conveying meaning as the grammar and words themselves that make up utterances. Intonation is one of the most difficult features of English pronunciation to analyse, and several new theories have been produced in recent years. A very simplified version is given here for introductory purposes.

The most important patterns of pitch change can be briefly described as follows. (It should be noticed that it is only on a stressed syllable that there can be a change of pitch during the uttering of a syllable.)

1 *Falling intonation.* Complete statements, utterances with no special emotional colouring, questions beginning with *where*, *who*, *why* (i.e. not expecting the answer *Yes* or *No*) and asked in a

down-to-earth unemotional way, and exclamations, usually take a fairly high level pitch on the first stressed syllable, a slightly lower level one on the next, and so on down a descending scale till the last stressed syllable, on which the pitch of the voice falls to its lowest normal tone. Unstressed syllables between the stresses may fluctuate slightly in pitch; if they precede the first stress they may in fact form a slight rise. If they follow the last stress, they remain at the bottom low level of the voice pitch. In long utterances, the voice pitch may go up a step on an intermediate stressed syllable, especially where there is a natural pause or where slight extra emphasis is wanted.

This description is considerably oversimplified. The need for special emphasis or contrastive stress may mean that a falling tone is shifted from the last stressed syllable to an earlier one.

Different textbooks use different devices to symbolize intonation patterns, but the use of dots to represent unstressed syllables, and of dashes, level or oblique, to represent level or falling or rising tones on stressed syllables, is the most common. The teacher should listen to the intonation he gives to different utterances and try to mark this in some way such as that suggested here. For instance:

    \ .

Thank you.

  . .   \

This is my friend.

  . . \ .

This is my sister.

 — . . —   \ . . .

These are the books I was telling you about.

2 *Rising intonation.* A similar pattern of pitch changes, i.e. a series of descending steps on stressed syllables, but with a *rise* on the last stressed syllable, is found in unfinished statements, in many questions where the answer is Yes or No, and in utterances where there is emotion involved – encouragement, warmth, impatience, fear, etc. In this pattern, if there are any unstressed syllables following the last stressed one, they are so pitched as to continue the rise. Compare with the patterns given in (1):

Thank you.

Is this your friend?

Can this be your sister?

These are the books, and I hope you enjoy them.

One, two, three, four, five.

We can call these patterns the two main 'tunes' of English intonation, and although there are others, this brief outline will suffice to introduce the reader to the subject. He should learn to listen to the pitch changes, the intonation contours of his own speech, and should in particular practise making sounds with level pitch (—), and then with falling ($\searrow$) or rising ($\nearrow$) pitch, and sometimes with a 'wavy' pitch ($\wedge$ or $\vee$), a rise and fall or a fall and rise, all on the same syllable.

Now too he should begin to see the reason for the un-English quality of his pupils' pronunciation. First of all, are their overall intonation patterns coming out correctly? When they say 'Thank you' politely, do their voices fall correctly on the right syllable or do they rise? In statements and different kinds of questions are their voices falling and rising where they should? And – a feature of much Indian and Pakistani speech – are they making pitch changes at wrong places in the sentence, and in particular using falling-rising tones on *all* or nearly all stressed syllables (sometimes producing a kind of 'Welsh' accent in their speech)?

Remedial work on rhythm and intonation cannot be divided into compartments. When it becomes necessary, the teacher should aim at getting his pupils to *hear* how his voice falls or rises; gestures with the hand, or, when they are at the reading stage, the use of symbols such as sloping arrows written above the words on the blackboard, will help. Rhythmic material, carefully chosen speech rhymes, can be practised softly in chorus, the teacher and pupils beating time. But the teacher will have to be careful to choose rhymes in which the metre follows the natural rhythm of the words; otherwise he may be defeating his own ends. It sometimes helps to practise stress and intonation without using words at all, e.g. by using '*m—m—*'*m*, '*da—di—*'*da*, etc., so that attention is directed solely to these features and not to meaning; but this may not be suitable for all pupils.

In this, as in all questions of pronunciation teaching, the greatest care and tact is necessary, so that the nervous pupil, from being over-corrected, does not become more nervous and inhibited. Chorus work, for this reason, is particularly valuable, though the teacher has to keep it rigidly controlled so that there is not too much laxness and imprecision in less able pupils. Choral speaking in groups and sections will always be a valuable technique but one needing careful handling. Both young and old pupils usually find great pleasure in saying rhymes but over-enthusiasm may be as detrimental or as unproductive of improvement as shyness or apathy. Some suitable rhymes for this kind of work will be given at the end of the next chapter along with other speech material.[1]

The sounds of English

It has been suggested, then, that for general intelligibility it is most important that the foreign learner of English should acquire correct habits of rhythm and intonation, and it is to this end that the teacher's effort should primarily be directed. But of course there will also be many occasions when the teacher will realize that he has to help pupils with their pronunciation of individual sounds. It should be stressed that this kind of corrective work is particularly difficult, and the more specialized aspects of it will largely only be relevant to work with older pupils.

It is always to be hoped that young pupils will learn best by pure imitation, and certainly they have the advantage over the older pupils in that their imitative faculties are generally sharper. Where it may seem feasible to concentrate on this type of corrective work with older pupils for certain periods of time, there will certainly be problems: boredom soon sets in if much time and attention is paid to individuals, and yet it is only by individual help that much good can be done. Moreover, unskilful or tactless

[1] See below, pp. 168 ff.

handling may do more harm than good. Although as a general rule every teacher should try to do some specific work on pronunciation every day, five or ten minutes at a time will probably be the maximum possible. (Again, some techniques and procedures for doing this kind of work are given in the next chapter and will perhaps suggest other ways and means to the teacher.)

We divide speech sounds into (1) vowels, (2) diphthongs (which to all intents and purposes are combinations of vowel sounds), and (3) consonants. All these sounds are made by air passing from the lungs up through the larynx and escaping through the mouth or nose; in vowels and diphthongs the vocal cords are set in vibration and the air is allowed to escape unimpeded through the mouth, the differences in qualities of sounds being produced by the position and shape of the tongue and of the lips, the mouth functioning thus as a resonance chamber. In diphthongs the position of the tongue (and sometimes of the lips) alters within the course of the sound, so a diphthong is really a glide from one vowel position towards another. Consonants are produced with or without the vocal cords vibrating, but always with some articulation of lips, tongue or teeth, so that the escape of air is prevented or impeded in some way; the friction thus produced forms an essential characteristic of the consonant sounds.

The twelve vowels of English are:[1]

[iː] as in bead	[ɔ] as in body
[i] ,, ,, bid	[u] ,, ,, put
[e] ,, ,, bed	[uː] ,, ,, boot
[æ] ,, ,, bad	[ʌ] ,, ,, but
[ɑː] ,, ,, bard	[əː] ,, ,, bird
[ɔː] ,, ,, board	[ə] ,, ,, about

The eight diphthongs are:

[ei] as in bay
[ou] ,, ,, bone

---

[1] The symbols given here and found elsewhere in this book are those of the International Phonetic Association used in Daniel Jones's *An English Pronouncing Dictionary* (see entry no. 69 in Bibliography) and in many other works of reference and textbooks.

[ai] as in b*y*
[au] „ „ b*ough*
[ɔi] „ „ b*oy*
[iə] „ „ b*eer*
[ɛə] „ „ b*ear*
[uə] „ „ p*oor*

and some people have a ninth,

[ɔə] as in b*ore*.

The twenty-four consonants are:

[p]	as in	*p*at	[θ]	as in	*th*in
[b]	„ „	*b*at	[ð]	„ „	*th*en
[t]	„ „	*t*on	[s]	„ „	*s*ue
[d]	„ „	*d*one	[z]	„ „	*z*oo
[k]	„ „	*k*ale	[ʃ]	„ „	*sh*op
[g]	„ „	*g*ale	[ʒ]	„ „	mea*s*ure
[f]	„ „	*f*an	[tʃ]	„ „	*ch*eap
[v]	„ „	*v*an	[dʒ]	„ „	*j*eep

[m]	as in	*m*ay
[n]	„ „	*n*ay
[ŋ]	„ „	si*ng*
[l]	„ „	*l*ead
[r]	„ „	*r*ed
[h]	„ „	*h*ot
[w]	„ „	*w*ild
[j]	„ „	*y*oung

Some of the above consonants are printed in pairs. The consonants in any one pair are made in the same way, i.e. with the lips, tongue, teeth, etc., in the same position for both, but with this important difference, that in the first consonant of each pair there is no voicing, while in the second in each pair there is. Voicing, as we said before, occurs when the vocal cords are set in vibration: this can be clearly 'felt' if you place a finger in each ear and make one of the voiced consonants that can be held for a time (i.e. a continuant) such as [z] or [m]. (Some consonants such as [b] or [d] cannot be prolonged and their voiced quality is therefore difficult to feel in this way.)

English then may be analysed into these forty-four or forty-five separate sounds. No other language has exactly the same sounds, either in isolation or in the combinations in which they occur in English. In this lies one of the foreign pupil's major difficulties, for:

1 Some English sounds will therefore be completely new to him. Few languages, for instance, have consonants like our *th-* sounds, [θ] and [ð].

2 Some English sounds will be deceptively similar to sounds in the pupil's mother tongue, and in trying to produce the English sounds he may use the approximate ones in his own language without realizing that they are not the same as the English sounds in question.

3 The pupil's mother tongue may not distinguish certain sounds in the way English does, and different sounds may even be interchangeable in certain positions without causing a change in meaning. The best known examples of this are [l] and [r] in Chinese, and [f] and [p] in some Indian languages. It applies to vowels as well as consonants, and means that not all foreign learners will see any significance in the distinction English makes between such sounds. This may mean that they then fail to make the necessary distinctions in their pronunciation of English, and that some groups of sounds converge, one being produced for several, or several being interchanged indiscriminately where they occur in different words.

4 English is particularly rich in clusters of consonants, both initially, medially and finally in words; these may be clusters of two or three consonants such as [tr], [θr], [str], [lvz]; or even in some cases of four. Because there are few, or dissimilar combinations in the pupil's mother tongue, these clusters may present great difficulty to many learners.

5 The vowels and diphthongs of English do not maintain the same length when they occur alone or in conjunction with voiced and unvoiced consonants: thus, if you listen carefully to the sound [i:] in *see, seed* and *seat*, you will notice that in the first two words it is longer than in the last word. As a general

rule we may say that vowels that are open (not followed by a consonant) and vowels that are followed by a voiced consonant such as [d] or [g], are relatively longer than vowels that are followed by a voiceless consonant ([t], [k], [p], etc.). These differences in length are made automatically by native speakers. Many pupils will not imitate these differences in length perfectly. Corrective work in this area is again extremely difficult.

Special problems in the pronunciation of vowels and diphthongs

It would be beyond the scope of this small volume to deal exhaustively with the many difficulties that foreign pupils of different nationalities find in the pronunciation of the individual sounds of English. An attempt is made here to deal only with those that seem to occur most frequently in the classroom and cause most problems for teachers of immigrants.

1 [iː] [i] [e] [æ]

There may often be confusion between the first three of these vowels, and sometimes between the last two as well. This is because they are all made in a very similar way, namely by the front part of the tongue being raised towards the roof of the mouth (highest for [iː], lowest for [æ], with [i] and [e] at intervals in between), and it is quite easy for neighbouring vowels (i.e. [iː] and [i], [i] and [e], [e] and [æ]) to be confused, especially where one or more of them does not occur in the first language of the learner.

Most pupils will pronounce [iː] correctly, but may make [i] too close to it so that *it* rhymes with *eat* and *fill* with *feel*.

Generally speaking, with school pupils there is no point in the teacher trying to *explain* the differences in sound, and he must aim rather at improving his pupils' pronunciation by trying to get them to imitate his own pronunciation more accurately. Pupils need to *hear* that there is a difference between these sounds. This 'hearing' is best brought about by the teacher introducing pairs of words that contain the contrasting sounds (such pairs – words

E

which are exactly alike phonetically except for one sound – are known as *minimal pairs*, e.g. *bean–bin* [biːn – bin], *peal–pill* [piːl – pil], *pig–peg* [pig – peg], *pin–pen* [pin – pen], *beg–bag* [beg – bæg]). If it can be demonstrated that misunderstanding or nonsense results from failing to make this contrast in sound, the pupil's attention will be drawn to this difference in the best way possible, i.e. through attention to meaning.[1] He will listen the more keenly to the different sounds, and try to produce them because it will have become necessary to do so. Unfortunately, it is not always easy to find such useful minimal pairs as *pin* and *pen*, or *ship* and *sheep*, which so readily fit into meaningful sentences, and listening practice with pairs of words whose meanings are not known to the pupils or which have no context is not a great deal of use. However, lists can be used considerably with older pupils and suggestions for such pairs will be given here and there in the account that follows.

For practising these front vowels, the following pairs might be found useful:

[iː/i]		[i/e]		[e/æ]	
feel	fill	fill	fell	met	mat
eat	it	it	ate	pet	pat
leap	lip	pit	pet	head	had
steal	still	tin	ten	bed	bad

As we have seen, it is difficult to talk about tongue position when trying to get pupils to produce these vowel sounds more accurately. It helps, however, to draw their attention to lip position, and with [iː] and [i] there can be a clear difference. For [iː] get the pupils to draw back the corners of their mouths, to smile a big smile, and so on; for [i] their lips should not be drawn so far back, and the teeth can be a little further apart – with space enough to place a pencil between the teeth – as the jaw relaxes.

For [e] and then for [æ] the jaw is a little wider open again. If pupils say [e] with one finger between the teeth, they can be asked to say [æ] with two fingers there, one on top of the other. With small classes of older children, the teacher may choose to dis-

[1] See below, p. 140.

tribute pocket mirrors in which they can watch their own lip and jaw movements.

2 [ɑː] [ɒ] [ɔː] [u] [uː]

These five vowels are made by raising the back part of the tongue towards the soft palate; it is raised only very slightly for [ɑː], the most 'open' therefore of these 'back vowels', but for [uː], the most close, it is raised nearly up to the back of the roof of the mouth. Generally speaking, these are not difficult sounds for most pupils to imitate, though [uː] is sometimes confused with [u] (i.e. by the tongue position not being differentiated enough); [ɒ] and [ɔː] are often confused with one another and with the diphthong [ou], and [ɑː] may be confused with the central vowels [ʌ] and [əː] (see below). For all these sounds, should one try practising them in isolation,[1] the position of the lips is most important: for [ɑː] the mouth should be wide open, the lips loosely spread; for [ɒ], the next vowel 'up', the jaws come a little closer together; for [ɔː] they are nearer again, and the lips rounded and a little protruded; for [u] the jaws again get closer together and the lips more and more rounded, and with [uː] finally the lips can be drawn right up to form a little round space, which can be practised by sucking the end of a pencil and then removing it from the mouth. If the pupils are not producing these sounds correctly or are, for instance, making [u] and [uː] too much alike, the teacher should draw their attention to lip rounding, contrasting the two positions, and again, as with the front vowels, get them to distinguish the two in contrast to one another as in the pairs:

> pull pool
> full fool
> foot food etc.

Lists of words which could be useful in dealing with confusions between back vowels and between back vowels and other sounds should be drawn up as follows:

[1] One must beware of producing vowel sounds in isolation that do not in fact correspond to the actual sounds when incorporated in words. It is often difficult to isolate vowels accurately.

cot	caught	coat
not	naught	note
shot	short	
pot	port	
barn	bun	burn
bard	bud	bird
card		curd
hard		heard etc.

3 [ʌ] [əː] [ə]

These three vowels are made centrally, by the raising of the middle part of the tongue towards the roof of the mouth.

[ʌ] presents difficulties to some pupils. For many it is a new sound. It may be confused with [ɑː]. Like [ɑː] it is produced with lips spread and jaws wide apart, though not quite so wide as for [ɑː]. Older pupils may be taught to alter their tongue position (by looking in a mirror) and to close their jaws slightly for [ʌ]. Many will also confuse it with the front vowel [æ]. The teacher will have to see that the following distinctions are clearly identified by the class:

cut	cart	cat
hut	heart	hat
bun	barn	ban etc.

[əː] is found difficult by some pupils. Often they produce a faulty sound by rounding their lips too much. One method of helping them to produce it correctly is to get them to say [e], which is usually found to be easier, and then, while still saying it, to touch the tip of the tongue with a finger, keeping it still, and then rounding the lips very slightly.

[ə] is not a difficult sound in itself, and young pupils usually make it fairly easily. It occurs very frequently in normal speech, but only in unstressed syllables, and pupils who hear their teacher using it naturally and normally will imitate it fairly easily. But older pupils with some knowledge of written English and who are then influenced by the spelling, or pupils who have been taught by a teacher who indulges in a 'spelling pronunciation' (often a foreign teacher), will tend *not* to use it where it should be used, especially in the weak forms of the words listed earlier in this chapter. Many teachers find it useful in fact to introduce this one phonetic symbol, [ə] ('upside-down *e*'), to their pupils, because in correction of pronunciation they need to refer to it so often. It will often need attention in words (other than weak forms) where it occurs – *banana, breakfast, cupboard, moment*, etc. – and where again a bad habit of spelling pronunciation may have already taken root.

4 The diphthongs: [ei] [ou] [ai] [au] [ɔi] [iə] [ɛə] [uə]

The most common mistakes in this area are for pupils to use clear vowels for diphthongs; for instance, they will often make:

[e] instead of [ei] (pronouncing *late* [let])
[e] instead of [ɛə] (pronouncing *Mary* ['meri])
[ɔː] instead of [ou] (pronouncing *boat* [bɔːt])
[iː] instead of [iə] (pronouncing *really* ['riːli]).

In addition, Asian speakers especially will tend to confuse [iə] and [ɛə]. If the teacher gets as far as analysing and identifying such deviations from R.P. as these, it is then for him to decide whether, and to what extent, these features of his pupils' pronunciation need correcting. Obviously where they make for misunderstanding or unintelligibility, help should be given, and one technique will again be to get pupils to hear and then make the distinctions in minimal pairs. Some of the above pronunciations are of course features of accepted accents of English and seem relatively unimportant.

If the teacher wants to teach his pupils to make a diphthong instead of a pure vowel, it sometimes helps if he first gets them to make the two elements of the diphthong separately; e.g. for [ei] in *bay* the pupil should be asked to produce the first element (near the sound in *get*) and then the second (near the sound in *bit*). To form the diphthong the two isolated sounds can be said one after the other with a shorter and shorter interval between them and with diminishing force on the second element, until the necessary tongue glide (and, usually, jaw movement) is obtained. (The teacher should draw attention to the movement of his own jaw.) The pupils must not be encouraged to hang on to the second element of the diphthong: this type of distortion is very common in attempts to produce some diphthongs correctly, especially [ou]. The second element must be cut off sharp or the sound produced will be overprecise and unnatural.

The diphthong [ɔə] may not be in the teacher's speech at all, as many people use the long vowel [ɔ:] instead of it.

Special problems in the pronunciation of consonants

In one respect consonants are easier to teach than vowels, because very often the articulatory process which produces them, e.g. the position of lips, tongue, teeth in relation to one another, can be clearly seen (whereas tongue position, which is one of the main factors in the production of vowels, is often hard to determine or correct).

One of the main difficulties in consonants lies in the difference between voiced and voiceless members of certain pairs. It was suggested earlier in this chapter how the vibration of the vocal cords can best be felt, i.e. by placing fingers in ears, though this only applies to continuants like [z], [v] or [ʒ]. The vibration of the vocal cords can also be felt if a finger is placed on the Adam's apple, though this is sometimes more difficult for pupils to detect. Although pupils may well be defeated by attempts at explanation, it is a good exercise – to be treated as a game preferably – for them to practise 'switching' the voice on and off, at the same time feeling for the vibration in their ears (or in the throat). Let them alternate thus:

s . . . s . . . s . . . z . . . z . . . z . . . s . . . s . . . s . . .

all in one breath. Later, if for instance [s] is produced for [z], a quick correction can be made in passing by the teacher making [z] and placing fingers in ears or on throat, encouraging the pupils to do so at the same time. The gesture, as much as the actual feel of the sound, can be used as a short cut to obtaining what is wanted.

A few hints on the pronunciation of consonants follow:

1 [s] and [z]
    (See immediately above.) The tip or blade (i.e. the very front

part) of the tongue is just behind the upper gums ('the teeth ridge'), i.e. towards the front of the mouth. Generally speaking it is the voiced sound [z] of this pair that causes most difficulty and to which most attention has to be paid. The two sounds can be drilled in contrasting pairs such as

hiss	his
bus	buzz
close	close (vb.).

(In pairs such as these attention will also have to be paid to variations in vowel length; see above, p. 120.) And, of course, pairs in which they occur initially or medially may also be found useful (e.g. *sip/zip; prices/prizes*). Some pupils will also confuse [s] with [ʃ] (see below under [ʃ]).

2 [θ] and [ð]

If these consonants cause difficulty, get the pupil to place the tip of his tongue between his teeth and then to blow through his teeth. Gradually he will learn to make these sounds with the tongue just against the upper teeth and not showing through; but always, when being corrected, he should be made to revert to 'biting the tongue'.

Many pupils will try to substitute [t] or [s] for [θ] and [d] or [z] for [ð], and the necessary distinctions should be made through contrasting pairs such as:

tin	thin	sin	thin
tick	thick	sing	thing
tree	three	sick	thick
breathe	breeze	day	they
clothe	close	dough	though
bathe	bays	den	then

Some pupils may be able to produce these consonants when they occur at the end of a word but not when they occur at the beginning, and vice versa. This will probably be because the sound occurs in the one position in their mother tongue but not in the other. The teacher should note this and get pupils to make the sound in words where they seem to find it easy to do so, and then in words where it occurs in the position that is more difficult for them.

3 [f] and [v]

For both of these sounds the lower lip is placed against the upper teeth. Some pupils make [v] by pressing both lips together and this type of articulation should, if possible, be cured. If a pupil holds his upper lip still with his fingers, while pronouncing [v], this may be found to help.

Some Indian and Pakistani pupils substitute [p] for [f] and vice versa. It will help if the teacher emphasizes the way [f] is formed as above, i.e. not with both lips like [p], but with lip and teeth. [p] should be contrasted with [f] in pairs such as

pool	fool
put	foot
pull	full

4 [w]

This is often substituted for [v] and a clear distinction must be made as in

west	vest
worse	verse
whale	vale

Both lips are used for [w] and they should be well rounded. This position can be exaggerated at first to distinguish the way [w] is made from that of [v]. If a pupil cannot say [w] at all, get him to make the vowel [uː] with rounded lips; substitute this vowel for the missing consonant, saying it very quickly and moving from it to the rest of the word: *oo–ite = white, oo–est = west.*

5 [j]

If this consonant also proves to be a difficulty, it can be approached through the vowel [iː] just as [w] can be approached through [uː]. So, to pronounce the words *young* and *yet* the pupil can first say *ee–oung = young*, and *ee–et = yet*, etc.

When [j] is confused with [dʒ], contrasting pairs of words should be practised such as:

jell   yell
Jew   you

6 [k] and [g]

This is usually an easy pair of consonants, but one is sometimes substituted for the other. [g] must be voiced, and not made too far back in the mouth so that it becomes throaty. It is pronounced with considerably less force than [k], as is true of most voiced counterparts of voiceless consonants.

Neither [k] nor [g] should be allowed to intrude where it is not required, for instance after [ŋ] at the end of words.

7 [ŋ]

Many foreign pupils find [ŋ] difficult, and as mentioned above, have a tendency to add [k] or [g] to it in final positions. This may lead to confusion between pairs of words such as *sing* and *sink*, *thing* and *think*, etc. One way of curing this fault is to get the pupils to prolong the [ŋ] sound at the end of a word and in prolonging it to weaken the force with which it is said.

8 [m] and [n]

These two consonants, like [ŋ], are nasals: the air from the lungs escapes through the nose and not through the mouth. This nasal quality should not be allowed to carry over to adjacent vowels. If vowels are nasalized, either in proximity to nasal consonants or elsewhere in words, the teacher should try to remedy this by practising such vowels first of all in words where no nasal consonants occur, only then returning to words which include [m], [n] or [ŋ].

Neither [m] nor [n] usually present difficulty. The lips are closed for [m] (as for [p]), whereas [n] is made with the tongue against the upper gums and with no lip movement.

9 [p] and [b]

These consonants do not usually present difficulty in themselves, though, as noted above, [p] may be substituted for [f] and vice versa. Both [p] and [b] are made in the same way: the lips are closed and then opened suddenly as the breath is expelled. [b] is voiced and produced with less force than [p]. Some pupils may have to be encouraged to pronounce initial [p] with a bigger puff of breath to distinguish it from [b], as they have a tendency not to aspirate it enough. This can be practised by letting them feel the little puff of breath on their hands as they make the sound [p] several times, or by letting them hold a little piece of paper up in front of the mouth while they make it; the paper should move just a little but not too much.

The two sounds [p] and [b] can also be practised in pairs of words in different positions:

pull	bull	cap	cab
pill	bill	rip	rib

10 [ʃ]

This sound should not be confused with [s] or with [tʃ]. Whereas for [s] the tip or blade of the tongue is just behind the upper gums or teeth ridge and the rest of the tongue is lower in the mouth, for [ʃ] the central part, technically known as 'the front' of the tongue, is raised towards the hard palate (see diagram below). This, of course, is hard to see in a mirror and hard to explain to pupils. All the same, an attempt should be made to stop Indian and Pakistani pupils substituting [ʃ] for [s] and vice versa. Practise:

see she
so show
sue shoe

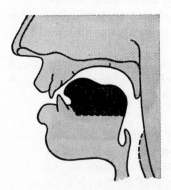 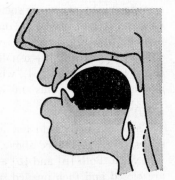

Tongue positions for [s] and [ʃ]
(The tip of the tongue may be lower in both cases.)

11 [tʃ]

To differentiate [tʃ] from [ʃ] let pupils who find difficulty make [t] first; then placing the tongue in position for [t] again, glide quickly to [tʃ] in one swift movement. Some phoneticians suggest that pupils should be taught to say words like *hat shop*, moving on from that to *hatchet*, and similarly from *what shop* to *watch*.

[tʃ] and [ʃ] should also be contrasted as in

watch	wash
catch	cash
which	wish

12 [ʒ] and [dʒ]

These two consonants are the voiced counterparts of [ʃ] and [tʃ]. [ʒ] only occurs in a few words and in a medial position, e.g. *measure, pleasure, treasure, usual*. If it causes difficulty, it is best to work to it from [ʃ]. [dʒ] should be drilled if necessary in contrast to [tʃ] with which it can easily be confused:

catch	cadge	cheap	jeep
etch	edge	chin	gin
chain	Jane	choke	joke

13 [h]

This sound, simple aspiration, is not usually found difficult though it may be missing where the teacher feels it is needed. To practise feeling the aspiration, pupils can be told to cup their hands and breathe into them; and then to do this while repeating pairs of words aspirated and unaspirated alternately:

hit	it
had	add
his	is
hall	all
hair	air

The teacher should not insist on the pupil making [h] at the beginning of pronouns when they occur in weak forms as this can often be detrimental to the natural rhythm of an utterance.

Some pupils may confuse [h] with a sound in their own

language rather like the final sound in the Scottish word *loch*. They may try to pronounce it with a lot of friction in the back of the throat, or too vigorously so that attention is drawn to it unnecessarily. They must be shown how to make it as a very light sound, with so little force that in fact paper suspended in front of the mouth is hardly moved by it.

14 [l]

In most parts of Britain there are two [l] sounds in English, a clear [l] made towards the front of the mouth which is used in initial positions and before [j], and a dark [l] made further back in the mouth which occurs in final positions or when [l] is followed by a consonant. Teachers could listen for the difference in the [l] sounds in, for instance, *live*, *life*, *love*, *million*, and in *vile*, *mill*, *mild*, *people*. It sometimes helps to be aware of these differences, for while it may not be necessary to correct pupils' pronunciation if they substitute one [l] for the other, it may be that this feature of their pronunciation explains part of the foreignness of their accent. Failure of pupils sometimes to hear dark [l] if, as is likely, it does not exist in their own language, may even result in their misunderstanding English on occasions. A dark [l] should particularly be practised when the sound itself constitutes a syllable (i.e. when the [l] is said to be syllabic) as in the second syllable of *people*, *settle*, *puddle*, *label*.

15 [r]

Many types of [r] can be heard in Britain, and the [r] of R.P. is particularly difficult for foreign pupils, who will often use a trilled or slightly rolled [r] sound instead. This is not a serious defect at all, though if it is vigorously pronounced in positions where in R.P. it is silent (as is often the case with older pupils who have been influenced by the pronunciation of bad teachers or by the written word) the teacher may go about trying to modify it a little.

16 Consonant clusters, e.g. [sk] [str] [θr]

It should be remembered that groups of consonants which occur in English at various positions in words, initially, medially and finally

stop, strap, throw, dry
under, it's a, mixture
shelves, pushed, danced, sixths

do not necessarily occur in such combinations in the mother tongues of the pupils and often therefore present special difficulties.

To cope with the pronunciation of these combinations of consonants, pupils may omit one or more of the consonants in the group; or they may make the articulation 'easier' by adding a vowel sound to split up the straight sequence of consonants; thus the word *stop* may become [ə'stɔp] (or [i'stɔp]) or [sə'tɔp], an extra syllable being created.

It would obviously be best to avoid such problems as these in the early stages of work by not introducing words which contain these clusters, but when they do arise, as inevitably they must, patient repetition and the breaking up and putting together again of the separate sounds in the cluster may help. With this problem, as with others, it helps if the pupils can be taught to hear the difference between the way they are saying the word and the way it should be pronounced. To do this, the teacher may briefly imitate their pronunciation, contrasting it with his own.

17 Retroflexion

One big difficulty which is met with in the pronunciation of English by Indian and Pakistani speakers, is their tendency to make many sounds *retroflexively*; that is, to pronounce them with the tip of the tongue turned up and back, so that the sounds in fact have a quality hard to describe but essentially un-English.

If the teacher practises retroflexion himself, for instance, by saying the word *hotel* with the tip of the tongue as far back in the mouth as it will go for [t], he will then realize what it is that characterizes some of his pupils' pronunciation of English.

To cure this habit, i.e. to replace the Indian type of articulation with the English, the teacher may, if he is sure of his ground, get the pupils to try articulatory exercises – 'tongue' gymnastics, e.g. pointing the tongue, sticking it out as far as it will go, etc. – before returning to the consonant sounds in particular which pupils have to learn to make without turning their tongues up. Pocket mirrors might also help if brought into use with older pupils.

But this is speech work which would need to be carefully handled and which, it is to be hoped, should not be necessary with young pupils, who usually prove to be the best imitators of their teacher's pronunciation from the beginning.

Finally it should be said that the teacher's knowledge of speech training as it is often taught in the training colleges is by no means irrelevant to his teaching of immigrants. All pupils need to learn such things as good posture and good habits of breathing, and obviously the more articulatory exercises – flexing of tongue, lips, etc. – that they are trained to perform, the better will they cope with the adjustments they have to make in their speech habits in order to produce the sounds of English. A minute or two of this sort of work in the course of each school day will pay dividends in the long run.

With the foreign learner's difficulties in mind, the teacher of immigrants should sift through his material for speech work with British children, selecting from it and adapting it to his present purpose.

BOOKLIST TO CHAPTER 3

ABERCROMBIE, *Problems and Principles in Language Study* (X)
A very clear statement of many of the problems connected with the teaching of oral English, and an especially valuable discussion of the question of the *kind* of English one should teach, the nature of dialect and accent, etc.

ALLEN, *Living English Speech* (X)
Really a textbook designed for teaching English rhythm and intonation to foreign learners. No knowledge of phonetics is required to use it. The reader will find it a useful book to study to teach himself the intricacies of the subject and to suggest ways of teaching it.

HILL, *Drills and Tests in English Sounds* (X)
A most useful reference book for the teacher to have, suggesting

a mass of minimal-pair work that could be adapted to teaching pronunciation at various levels. Two tapes accompany the book.

JONES, *The Pronunciation of English* (X)
Standard introductory work which gives a very clear outline of English pronunciation in all its aspects though with not a great deal on intonation.

LEE, *An English Intonation Reader* (X)
A fairly recent publication on intonation, which is a good straightforward introduction to the subject without being too difficult in use of technical terms. Especially see Chapter III, 'Intonation at work'.

MCCALLIEN and STREVENS, *English Speech* Bks. 1, 2, 3 and Teachers'
Books 1, 2, 3 (X)
Written originally for use in West African schools, it describes simple speech-training exercises and pronunciation work that can be carried out with young children learning English as a second language. Strongly recommended for the techniques suggested and for the wealth of illustrations.

MCALLISTER, *The Primary Teacher's Guide to Speech Training* (X)
Useful for description of speech-training techniques (breathing exercises, tongue exercises, etc.) and for outline account of speech defects. Not so useful on the phonetic side.

O'CONNOR, *A Course of English Pronunciation* (X)
A handbook intended to accompany a set of gramophone records, but very useful in its own right. Especially valuable for exercises on vowel length, and for very simple outline of English intonation.

WARD, *The Phonetics of English* (X)
Covers much the same ground as the shorter book by Jones, but with special reference to problems of English speakers, and is therefore useful for the ordinary teacher as well as the teacher of immigrants; includes useful discussion of accent and dialect.

4

Techniques and procedures in oral teaching

General procedure

A good teacher can become a good language teacher, and it has already been suggested in this book that much excellent teaching of English to immigrants is being carried out by teachers who have developed their own ways and means of coping with the problem by virtue of their own natural 'teaching instinct'. Many of the techniques and procedures they use have developed out of their own personal inventiveness; many of them are modifications of what one might call 'ordinary' teaching practice, especially the activity methods of the primary school. It is hoped that the hints given in this booklet will set other teachers on this same track: they know how to teach, but they have to make their teaching into *language*-teaching. By understanding the nature of language, and by themselves learning something about the processes of language learning and language teaching, they can begin to do so. The new ideas they must themselves develop, and the modifications of their old techniques that they must come to make, should all be directed to this one aim – to teach English language as effectively and economically as possible to these particular pupils in their particular situations.

But it is precisely because teaching is a personal thing, and because details of techniques and procedures are often personal too, that books of practical hints are difficult to compile or to read and apply. It is a common experience that what 'works' with one teacher, fails dismally with another, and this is not only true of techniques in the classroom but also of textbooks used and set exercises performed. However, a scientific attitude to language teaching, and the approach suggested in this book, imply that certain general procedures will be followed (e.g. in the pattern and extent of oral work, the use of imperative drills, for example, at an early stage, the use of questions and answers by the pupils, etc.), and some hints on these are included in the teacher's notes to the scheme of work. In this present chapter it is proposed to give further advice and ideas about such procedures, with illustrations of the sort of language activities that can usefully be employed for teaching purposes, and some suggestions too about the sort of material and methods that can be applied more strictly to the teaching of pronunciation. There is a separate chapter on apparatus and teaching aids; their use is obviously very closely connected with the choice and development of procedures in language teaching.

But first a word about general procedure as distinct from procedures. This of course varies considerably with the type of immigrant class the teacher is faced with, its position within the school, its size and composition – whether made up of pupils of one language group or of many, of children of approximately the same age or of varied ages, etc. – together with the amount of time the teacher spends with it, which may vary from one or two hours a week to practically the whole of every day. If the teacher has an infant class on a full-time basis, he may feel that he can proceed slowly and cautiously, giving the pupils all the time he likes to allow them to develop at their own rate, jointly and individually, in the various language skills. But many teachers will be subjected to much greater pressure than this, to get their immigrant pupils understanding, talking and grounded in the rudiments of reading and writing as quickly as possible, so that they may be integrated into the main part of the school, or, where there is pressure of new numbers coming in, simply to make room for others. These are the variables that will determine how much time the teacher can give to individuals or to groups, and which will also, as a consequence, influence much of his choice of procedures and the length of time that he can reasonably spend on certain activities.

Whatever the pressures, he will always have in his mind the need to see that at each stage of the work the language is learnt as thoroughly as possible before moving on to the next; passing on to new items as quickly as possible, leaving old ones only half mastered (and *mastery* should be the key-word always) is a false economy. It also proves to be a false economy to expect too much of pupils too soon; especially in the early stages it is easy to underestimate the amount of repetition the teacher has to give to a new item before the pupils have made it part of their active use of language. They need to hear things repeated by the teacher very many times, and they themselves, when they then come to practise them, need to have very many chances of doing so. This cannot be overemphasized. New patterns of words and new items of vocabulary are only mastered when they slip automatically from the tongue. With small numbers the teacher may be able to go round and round the group individually, using varying techniques, games and games-like drills such as those suggested on pages 148–157; but in a large class he will have to replace much of the individual work with chorus work, first, for instance, getting the class as a whole to repeat what he wants, then signalling to rows or groups in turn, occasionally if he chooses breaking up the procedure by picking on an individual who he knows from experience is likely to get it right.

A word of warning should be given at this point about chorus work, for in English-language classes, as in others, it can soon get out of hand and result in a noisy or ragged babble, doing more harm than good to all concerned. Pupils have to be trained to keep their voices down and to keep time together, neither dragging the words out nor racing too quickly through them. In a well-taught class a starting signal from the teacher may be enough to achieve all this, but more often the teacher will need to beat time. He will also need to watch for pupils who do not actually join in the chorus work but merely move their lips in time with the others.

Moreover, in chorus work and all repetitive work there is the great danger of going on too long. The teacher's discretion and sense of timing must tell him when to stop. It is very often the case that the type of pupils he has, their age and disposition, and even their national grouping, may make chorus work impossible unless it is introduced in some disguise, again as a game or competition.

Throughout the day the teacher's use of English is the model that the class bases its own English on. He will be aware of the need to correct errors in pronunciation or grammar, but at the same time will know that he must at all costs avoid discouraging the weak or insecure pupils. If a mistake is made by a pupil, it may, for instance, be best for the teacher to say the correct form himself without further comment, then to pass on to other children in the hope of obtaining a repetition of the correct form from them, finally coming back to the first child when he has thus had the opportunity to hear the correct form repeated and repeated. Telling a child crossly that he is wrong, grinding away at him to make him correct himself, will often only make him nervous. He needs to hear the correct form from his teacher and fellow pupils as often as possible. (Of course, the lazy or careless child may well require handling in a different way.)

When a pupil is known to find difficulty or to be shy, or when the teacher is working with new material, it is a good technique to prompt – either by whispering, or by giving the first part of the required response – in order to get the pupil going. Correct language habits will not form in long threatening silences, but only after the correct form has been heard several times or by helpful stimuli setting the necessary mechanism in motion. This is particularly true of all language work with young children, who should never be expected to 'sit and think' about language.

One technique in particular may be added here, which is of special reference to the teaching of pronunciation but also relates to other areas of language work. Sometimes it seems that the pupil has to be helped to *hear* the mistakes he persists in making; some teachers achieve this by pronouncing the form correctly and then very briefly imitating the pupil's mistake in juxtaposition to it. If this is done in a good-natured way, it often drives the point home (as does listening to oneself on a tape-recorder sometimes), and the pupil will then make greater efforts to approximate to the correct version. But obviously this particular technique must be carried out with both tact and skill.

Language-learning opportunities

Referring now to what was said in Chapter 1 about language and meaning, and the pupils' motivation in learning, we pass to the general consideration of the techniques by which language can best be used and taught in the classroom. 'Using' language and 'teaching' language should not be thought of as necessarily separate activities: although we need to be clear about what we are teaching and how we are teaching it, we should not be blinded by a rigid compartmentalization which stops us seeing language in its true perspective. This perspective must always include meaning.

The language that will in fact be learnt first and most quickly by the immigrant pupil is the language that is essential to the moment, the bits of English that he cannot do without, hence even the youngest immigrant's pre-knowledge of how to answer questions like *What's your name?* and similar demands for such data that he knows he may have to produce for those in authority. The area of language suggested early in Chapter 2 as being essential to the conduct of a class – *Sit down, Give out the milk, Please may I leave the room?* etc. – is also of this nature. This is language that, in the terms of the linguist, is fully contextualized: it has to be used at the moment it is used because the situation, the pattern of events, of human desires and demands, needs it for expression.

Clearly there is a limit to language that is learnt in this way in the classroom, but it is probably the area of language that is most thoroughly and quickly learnt by the pupils because they themselves, their wants and needs, their feelings and senses, their participation in their little bit of society, are involved in it to the fullest extent. In this category I would place all the language used in the general activities of the class (i.e. outside the English-language period), activities which immigrants can often share in with British children, especially, of course, P.E. and games, and handwork, and also the activities of the so-called activities-period in the junior school (such as ludo, snakes-and-ladders, tracing, cut-out work, sticky-paper work, modelling, etc.). In this kind of work – or play – the pupil will be doing something that he enjoys and finds interesting; his mind and body will be occupied while he experiences pleasure in movement, or creative or patterned activity. The language associated with this, which is necessary for conducting it or participating in it, or for communicating with others about it, will be 'English with a purpose'. As suggested elsewhere, the teacher should make the most of this kind of opportunity for language work. He should be aware of the structural items and vocabulary that are, or can be, used on these occasions, and should see how they relate to the scheme of work he is pursuing in his formal English periods.

Obviously it is desirable that the language formally practised in English, and the language of these other times should be closely linked. The type of work that can be done to consolidate the pupils' language learning will be obvious from a few examples. If, for instance, in the early days of P.E. the children learn to respond to the teacher's commands *Run! Skip! Hop!* etc. and perhaps to give the command themselves on occasions, they should at the appropriate moment be encouraged to use the present continuous tense of the same verbs to describe what they themselves or their companions are doing at the actual moment of doing it, and at a later stage should move on to using the same verbs in the simple past to describe after the lesson what in fact they did. This will be language meaningfully and speedily learnt. Many prepositions can be learnt and practised in the same way:

> Run round the room
> Jump over the box
> Run in and out the benches;

similarly, numerals, especially the ordinals and series:

> I want the first boy to run . . .
> Run twice round the room

and adverbs and adverbials:

> Walk slowly
> Hop on one foot.

In art and craft, the necessary language, not just the isolated lexical items such as *paper, nails, red wool, blue raffia, small hammer*, but the structures and patterns of language which occur in the context of the lessons

I can't find a big needle
Can I have another piece of cotton?
Use the scissors, not a knife

will again be amongst the language items most securely learnt if the teacher takes every opportunity presented to see that pupils' passive *and* active knowledge is exercised. This of course will best be done by individual questioning as the teacher supervises such work and moves round the class.

It is fairly obvious from this that the most rapid and efficient language teaching will probably be carried out if the same teacher has the class for all periods, so he will know what language work he has introduced in the course of the day in one context and can thus take or create opportunities to practise it in other periods. But if different teachers take the class for P.E., etc., then, as suggested above, it would be a great gain if they could always be briefed in advance as to what language the children are supposed to know or to have a passive knowledge of.

Fully 'contextualized' language learning does not end there. For at odd moments throughout the day the teacher can create opportunities for furthering it. There will be moments, for instance, when a child makes an error and the teacher may find it convenient to feign a misunderstanding that does not really exist. The pupil whose vowels are uncertain may ask for a *pin* when he means a *pen*. If the teacher presents him with a pin, and then, when the pupil objects, allows the misunderstanding to be cleared up by saying 'Oh – a pen. *This* is a pen – that's a pin. Do you want a pin or a pen?', a significant point should have been got across, i.e. the pupil will at least have learnt the necessity to produce an accurate sound even if he is still not quite able to do it, and his ears may begin to respond that little bit more to the slight phonemic difference between [i] and [e].

One of the teacher's most useful techniques then is to feign emotions which he may not really feel: puzzlement, mock anger, surprise, dismay. Working along the same lines, he may contrive sudden little situations simply to provoke some response from his pupils which they need practice in. He can for instance – an old favourite but a well-tried one – pretend to be slightly deaf; or he may contrive a search for some 'lost' object, his glasses or his pen (*They're in your bag, sir – It's on the top shelf*); or he may deliberately muddle the giving out of books (*This isn't mine; it's Antonio's*), and so on.

The alert teacher who knows his class will not only use every opportunity that presents itself for this 'natural' language practice, but will invent such opportunities. On the whole, the language used on such occasions will be language that has already been presented and which is now needing to be practised; but it may well be that on some particularly promising occasion, when the attention and imagination of the class are likely to be captured and held, some quite new item may be introduced and, through the magnetic quality of the moment, be half-way to being learnt on its very first introduction. The language teacher must above all be an opportunist.

Language drill

The main theme of this book has been the idea that a methodical approach to language teaching is likely to be the most economical and the most effective one; and so the teacher, while making the most of every opportunity that occurs, or, as suggested, while actually creating opportunities for the practice and use of language items, will at the same time be working through a syllabus or scheme of work in language, thus trying to ensure that his pupils develop accuracy in the use of the structural patterns of English.

The rule is always that when the teacher presents a point of grammar, he does so by introducing it meaningfully in a situation, holding up different objects in turn if he is dealing with the naming of things (*This is a book, This is a pencil* . . .), handling actual groups of different objects if he is introducing plurals, performing and making pupils perform actions when dealing with the present continuous tense, and so on. The meaning of the language thus presented is 'visible' in the situation: it does not have to be explained by anyone having recourse to the pupils' mother tongue or to a dictionary.

In the teacher's notes to the Scheme of Work put forward in

Chapter 2 some suggestions on presentation of items in this way are included, and reference is made in the Book List to the present chapter to other sources where help in devising such procedures can be found. Teachers will work out their own methods with a little practice. But the mere presentation of the language item being taught is not of course enough; what has to follow is plenty of opportunity for the class to practise the form or forms in question, rapidly and in quick succession, so that these become absorbed into the automatic language habits of the pupils.

This repetitive and very important part of language learning is most usually known as *drill*. It is the element that has till recently been most often lacking in the teaching of languages in British schools. In essence, language drill has to provide the pupils with the opportunity of using the language items correctly as often as possible; i.e. it should be a time when pupils are given the opportunity to get things right, not wrong, and it should not be confused with testing.

With a co-operative class even the most repetitive and apparently tedious drill may succeed if conducted with enough life and enthusiasm by the teacher. At its simplest, for example, Pupil A will turn to Pupil B saying, 'My name is ——. What's yours?' B answers, saying, 'My name is ——,' and, turning to Pupil C, asks 'What's yours?', and so on, right round the class. This is what is known as a circular drill. When there are several failures or mispronunciations, the teacher may switch to general or group chorus repetition to pull the standard up and break monotony, and may then resume the individual drilling at a different point.

Much drill can be incorporated into a lesson by getting the class used to giving chorus repetition after individual responses:

TEACHER: Where's your book, Rashid?
RASHID: It's in my desk.
CLASS: It's in his desk.
TEACHER: Where's your money, Nina?
NINA: It's in my pocket.
CLASS: It's in her pocket.

The action-chain drill (outlined on pp. 60 and 101 above) can be used in the same way to practise different persons and different tenses of the verb, and can be varied in many ways by the teacher, or a pupil, asking additional questions (*Is he going to the door? – No, he isn't. He's going to the cupboard*).

Another basic form of drill can be arrived at by simply cueing in content words, the cued word to be substituted by pupils, in chorus again or individually, in the chosen pattern, e.g. to practise *There's a* —— the teacher, having established the pattern, would call out the names of things or hold up different items (or at the reading stage even point to words on the blackboard or hold up flashcards):

TEACHER: Box.
CLASS: There's a box on the table.
TEACHER: Pen.
CLASS: There's a pen on the table.

and might vary this at a slightly later stage by using plural cues as well as singular ones:

TEACHER: Two books
CLASS: There are two books on the table.
TEACHER: Penny
CLASS: There's a penny on the table.

A teacher can remind himself of the 'substitution drill' he wishes to practise by preparing a little table beforehand to show the structures together with the content words which form the items where the substitution(s) can be made. Thus for the above drill, he would have prepared something like:

There's	a box a pen a penny	on the table.
There are	two books three matches	

Older pupils at the reading and writing stage can be given both oral drill practice (from the blackboard) and written practice (copying sentences into their books) through substitution tables such as the above. They will be found in many textbooks nowadays[1] and provide a good basis for this necessary repetitive work. They are often more enjoyable for the pupils if the choice of items from the different columns involves an element of sense or nonsense which the pupil has to see through and select or discard accordingly:

This book The teacher's hat Ali's bicycle The desk	is is not	made of	tin wood felt steel

Where the teacher feels that this kind of drill work will go down, he will develop other ideas of his own using, for instance,

Mr. Brown   Mr. Smith

cues and substitutions from pictures, or from facts or figures written up in readiness on the blackboard. Simple sketches can be used to obtain, for example:

Mr Brown is richer than Mr Smith
Mr Smith is fatter than Mr Brown
etc.

[1] e.g. See French, *English in Tables*, and textbooks such as *The Oxford Progressive English Course* (item 13 in Bibliography, p. 243).

Mr Smith has got a car
Mr Brown hasn't got a car
Mr Brown has got one cat, but Mr Smith has got three
cats
    etc.

Drill in which the language items being drilled thus have considerable 'meaning' (because they describe a picture or a person – something tangible) will on the whole be enjoyable and therefore the more effective as a teaching device.

But whatever type of drill is used, it will be necessary to keep the whole procedure short and sweet. Five to seven minutes may be the very most for young pupils; older pupils may have slightly longer periods, but even with them it will usually be necessary to switch from one type of drill to another in order to keep the procedure brisk and lively. Drills have obviously to be very carefully planned beforehand.

It is usually found that the older learners of a foreign language will work hard and co-operatively at language drills without becoming too bored (though admittedly they will often become very tired), and if they do get bored, at least they will know why they are being made to perform the drills. But experience has shown that on the whole very young pupils do not readily take to drill work unless the whole procedure is essentially meaningful and the drill element more or less completely concealed. For most of them, using English in class has to be part of purposive activity; there must seem to be some point in saying what the teacher wants them to say. An example may remind some teachers of their own experiences. A teacher wanting to drill the plural demonstrative pronouns and verb forms, might choose a simple drill such as:

These are red pencils
Those are blue pencils
These are yellow pencils
Those are green pencils

Obviously, unless the pupils could see the different coloured pencils in question each time, the whole activity would be puzzling and nonsensical. The teacher would therefore assemble his sets of different coloured pencils, and with older pupils would probably find he could obtain the responses he wanted simply by getting individuals to touch or point to the different pencils. But for younger pupils, this would be inadequate; the drill would not come to life. For them to respond fully, they would need to have the whole procedure turned into a kind of game by, for instance, the pencils being hidden under a duster so that they had to guess the actual colour of the different sets; as they felt or pointed to the hidden pencils they would then, it is hoped, be drilling the required item – *These are . . ., Those are . . .*, etc. For them it would in fact be the colour of the concealed pencils that was the really important part of what they were saying. In the former case, the colour would have been of relative unimportance; in the latter it would be all important as providing the point of interest in the guessing game.

This example will have served to point to the sort of activity, called here a 'structural game', which can be utilized to involve pupils in a kind of painless grammar practice. Some suggestions along these lines have in fact already been made here and there in the teacher's notes to the Scheme of Work (Chapter 2), and a few others are now given below. It is hoped that once set on the right road, the teacher will find it fairly easy to invent others to add to his own personal list.

GAMES FOR IDENTIFYING OBJECTS AND PEOPLE, USING SIMPLE INTRODUCTORY STRUCTURES

Is it a . . .? Is it an . . .? Yes, it is. No, it isn't.

(1) The teacher holds a small object concealed in his fist (or in a bag, etc.). Pupils guess in turn: *Is it a penny?* etc. The child who guesses correctly takes the teacher's place. Objects should be chosen to include practice of *an* as well as *a* (an egg, an apple, etc.).

(2) One child goes out of the classroom, and the class decides on a certain object. The child comes in and tries to guess what it is, asking pupils individually, who reply *No, it isn't* until the correct object is arrived at. If

teams or groups are established, this game can be played as a competition and scores can be kept; one child from each team can go outside, and when they come in they have to take it in turns to guess.

Is it Ali's?

(3) To practise the possessive forms, follow the procedure in (2) but the class chooses an object which must be something that several or all have in common (pen, book, bag, etc.); the questioner can be told *what* the object is, but has to guess *whose* it is: *Is it Ali's?*, etc.

Is it on . . .? Is it in . . .?

(4) *Hunt the thimble.* A small object such as a ring or a thimble is chosen, and while one or two children go outside, the class decides where it is to be hidden. The child outside then comes in and asks questions with prepositions: *Is it on — ? Is it in — ?*, etc.

Is it Nassif?

(5) *Blindman's Buff.* A blindfolded child has to catch children as they go past. When this is played in the classroom, the teacher can simply beckon to pupils to creep out and slip past the one who is blindfolded, and there is no need for the whole class to be in motion. When someone is caught, he must guess who it is he holds captive: *Is it Nassif?*, etc., and the whole class answers accordingly. If he guesses correctly, the child who is caught takes his place.

(6) *Twenty questions* (simplified form). The teacher or a pupil selects an object (something in the classroom, to start with) and the rest of the class tries to guess what it is by asking simple questions:

Is it small?
Is it red?
Is it near the door?
Is it Ali's pencil?

The answerer can only respond with *Yes, it is,* or *No, it isn't,* and the score should be kept to see if the class can guess correctly in fewer than twenty questions.

These first six games are prototypes and can be varied in many ways by introducing or varying the competitive element, by changing the required patterns of questions and answers, etc., and sometimes by being combined with one another (for instance, (1) with (2)). *Twenty questions* can be played throughout an English course, becoming more complicated as more language is learnt, the class asking questions which practise new structures and vocabulary, new tenses of the verb, etc.; e.g.

> Is it an animal?
> Does it eat fish?
> Does it live in . . .?
> Can it swim?
> etc.

GAMES FOR PRACTISING SLIGHTLY MORE ADVANCED LANGUAGE, INCLUDING PLURALS, UNCOUNTABLE NOUNS, PARTS OF THE VERB 'BE', PRONOUNS, ETC.

This is for you.
What is it?   (What have you got?)
It's a . . .   It's an . . .   It's . . .   It's some . . .

(7) *The postman* (especially useful for going over vocabulary learnt in connection with one centre of interest, such as items of furniture, food, groceries). A pupil, who is chosen to be postman, is given a bag containing several small articles wrapped separately (such as doll's house furniture, small quantities of rice, sugar, etc., done up loosely in polythene; or pictures of related items, animals, clothes, etc., on separate cards).

The postman hands out one item to a pupil: *This is for you.* The pupil feels the package he has been given and the others ask him *What is it?* or, at a later stage, *What have you got?*

The pupil guesses, and then opens it to check. Answers should be the simple formula *It's a/an* . . . or, if uncountable nouns are involved (foodstuffs, substances), may simply be *It's* . . . or *It's some* . . .

Where does it go? What does it say? How does it taste?

It goes in . . . **It says** . . . **It tastes** . . .

As an extension to this, if, for instance, the simple present tense of some verbs has been learnt, pupils can ask further questions, e.g. if furniture is used: *Where does it go?* and the pupil must answer *It goes in the* . . . *room*, or with animals, *What does it say?*, with foodstuffs, *How does it taste?*

Packages or cards are finally collected by the postman and another pupil can take his place.

There is . . . **There was** . . . .

(8) *Kim's game.* The teacher shows the class a picture, or a drawing on the blackboard, consisting of several objects which they know; or the objects themselves can be placed on a table or tray. These are covered up after a few minutes and pupils have to say, or write down, the ones they remember (*A rubber, a ring, an orange* . . .). As in game (1), objects should be selected to include practice in *an* as well as *a*.

At a later stage the same game can be used for practising *There is* . . ., and later again, *There was* . . . .

If it is played orally, the game can be varied by letting each pupil name one object only. This can be turned into a competition by taking answers from different teams in rotation.

There are . . . **There were** . . .

The collection of objects can be made to include the practice of plural forms of nouns, with numerals and/ or colours: e.g. two blue pencils, one black pen, four red buttons, two orange stamps. This could later involve pupils in the use of *There are* . . . and *There were* . . .

ADJECTIVES

The teacher's cat is a black cat.

(9) *The parson's cat.* A simple version of this game can be played at first to practise adjectives. The first child says, for instance, 'The teacher's cat is a *black* cat'; the second child simply substitutes another adjective of his own choice for *black*: 'The teacher's cat is a *big* cat', and so on round the class.

Later the more difficult conventional version can be played, pupils having to choose adjectives in alphabetical order (e.g. *awful, big, clever, dirty* . . .) and repeating all those that have already been said so that the list is cumulative.

Are you sleepy?   No, I'm not.   (Yes, I am.)

(10) *Miming* (adjectives). The teacher, or a pupil, selects an adjective known to the class and mimes it in some way; the class has to guess what it is, by asking questions:

Are you sleepy?
Are you sad?
Are you ill?
   etc.

The mimer answers *No, I'm not* until someone guesses correctly and takes his place, choosing another adjective to mime.

Is he sleepy?   No, he isn't.   (Yes, he is.)

This game can also be played in such a way that it includes practice in third-person forms: the mimer whispers his chosen adjective to a pupil (or the teacher) and the class do not then question him directly, but ask instead *Is he sleepy?*, etc. The pupil (or teacher) replies *No, he isn't* until the correct adjective is found.

PLURALS OF NOUNS, NUMERALS, ETC.

We have 50 beans . . .

(11) *Collections.* The teacher hands out collections of objects to different groups, who have then to enumerate the items they have been given: *We have 50 beans, 10*

stamps, and 6 pins. This game can be varied by letting teams first guess the numbers of articles they have before they start counting them. Alternatively, groups can make a guess at the numbers of articles in the collections given to other groups before the counting begins.

Is it in Rashid's hand?   Is it in your hand, Rashid? No, it isn't.—Yes, it is.   Has Antonio got it?   Have you got it, Antonio?   No, I haven't.

(12) *Where's the penny?* The pupils in one team stand in a row very close together and pass a penny from hand to hand behind their backs. The other pupils guess where it is. The members of the first team must keep absolutely still as soon as a question is asked, and the pupil named in the question must answer appropriately according to the wording of the question. If this game is played at an early stage, questions could take the form *Is it in Rashid's hand?* or *Is it in your hand, Rashid?* and the answer would be *No, it isn't,* or *Yes, it is.* At a later stage, *have* or *have got* could be used: *Has Antonio got it?* or *Have you got it, Antonio?*, with suitable replies from the pupils named by the questioners.

Is he a . . .?   Are you a . . .?   Are they . . .?

(13) *Occupations.* Individual pupils or members of one team or group mime different occupations and the others guess what they are meant to be: *Is he a bus driver? Are they soldiers?*, etc. This can provide practice in the different persons of the verb *be,* and also in the use of the 'zero' indefinite article plural (see p. 54 above). Answers should include *Yes, we are, No, I'm not.*

GAMES INVOLVING PRACTICE OF VERB FORMS, PRESENT CONTINUOUS AND OTHER TENSES

Is he (she) running?   Yes, he is.   No, he isn't.

(14) *Actions.* The teacher draws a quick sketch of a pin man performing an action; the pupils try to guess what

the man is doing: *Is he running?*, *Is he jumping?*, etc. The one who guesses first then provides a drawing for the others to guess about (or, if the pupils are not up to drawing quickly and recognizably, let them simply score points for correct answers while the teacher goes on providing the drawings). Picture cards (drawings or cutouts) exhibited like flashcards can be used for variety or for greater speed.

Is he marching?   Are they building . . .?

(15) *Silent actions.* The teacher whispers instructions to a pupil who then performs an action as required. The class questions, as in (14). Pupils may themselves choose the actions they wish to perform. Group mimes should be included to afford practice in plural forms: *Are they marching?*, *Are they building a house?*, etc.

I'm going to put . . .

(16) *Packing the bag.* This old party game can be simplified in various ways, though it will be of most use if pupils actually handle the objects they choose, e.g. as a pupil adds a new item, he picks up the object, or a picture of it, and actually places it in a bag in front of the class. This game is perhaps best played cumulatively, the first pupil for instance saying, *I'm going to put a hat in the bag*, the second saying, *I'm going to put a hat and a pair of shoes in the bag*, etc. Pupils should be chosen alternately from different teams if this is to take the form of a competition, teams losing points if their members slip up in repeating the list as it gets longer and longer.

I packed my bag and in it I put . . .

Later, pupils can revert to the authentic version, using the past tense: *I packed my bag and in it I put . . .*

Yesterday, I bought . . .

The formula itself can be varied to introduce other verbs and the vocabulary of other situations, e.g. *Yesterday, I bought some butter. Yesterday I bought some rice and some butter*, etc.

SPELLING GAMES

A word should be said about spelling games within the context of the English lesson. On the whole these are not as useful for language practice as the structural type of game suggested above, but they can find some place in the language class. Spelling games cannot be played until the pupils have learnt the alphabet, and the alphabet is not an item to be learnt at an early stage.[1] If some work on letter sounds is included as part of pre-reading activity, it may be possible to base some simple games on this, such as competitions in which pupils have to select a picture or an object, the name of which begins with a sound pronounced very clearly by the teacher. For example, the teacher would say 'Now who can find me a picture of something beginning with [b]?' and pupils would then go and select a picture from a set of cards which might include pictures of buses or bags amongst several other things.

Once the alphabet is mastered and reading and writing begun, simple spelling games such as *I spy with my little eye* can be played with variations.

Word-games, such as *Hangman*, team spelling-bees, building word-squares, crossword competitions of different kinds, building as many words as possible out of the letters that make up one long word, and games on the lines of *Scrabble* are enjoyed by the average class. But as in all the games described above, the teacher needs to exercise control over the vocabulary used, to see for instance that the right names are given to the letters of the alphabet when they are used, that everyone as far as possible has a turn, and that within the framework of the game learning opportunities are not wasted.

TRADITIONAL PLAYGROUND GAMES

Many traditional children's games involve a language element which can be utilized for the present purpose. These are mainly running-about games which are probably more suited to the playground, gymnasium or hall than to the classroom, and would be suitable for inclusion in P.E. periods with younger pupils.

[1] See below, Chapter 5, p. 184.

The language practice provided for instance by the popular *What's the time, Mr Wolf?* is obvious:

What's the time?   One o'clock.

(17) *What's the time, Mr Wolf?* One child is chosen to be the wolf, and walks around with the other children following at a distance chanting *What's the time, Mr Wolf?* Every so often the wolf stops and replies *One o'clock, Half past three,* etc. (In some versions everyone must freeze each time the wolf replies, in others everyone goes on walking.) When eventually the wolf says *Dinner time,* or some other mealtime, or a chosen formula such as *Time to eat you,* he turns and chases the others until he catches one, who then takes his place as wolf.

What are you doing?

Other versions of this game could be played to practise different language items, such as:

What are you doing, Mr Wolf?
  I'm walking.
  I'm running (*suiting action to words*).
  I'm skipping.
  I'm going to eat you . . . (*beginning to chase the others*).

Does the tiger live here?   No, he doesn't . . .
You must go further through the forest . . .
Yes, it does.

(18) *Hunting the tiger.* One child is chosen to be the hunter, and is given a den, a chalk circle in the middle of the playground. The others stand in a ring around him (or, if there are not very many in the class, in a line close together, facing the hunter's den). They pass a small object from hand to hand (such as a very small ball, or a piece of chalk) without the hunter seeing. He then leaves his den and questions each child in turn: *Does the tiger live here?* Children answer in the negative if they do not have the object at that moment, saying *No, it doesn't,* and adding, according to their knowledge of the language, a formula such as *You must go further through the forest* (or *You must go on down the road,* etc.).

The child who has the object answers *Yes, it does*, and chases the hunter back to his den. If he catches him before he reaches safety, they change places.

The invention and adaptation of games such as those listed above is a fairly simple matter. The teacher should certainly not look on them – least of all on the kind suggested for use in the classroom (nos. 1–16 above) – simply as time-filling activities reserved for Friday afternoons. The motivation of pupils in games and competition-like activities, is high, and if the language used in them is carefully guided and controlled, they can form a very enjoyable practice-ground for the unavoidable repetitive work which in one form or another is a most vital part of language learning.

Towards free language activity

Language teaching, to be successful, must provide the learner with very many opportunities to hear and repeat the same item, or related items, of structure and vocabulary; he has to hear and say them himself so often that he can produce them automatically when required. A set of language habits must be formed.

But language learning cannot stop at this, because in the end mastering a language is more than mastering a set of habits. The teacher has to try to ensure that the responses his pupils give automatically in the drill or structural-game situation, are also produced in the 'real-life' situation. He has to make a connection between the language of the English class and the living language – 'verbal behaviour' as it has been called – of the thousand and one situations in which it is used outside the classroom. (Earlier in this chapter it was stressed that there should always be a connection between the language of the English class and that used in other lessons such as P.E., etc., and collaboration between teachers – or deliberate planning by the one teacher – was recommended.) Within the language class itself, the teacher must take steps towards linking classroom English and 'real' English; the pupils must be brought to see that the way they have learnt to talk about pens and books and desks, or about themselves, in the classroom, is extendable to the way people talk in shops, at the doctor's, in restaurants, or in their own homes. The teacher has to help them make this transference.

To do so, he has to get his pupils using English in which control – as in the drills and structural games – is still exercised to a very great extent, but in which the drill element is submerged while the language seems increasingly purposive.

DIALOGUES

Short dialogues are probably the most effective form that this kind of language work can take. It is suggested that teachers should consider using them very frequently as a teaching device and from as early a stage as possible, basing them firmly on the structures and vocabulary which are taught to the class at each step, but including too the sort of language items which can hardly ever be formally taught (like the conversational *then* and *perhaps* used in the incidental questions suggested in the Scheme of Work, p. 80 above), and the many exclamations, pause-words, etc., which form part of the give and take of normal spoken language.

Here is an example of such a dialogue using simple introductory structures and based on an everyday scene familiar at home or school:

MOTHER: (sweeping the floor): What's this? What's this?

ALI: What are you doing, mother?

MOTHER: I'm sweeping the floor. Now, what's this?

ALI: It's Nassif's book.

MOTHER: And oh! what's this?

ALI: It's Nassif's shoe.

MOTHER: Nassif's a naughty boy. Put them in the cupboard, please.

Ideally a dialogue should be memorized and acted by groups of pupils (in the above, for instance, in addition to the Mother and Ali, non-speaking parts could be assigned to the Father and to Nassif, the untidy brother), different groups taking it in turns to give a performance. If the dialogue is short and interesting (the Mother's emotions of anger or impatience in the above would make it interesting 'dramatically'), it will be more easily enjoyed and memorized. As different pupils take part, they can be encouraged to make their own variations in the language of the original:

MOTHER: What's this . . . and this . . . and this?
ALI: What are you doing, mother?
MOTHER: I'm tidying the cupboard. Now, what's this?
ALI: It's my coat.

(The use of substitution in dialogues in this way should not be confused with language drill, but it has obvious potentialities which can be exploited.[1])

Memorization of dialogues and frequent repetition (carried out as naturally as possible) are the two main features of this form of work. Both are reasons for the dialogues being kept short, in the early stages anyway. Teachers may write their own, or after a while find that a class can compose its own, often as a co-operative effort. But, however composed, neither the individual lines nor the dialogue as a whole should be long, otherwise it will be neither memorized easily nor used naturally by the 'actors'. Four or six short lines may be all that can be mastered at first.

Dialogues can be devised in different ways according to the required language content. Some, for instance, can be between pupils themselves in a school setting (e.g. bringing a new boy to class, giving a present to a friend, showing an object of curiosity to the teacher, complaining of a hurt received in the playground, etc.), others may relate to the out-of-school environment, such as the home or the street, bringing in characters such as visitors, lost passers-by, a policeman, shopkeeper, etc. It should be noted that an element of emotion (anger, grief, pity, etc.) and of colourful characterization (forgetful old man, nervous young lady, etc.) can be telescoped into quite a short space and makes this kind of work twice as lively and enjoyable.

It is obvious that work of this nature can very usefully help the immigrant pupil to cope linguistically with some of the problems

[1] A most useful textbook which in fact provides a set of dialogues together with built-in substitution practice is *Conversation Exercises in Everyday English* by Jerrom and Szkutnik (entry no. 28 in Bibliography).

of living in a new community. All involved in the education of immigrants have ultimately a wider objective than simply teaching them to speak English; the immigrant pupil has to learn how to live and to deal with many features of British life that are strange to him, from shopping, or travelling by public transport – daily occurrences perhaps – to situations like using a public telephone, going to a cinema, visiting a doctor or hospital, posting a parcel, and so on. Many of these situations cannot be fully dealt with until the pupil has a moderate command of English; but many can be introduced in the classroom in some form or other – e.g. through work on projects or centres of interest[1] – and some of the necessary vocabulary and structures essential to related situations can enter the language scheme.

Dialogues can obviously be used with this type of work to a large extent. Through dialogues, for instance, the acceptable patterns of language for use in shops can be practised – for buying bus tickets, asking the way, and so on. With all dialogue work the teacher will find that attention to the following points will make the whole procedure the more valuable:

1 The dialogue as a whole should be presented as clearly and dramatically as possible to the class. The teacher should 'set' it, using pictures, or models, or articles of furniture; he should act it out as expressively as possible, and consider using cut-out figures, pictures, or – perhaps best of all – puppets, to indicate who is saying what. The better the initial presentation, the more complete will be the pupils' involvement in it.

2 The whole class, then groups, then individuals, should be thoroughly rehearsed in the dialogue and helped to memor-

[1] The use of 'centres of interest' as a basis for language work and for activities such as drawing and modelling in other periods, is highly recommended in work with immigrant pupils. Starting with the classroom itself, moving outwards to the home, the rooms in it, meals, etc., and then going further afield to shops, the doctor's, the hospital, the park, transport, etc., the teacher should easily find enough topics to last him the year. In the techniques associated with work based on centres of interest and projects, primary-school method and practice has again a great deal of relevance to the teaching of immigrants at all stages, and teachers who have not had this kind of experience would benefit from a visit to a primary school where they could observe such techniques being used.

ize it. If a written text is used (books, or the blackboard), it should be memorized before pupils are asked to perform it.

3 A few necessary or suitable props should be provided, especially rudimentary dressing-up items such as hats, spectacles, newspapers, etc.

4 Pupils taking parts should be encouraged to speak clearly and accurately. Special attention will need to be paid to intonation. All the rest of the class should listen attentively. (Attentiveness can be encouraged by awarding points to rows or groups whose members give the best rendering.)

5 Dialogues once learnt should not be performed to death, but neither should they be dropped too soon and forgotten. New ones can be invented as extensions of old ones and with the same characters; old ones should be revived and the language in them freshened up and corrected if there are lapses.

Dialogue work is certainly not confined to use with young pupils only. It will be found effective with pupils at secondary school and with adults. Older pupils are particularly glad to learn dialogues that relate to their everyday life in the community. They may also learn rather longer ones than juniors. But length is not always a gain: dialogues should go to the heart of a situation as briefly and expressively as possible.

PLAYS, DRAMATIZATION

From dialogue work it is only a short step to the use of plays, puppet plays, dramatization of episodes from stories, and so on. This kind of work also meets with a great response from most pupils and can be turned to good use in this transition stage between control and freedom in the use of grammar and vocabulary.

Shortness is again a great virtue, and although the teacher may sometimes feel it necessary to aim at a proper 'production', using the best actors and speakers, he should see that all the class are involved in some capacity or other and that opportunities are given for all to learn in it and through it.

Although many teachers will find it best to write their own, it is possible to obtain texts of short plays in which the language carefully graded and controlled and in which especially there is considerable repetition of simple structures, a feature which helps pupils to memorize the lines much more easily and which often has considerable charm.[1]

The tape-recorder, which has many uses in language teaching (see below, p. 227), is particularly valuable in connection with all of the above work. Recording and criticizing different renderings usually holds the attention of pupils and can often be an incentive to better performance. The teacher may also find it useful to present his pupils with pre-recorded versions of material they are working on in class: dialogues, or extracts from plays, recorded with sound effects, are especially useful.

STORY TELLING

The teacher should consider the possibilities of story-telling, remembering how much this appeals to pupils of all ages, and how, regrettably, the immigrant pupil at school is often cut off from the enjoyment of the pleasures of the imagination because of inadequate language, and this in many cases at an age when he would most naturally be experiencing and benefiting from it.

How soon can the teacher start story-telling with young immigrant pupils? There must obviously be an interval between the pupil's starting English and the time when he knows enough to follow a simple narrative, but the teacher should not put it off unnecessarily long. It is, for instance, perfectly feasible for a story to be told before the class learns the simple past tense, the tense most often associated with narrative; this can be managed by using the present continuous and where necessary the simple present (this will be long before the class has learnt the 'historic' use of the present as such).

Stories in the early stages need a lot of preparation, but the interest and pleasure and – which is why we include this discussion in the present section – the purposiveness pupils find in their telling, well justifies this. It is best if any essential key words needed for the story are taught beforehand; it should never be necessary to stop in the middle of a narrative in order to explain a new word. Simple pictures of the characters and the main scenes

1 Some titles are suggested in Section V of the Bibliography, p. 247 below.

will be found to be almost indispensable; puppets or dolls to represent the main characters and to be held up when they speak, are also very valuable aids to story-telling.

Large picture-stories, if the pictures can be found or prepared beforehand, are also most useful for the teacher to base his early story-telling on.

Two examples of simple stories are given below; first, one from a language course in which no past tenses are used at all. It is written within a very limited vocabulary and confines itself to the present continuous, simple present and simple future (using *'ll*). It will be obvious that even further simplifications could be made in it, and also that a few simple pictures would help considerably in the narration:

A CLEVER MONKEY

Here is Kitoto. He's a pet monkey.
He's Martha's monkey.
Martha likes him very much.
He isn't very big. He's a little monkey.
He wears a white piece of string round his neck.
He plays with Martha in the *shamba*.[1]
He sits on a chair in the sitting-room.
But he doesn't talk.
He can't talk.
Every morning Martha walks to school.
Every morning Martha says good-bye to her pet monkey.
The monkey wants to go to school.
He can't go to school.
Martha says, 'Good-bye, Kitoto. I'll come back soon. Then I'll play with you in the shamba.'
The monkey looks sad.
He runs to the gate.
He watches Martha walking along the road.
She waves to him.
Then he runs behind the house.

[1] A word which would be edited out by the teacher; it means yard, and, like the monkey itself, and the mangoes later in the story, occurs in the original because it is from a text designed for use in East Africa.

He climbs into a tree.

He goes to sleep.

At 12 o'clock he wakes up.

He runs to the front of the house.

He jumps on to the fence.

He sits there. He watches the road.

He sees Martha. She's running down the road.

She's playing with a red ball.

It bounces into the middle of the road.

Martha runs after it.

She falls down. Now she's crying. She can't get up.

Her pet monkey runs quickly into the house.

Martha's mother is there.

The monkey tries to speak to her.

He can't speak.

He tugs her dress. He pulls her to the door.

Martha's mother knows something is wrong.

She runs to the gate.

She sees Martha. Martha is lying in the road.

Her mother runs out. She runs very quickly. A bus is coming.

She's just in time.

She picks Martha up.

She takes her home.

Martha is crying.

Her knees are bleeding.

Her hands are bleeding, too.

Mother washes Martha's knees and hands.

She puts bandages on her knees. She bandages her hands.

Then she puts Martha to bed.

Her pet monkey runs into the bedroom.

He has a red ball in his hand.

He jumps on to the bed.

He gives the ball to Martha.

'Oh, you clever monkey,' says Martha.

'That's my ball. Thank you! Thank you!'

Martha's mother says 'I'm going to give him a present. I'll give him some mangoes.'

'Oh, yes, please,' says Martha. 'He loves mangoes.'

'Now go to sleep, Martha,' says Mother. 'You'll feel better in the morning.'[1]

The second example, in more difficult English, is from a reader in a series not originally designed for second-language learners but which is in many ways ideally suited to them. With a certain amount of editing it could be read to young immigrant pupils.

THE OLD KETTLE

This old kettle was lying in the hedge.

He was very sad.

'Oh dear,' cried the kettle, 'I have a big hole. I am old and no good to anyone. Soon I'll be rusty and crusty and fit for nothing.'

One day a robin hopped into the hedge.

He peeped through the hole in the kettle and called, 'May I come in and rest?'

The old kettle was so happy.

'Come in,' he cried. 'Come right inside.'

So the robin lived in the kettle, and they were very happy.

Then a mouse came past, and she peeped through the hole in the kettle and called, 'May I come in and rest?'

'Come in,' they cried. 'Come right inside.'

So the mouse lived in the kettle with the robin and they were all very happy.

A lizard came along, and he, too, peeped through the hole in the kettle and called, 'May I come in and rest?'

'Come in,' they cried. 'Come right inside.'

So the lizard lived in the kettle with the robin and the mouse, and they were all very happy.

Out of the wood came a rabbit. He peeped through the hole in the kettle and called, 'May I come in and rest?'

'Come in,' they cried. 'Come right inside.'

So the rabbit lived in the kettle with the robin, the mouse and the lizard, and they were all very happy.

'There is very little room left now,' said the old kettle one day.

[1] *The New Peak Course*, Standard 2, Volume 1, page 29. (See Bibliography, entry no. 10.)

'There is not room for anyone else unless it is someone very small.'

Just then, a little beetle peeped through the hole in the kettle and called, 'May I come in and rest?'

'Come in,' they cried. 'Come right inside. There is just room for a little one in the spout.'

So the beetle lived in the kettle with the robin, the mouse, the lizard and the rabbit, and they were all very happy.[1]

The repeated formulas, the patterned nature of the story (as of all the stories in the series), is the sort of feature that makes it highly suitable for use with language learners, and the teacher might well think of how he would adapt this and others like it to his purpose. When 'editing' such stories, he should of course look out for difficulties of all kinds. He might, for instance, alter 'rusty and crusty and fit for nothing' in line 4 to something much simpler; or, if he decided to leave it in on the grounds that it is one of the most appealing lines in the story, he might make a mental note to see that *crusty* was not misused by enthusiastic pupils on future occasions. There are several other difficulties which might not be so obvious at first glance, such as the inversion in the line 'Out of the wood came a rabbit'.

For older pupils who need more sophisticated subject matter, the teacher should turn to some of the simple readers listed in Section VI of the Bibliography (page 248 below).

Techniques and procedures for the teaching of pronunciation

As suggested in the chapter on pronunciation, it is largely in questions of rhythm and intonation that bad speech habits and mistakes cause unintelligibility and misunderstanding. But bad speech habits can also be of a more general nature, exactly like those of many British children if they have not been well trained, and the teacher should ensure that his pupils get into the habit of listening attentively to him and to one another. Pupils have to be taught to keep their voices up when answering individually, and to speak with control of volume, pitch and speed at all times.

[1] From the series *Reading with Rhythm*, Set Two (Longmans).

Many teachers give up in despair at the machine-gun-like patter of some of their pupils, who when excited are vocal but almost incomprehensible. It is essential therefore from the beginning that they should learn to respond to discipline for the sake of quickness and order, and that the teacher should also train them – as British pupils have to be trained – to sit correctly and breathe well, using the muscles of chest and diaphragm, and learning control of movement of lips and tongue. As suggested in Chapter 3, it would be valuable to spend a few minutes on this work every day.

But then to return first to the question of incorrect rhythm and intonation which, it is suggested, will be the teacher's biggest problem in work on pronunciation: how is one to deal with this? At root, the answer lies in cultivating a sensitivity in the pupil, an awareness of patterns of rhythm and pitch in what he hears and tries to imitate. Obviously as much rhythmical work as possible, with attention paid to the rhythmical element by way of beating time, marching or performing actions to the rhythm, etc., needs to be incorporated into each day's work. The teacher's problem is to select suitable material for this sort of work.

One of his main sources will be traditional nursery rhymes and action songs. Many of these appeal not only to the very young but often – if treated unsentimentally – to older pupils as well. The teacher should try to avoid any of these in which the natural rhythm of speech is badly distorted, for instance where a strong beat occurs on a normally unstressed preposition or weak form of verb or pronoun. And he should also take into account the structures and vocabulary of any rhyme he decides to use. Fortunately, in many of the most suitable there is a structural simplicity, and sometimes a repetitiveness, which makes them ideal for classes learning English. But there are also quite often words of low frequency in present-day English (such as 'crown' in *Jack and Jill*, and 'tuffet' in *Little Miss Muffet*), and some archaisms and inversions, and with these the teacher must use his judgement. He may be able to edit the text slightly – in the very useful song *Here we go round the mulberry bush* it is simple to substitute a local place-name or landmark for the words 'mulberry bush' – or he may feel that such difficulties are slight enough to be ignored.

Some of the most suitable of the action songs and rhymes are listed in the section on singing below. Teachers will not need to be reminded of the words of most of the traditional material of this kind. In the present section we give examples of some of the less commonly known rhymes which are also suitable, especially for this all-important work on rhythm.

First, some counting rhymes, ranging from fairly simple to more difficult. When using these with young pupils, it would be a good idea to let them see the actual objects enumerated, or pictures of them, and actions or mimes could be performed where appropriate:

1 One, two! This is my shoe.
Three, four! That's the door.
Five, six! A bundle of sticks.
Seven, eight! A big white plate.
Nine, ten! Say it again.

2 One, two! Tie your shoe.
Three, four! Shut the door.
Five, six! Pick up sticks.
Seven, eight! Lay them straight.
Nine, ten! A big fat hen.

3 One, two, three, four!
Come in, please, and shut the door.
Five, six, seven, eight!
It's time for school; you're very late.
Nine, ten, nine, ten!
Don't be late for school again.

4 I've got ten little fingers,
I've got ten little toes,
I've got two ears,
I've got two eyes,
And just one little nose.

5 One, two, three, four, five!
I caught a fish alive.
Six, seven, eight, nine, ten!
I let it go again.

While rhymes such as these are chiefly of value for their rhythmical content, they also provide practice in other features of pronunciation work. Many structurally simple rhymes can be found that depend for their effect partly on alliteration, or on echoic devices; these can be utilized to give special practice of the individual sounds used in these devices, especially if they are sounds that pupils find difficult. Teachers should learn to examine their anthologies[1] and notebooks with an eye for the potential pronunciation-teaching value of such rhymes and jingles. A few examples are given below:

6 *The rain*
   Pitter-patter,
   Pitter-patter,
   Listen to the rain!
   Pitter-patter,
   Pitter-patter,
   On the window pane.

[p]   [i]   [ei]   etc.

7 *Silly Billy*
   Silly Billy! Silly Billy!
      Why is Billy silly?
   Silly Billy hid a shilling;
      Isn't Billy silly?

[i]   [l]   [s]   [ʃ]

8 *Skipping is fun*
   Skipping is fun, skipping is fun,
   Skipping is fun for every one.
   The longer you skip, the better you skip –
   So skip, skip, skip!

[i]   [sk]   [f]   [ʌ]

9 *Motoring*
   My motor is humming,
   I'm coming, I'm coming,
   Make room, make room, make room!

[1] See booklist at end of chapter.

Not a minute to wait,
I'm late, I'm late,
Make room, make room, make room.

[m]   [ŋ]   [ei]   [ʌ]

10 *Hush, children, hush!*
Hush, children, hush!
Baby's fast asleep.
Sh! sh! sh!

'Sh!' says the mother.
'Sh!' says the father.
'Sh! sh! sh!'

[ʃ]   [h]

11 *Guessing game*
'Guess what is making the sound you hear:
    zzz . . . zzz . . . zzz.'
'A bee is making the sound I hear:
    zzz . . . zzz . . . zzz.'

'Guess what is making the sound you hear:
    sh . . . sh . . . sh.'
'The sea is making the sound I hear:
    sh . . . sh . . . sh.'

[s]   [z]   [ʃ]

The last rhyme would be best said by the class divided into two
groups, asking and answering the questions alternately; or with
one child or the teacher asking the questions and the rest answering; obviously other sounds can be added to the list and the whole
thing turned into a kind of guessing game as its title suggests. A
similar procedure can be followed with 'animal rhymes' such as
the following:

12 *What does the crow say?*
What does the crow say?
    Caw, caw, caw.
What does the pigeon say?
    Coo, coo, coo.

What does the cat say?
Miau – miau!
What does the dog say?
Bow – wow!

(If relatively unknown animals or birds, such as the crow, are used in this sort of rhyme, the teacher should introduce it first by means of pictures, and, as a preliminary to the chorus work, teach the class that the bird in question says *Caw, caw*, etc.)

'SOUNDS'

Speech rhymes such as nos. (6) to (12) above have an obvious connection with remedial work on the individual sounds of English. This area of pronunciation teaching, especially with young children but also with older pupils who have already acquired some knowledge of English, is a particularly difficult one. In the first place, it is quite often hard to convey to young children the idea that they are only approximating to the sounds in question and that they need to make small adjustments in their articulation; in the second place, where habits have already formed, these cannot easily be cured. But the teacher has to try to do something, and, without boring or frustrating his pupils he has to persuade them to make deliberate efforts to be as accurate as possible in their production of the individual sounds. To do this, he has to train them first to listen, as with the other features of pronunciation, and then has to devise ways of encouraging them to make the necessary effort to achieve accuracy. Many of the so-called techniques therefore in this work are really methods of providing incentives to accuracy. The following are some suggestions.

(1) *Twiddle thumbs* (for use with very young children). The teacher gives ample opportunity for the children to hear a word containing a sound with which they have difficulty, e.g. [ei] in *name*. The class can be asked to repeat it in chorus a few times. Then the teacher tells the class that he and they are to listen very carefully. If a pupil can say the word perfectly, the teacher will twiddle his thumbs; but if the word is mispronounced

ever so slightly, the teacher's thumbs will stay still. (Other devices instead of twiddling the thumbs can be substituted.) The idea is that the whole attention of the class will be focused on the sound itself, and on the device that signals that it is correctly pronounced, rather than on the individual performer. Points can be awarded to individuals or teams.

(2) *Ball game*. Ideally two throwable objects should be chosen, the name of each of which should contain a sound that has so far been found difficult by the class, e.g.

a *ball* and a *doll* (contrasting [ɔː] and [ɔ]),
a *thimble* and a *threepenny-bit* ([θ] and [θr]),
a *pig* and a *fish* ([i]; [p] and [f]; small toys or models can be used).

Each child in turn must ask for one or the other of the chosen pair of objects. If he pronounces it correctly – and *only* if he pronounces it correctly – the teacher throws the object to him and that child's group or row scores a point. The object is then brought back to the teacher; the group that has scored the most points by the end has won the game.
If it is difficult to find throwable objects, balls can be used instead – preferably of different colours or sizes – to represent them.
This game lends itself to many variations.

(3) *Up the stairs and into the house*. A house can be drawn on the blackboard with steps leading up to it; or a picture or flannelgraph set can be used. A group of two or three difficult words, or a recently taught formula (such as *Excuse me, please*), is chosen. Children who say the words or formula absolutely correctly, go up the steps and enter the house (e.g. by writing their names inside it or drawing a pin man to represent themselves, if it is a blackboard drawing; or by using cutouts if it is a picture). Children who get it nearly correct are placed accordingly on the steps of the house.

Again, this kind of 'game' can be turned into a competition.

Many experts would rate listening to and discriminating between different sounds of more importance – at least to start with – than actually trying to make them. It is certainly important to train pupils to hear significant distinctions, and while drill to achieve this end can be practised with older pupils ('minimal pair drill', as suggested above, p. 121), it needs to be approached in a more disguised way with younger children. A few suggestions for turning work on aural discrimination into play are given:

(4) *Hands on heads, hands on desks*. The teacher decides on a short exercise based on five or six minimal pairs. These should consist of words with which the pupils are already familiar; for example, for the sounds [e] and [ei] the teacher might draw on the following pairs:

sell	sail
tell	tail
let	late
get	gate
men	mane

He tells the children to put their hands on their heads when they hear a word with the [e] sound, and to put their hands on their desks when they hear the [ei] sound. He then picks words at random from the above pairs. Different actions may be substituted (eyes open, eyes closed; twiddle thumbs, thumbs still, etc.).

(5) *Yes, no*. A slightly more formal use of minimal pairs may be made as follows. The teacher goes over words in different columns with the class (first taking the words from one column, then the words from the other); then he tells the class that he is going to say two words, one after the other. If they are the same, the class will say *Yes* (or, if preferred, *The same*), but if the two words are different the class must say *No* (or *Different*). After a few trial runs, quite young children understand what is

required, and once the technique is established, the teacher can ask individuals to respond, and then ask the class as a whole to confirm whether they are right or wrong. Pairs of words the same or different, should be given in random order, and like all these activities, the procedure should not be allowed to go on too long. When the pupils have done enough listening practice in this way, they can be asked to say the contrasting pairs individually.

(6) *Snakes and bees*. The teacher prepares pictures of a snake and of a bee. Showing them to the class, he says words to this effect:

This is a snake. A snake hisses. It says 's...s...s, s...s...s, s...s...s'. What does it say?
This is a bee. A bee buzzes. This bee is buzzing. It says 'z...z...z, z...z...z...z, z...z...z.' What does it say?

The teacher then gets the class to make the appropriate sound as he holds up one picture or the other. Suitable variations and other pictures and sounds can be introduced.

The above are given as some suggestions for a 'play-way' approach to the teaching of pronunciation to young pupils. The younger the pupil, the easier he should find it to imitate the teacher and to acquire a good pronunciation of English from the beginning; all the same, he may still need help with certain features of pronunciation. But the younger he is, the less easy is it to do formal pronunciation work with him. With older pupils it is presumed that larger doses of straight teaching will go down more easily, the play-way approach can be dropped, and some of the techniques outlined in the chapter on pronunciation can be adopted.

Songs and singing games

Songs and singing also have a place in the teaching of English to immigrants. It is obvious that singing is usually enjoyed by pupils for its own sake, just as games and competitions are; this is found to be true of Asian pupils as much as of European, although the former often find considerable difficulty in learning English melodies and in keeping the rhythm. Many teachers have to resign themselves to modifications in the melody of English songs, invented and insisted on by classes of immigrant pupils with an irresistible enthusiasm that defeats correction. This enthusiasm and enjoyment should be fostered, because obviously through the singing of well-chosen songs a form of language practice takes place. Songs provide opportunities for repetition of new structures and vocabulary; and it is well known that singing is a particularly good way of making things stick in the memory. But songs, like the rhymes discussed above, can also help pupils to respond to and master the rhythms of English. They should be said as well as sung when they are first being learnt, and the teacher should encourage pupils to beat time, to help them make as full a response to the rhythm as possible. As with rhymes, the teacher should try to avoid any songs in which the natural rhythm of speech is too distorted, and should also pay attention to the structures and items of vocabulary used.

Action songs are most popular and useful with young pupils; suitably simple ones are:

> *The farmer's in his den*
> *The noble Duke of York*
> *Looby Loo*
> *London Bridge is falling down*
> *Here we go round the mulberry bush*

Of the traditional nursery rhymes, some of the most easily learnt are:

> *Baa, baa, black sheep*
> *Polly put the kettle on*
> *Hot cross buns*
> *Hickory dickory dock*
> *Pussy cat, pussy cat, where have you been?*
> *Humpty Dumpty sat on a wall*

With older pupils, as with young, it is usually found helpful to teach one of the many *Alphabet* songs. Older pupils who may find the nursery-rhyme type of song too childish, enjoy repetitive or cumulative songs such as:

> *One man went to mow*
> *Ten green bottles*
> *Ten in the bed*
> *This old man*
> *Old MacDonald had a farm* (more difficult)
> *There was an old woman who swallowed a fly* (more difficult again)

There are in addition certain traditional songs which may be considered almost essential in any repertoire, such as *For he's a jolly good fellow* and *Happy birthday to you*, which again should be taught – and used – on suitable occasions.

Teachers should also consider the possibility of putting their own words to traditional or popular melodies. The melody of *This old man* (made popular all over the world by its occurrence in a film) is often found to be excellent for this purpose, and is easily remembered by pupils of different nationalities. This procedure, the fitting of new words to an old tune, has been very successfully followed in some well-tried language courses[1] and teachers should see if they can do the same. The enthusiasm roused by singing simple interesting words to easy melodies well repays any effort the teacher may make in this direction.

Finally it should be said that the learning of traditional rhymes and songs has another aspect which should not be forgotten, and that is its significance as a part of our general culture. The more the immigrant pupil learns of this, the better will he be able to understand and participate in the life and activities of the British children around him.

BOOKLIST TO CHAPTER 4

Note. Several titles listed at the end of Chapter 1, and most of those at the end of Chapter 2, include material highly relevant to some of the topics discussed in this chapter.

[1] See teacher's handbooks to *Absorbing English* and *Modern English for Malayans* (Bibliography, nos. 1 and 6).

General techniques, etc.

BILLOWS, *The Techniques of Language Teaching* (X)
A book full of practical advice based firmly on classroom experience. Full of stimulating ideas on all aspects of language work, and especially good on activity in the English lesson group work, the use of aids, etc.

FINOCCHIARO, *Teaching English as a Second Language* (X)
A book for American teachers written mainly with reference to American schools with Puerto-Rican immigrant pupils, and relevant therefore to the problem under discussion. Particularly useful on curriculum planning, classroom management and techniques, ways of 'vitalizing' learning and of relating English language-teaching to general educational activities.

FRENCH, *Teaching English as an International Language* (X)
A more condensed work than Billows, but again of a strictly practical nature. Has a very good brief section on language drills, games and activities, and the use of the blackboard.

Drills and substitution tables

BYRNE, *Oral Practice for Foreign Students* (III, 20)
A book of elementary drills, providing systematic practice in the basic structures of English, mainly using question-and-answer techniques. Fairly simple vocabulary.

FRENCH, *English in Tables* (X)
A set of substitution tables and exercises based on them, which cover all the structural patterns up to an intermediate level. Not usable as a textbook, but a guide to the teacher in planning tables and drills for use in class.

MONFRIES, *Oral Drills in Sentence Patterns* (III, 19)
A set of drills based on essential conversational responses; usable as they stand with adults, but would need editing for use with younger pupils.

PALMER, *The Teaching of Oral English* (X)
A brief outline of an oral direct method of teaching English, with suggestions for extensive language drills based on actions

and on a kit of objects collected by the teacher. A source of ideas for teachers.

PALMER and PALMER, *English through Actions* (X)
A more detailed compendium of drills for use in the classroom; the action chains and imperative drills are especially useful. The wealth of material in the book as a whole is perhaps a little bewildering.

Activities, language games, dialogues, etc.

DANIEL, *Activity in the Primary School* (X)
GAGG, *Common Sense in the Primary School* (X)
HUME, *Learning and Teaching in the Infant School* (X)
None of these three books was written with the second-language teaching situation in mind, but all are full of ideas about the use of activity in language work which are highly relevant to the immigrant pupil's situation in the junior school and beyond.

The Peak Course. Course books for the teacher (I, 10)
Standard I, Vols. 1, 2 and 3; Standard II, Vols. 1, 2 and 3. Excellent notes on the use of activities, centres of interest, etc., in the second-language-learning situation.

LEE, *Language Teaching Games and Contests* (X)

JERROM and SZKUTNIK, *Conversation Exercises in Everyday English* (V, 28)
WEST, *Easy English Dialogues*, Books One and Two (V, 29)
WEST, *Improve your English* (X)
The above three books of short dialogues are all designed for the adult learner and are mostly too sophisticated for use with young pupils. Some of the dialogues could be adapted, and teachers would get helpful ideas from them for composing their own.

Speech rhymes, songs, etc.

There are very few books of this kind of material especially designed for the teacher of English as a foreign language. Teachers should look for suitable material in standard collections of rhymes and songs; the titles selected here contain relatively large amounts of suitable material.

AICKMAN, *Rhymes for Speech and Action*, Books 1 and 2 (**X**)

ALLEN, *Living English Speech* (**X**)
Includes a small section on rhymes, printed with very clear rhythm and stress notation.

BARNARD, *Better Spoken English* (**X**)

KINGDON–WARD, *A Book of Rhymes and Jingles* (**X**)

LEE and DODDERIDGE, *Time for a Song* (**X**)
A collection of traditional songs and nursery rhymes selected for teaching to the foreign learner.

SANSOM, *Acting Rhymes* (**X**)

SANSOM, *Speech Rhymes*, Introductory Book, and Books 1 and 2 (**X**)

SMITH, *Rhymes for Rhythm* (**X**)

SWANN, *Trippingly on the Tongue* (**X**)

5

Reading and writing

There are several important points to be made about the teaching of reading and writing to immigrant pupils. The first, mentioned in an earlier chapter, is that reading should follow and not be introduced simultaneously with the teaching of the spoken language. Next, when it *is* introduced, pupils should only be required to read language that they already know orally. Writing should follow reading, and should in turn be based on what pupils can read. Finally, it should be stressed that with both reading and writing, the immigrant pupil, however old, will often be in the position of the primary-school child learning these basic skills for the first time. If he can read and write his own mother tongue this may not always be very helpful, and his eye and hand movements may need to be completely retrained. The teaching of the basic skills of reading and writing is one of the most debated areas of educational theory and practice, and many teachers will realize that they learnt to read and write in a very different way from that followed in the schools today. There has been both a change of attitude, and a change in methods and materials. These may not all be suitable for use with immigrants at all ages, but they certainly need to be understood and, where suitable, adopted. Some useful titles are given at the end of this chapter.

Above all, because the immigrant pupil seems slow 'for his age' at reading or writing he should not be dismissed as stupid or backward. He is coping with the acquisition of many new skills and patterns of behaviour, and he has not the advantage of the British child who is learning to read and write English: by the age of about six the British child can say almost anything he needs to say, but the immigrant pupil has mastery of only a small area of spoken English and may not feel very sure of the words he is trying to read. They are not yet a part of him in the way they are a part of the British child of the same age.

It is clear that the sounder the pupil's command of spoken English, the securer he will be when he comes on to reading it. In some countries abroad a whole year or even two of purely oral English is taught before reading is started, and all the evidence points to there being a great gain from postponing the introduction of reading for a good while in second language teaching. But in dealing with immigrants it is impossible to draw a hard and fast rule. The good teacher will not hurry the introduction of different language skills unwisely; yet at the same time his pupils may have a very strong desire to be able to read and write and it could be both dangerous and foolish to frustrate this. Both adults and children may have this desire: the most rudimentary knowledge of reading and writing may give them a feeling of security, a feeling perhaps of belonging just that little bit more to the new society in which they find themselves and in which the adults, certainly, find themselves constantly confronted with written English and the need to be able to read it. And again, the premium set on literacy in countries abroad is hard for us to imagine in Britain, where illiteracy is now a limited problem; we should perhaps allow for an emotional factor in this which may again make the immigrants' urge to read and write very strong. These are points which it may be necessary to take into account when deciding on the timing of the introduction of these skills.

The issue is further complicated by the pupils' own experience of reading and writing in the mother tongue. An adolescent or adult pupil from Italy or Spain will probably be literate in his mother tongue, and will thus be used to reading Roman script from left to right. Greek Cypriot pupils will be used to the left to right progression, but not the same alphabet. Indian and Pakistani pupils will, if literate, be used to a variety of scripts, some of which go from left to right, and some from right to left. Obviously pupils with the latter type of reading skill will have the biggest problem when transferring to English, because here their basic motor skill in reading their mother tongue may actually interfere with their acquisition of reading or writing a new script. Pupils who are completely illiterate may therefore be easier to teach – except of course that there may be additional problems in rudimentary matters such as training them to hold a pencil or pen and to move it smoothly across the page.

Probably in all this elementary teaching of reading and writing, the most useful information the teacher can turn to is the literature written originally for primary-school teachers who have to deal with these problems, the teaching of basic reading and writing skills, in the ordinary British primary school. There are obviously different schools of thought about the approach and general method, but there is at the same time a core of solid agreement on fundamental principles. Teachers who are meeting these problems for the first time in teaching immigrants, might also turn to their colleagues in the primary school for advice.

If they are teaching multi-national classes of immigrants, or classes in which there is a wide age-range and possibly therefore a range in pupils' ability to read and write their mother tongues, then the teacher may well have to be prepared for considerable differences in rate of progress once his pupils start reading and writing. It will be impossible to deal with all these variables here, and so an outline discussion of the main problems follows, taking in detail only the most extreme case – pupils who are not literate in their mother tongue or whose mother tongue is not written in Roman script.

Preparation for reading

If the teacher has based his preliminary oral work on a published course and has taught the vocabulary and structures that occur in it so that they are used accurately by the class, he will naturally base his first reading lessons on the course. But even so, the beginning of reading will not consist of turning to 'Book One, page 1' and going through it with the class. There is preparatory work even to this – work which may be called 'pre-reading' and which is aimed at familiarizing the pupils with the notion of reading and with some of the muscular-sensory activities that are involved in the whole process.

Many elementary courses do in fact include a pre-reader or picture book which can be used with the class if pupils' copies are available, or which can at any rate be used as a source of ideas for pre-reading work. It should include exercises for training pupils to discriminate between visual symbols and at the same time to pay attention to detail. Teachers can devise wall-charts for this work as well as using ready-made apparatus and the pictures in pre-readers; charts, for instance, can be made consisting of sets of pictures in one of which a small detail is different from the others, or in which there is a deliberate 'mistake' (a flower with leaves of two different kinds, an animal with one leg missing, a cup with the handle on the wrong way, etc.). Simple story-sequences, and single *What is happening?* pictures also serve the same purpose. Games-like apparatus for individual use, made by the teacher or bought from educational suppliers, includes matching pairs of pictures or cards with similar designs, picture-dominoes, lotto sets, etc., which again all provide training in visual perception, visual memory and attention to detail. (See illustration, p. 219.) Published pre-readers often include 'long' pictures in which left-to-right eye movement is encouraged, e.g. pictures of a boy kicking a ball into a net, the path of the ball being traced by a dotted line across the page. Pupils following the line with their eyes, or tracing it with their fingers, learn thus to look at the left-hand side of the page first. When they move on to picture-strip stories, in which a little episode is told in pictures as in comic strips, they are acquiring the same habit.

Equipment such as the above is available not only in pre-readers as such but, as suggested, in the average primary-school equipment cupboard, and its use, even with pupils of secondary-school age, should not be considered out of place. At any rate, teachers should be aware of its purpose, and of its availability, and should consider buying or making their own collection.

'LETTERS' AND 'WORDS'

Pre-reading activities lead up to and include the introduction of print, again as a preliminary to the reading of the printed page. And this is the moment at which the teacher must be quite clear about exactly how he is going to teach his pupils the mechanics of reading. There are two things he must avoid – at least, one he must avoid and one he must be wary of. He must avoid, to start with, confusing learning the *alphabet* with learning to read. Memorizing the alphabet – the string of names we give to the twenty-six symbols with which we spell – can in the early stages be a waste of time, and even a step backwards, since it has little or no relation to the immediate task. Similarly, learning to spell out words in terms of letter-sounds ('phonics') may also be wasteful to start with. Many people who themselves learnt to read by this method may feel an instinctive preference for teaching by it. But English is not a 'phonic' language – the sounds represented by certain letters or groups of letters do not all fit neatly into readily observed and easily learnt patterns (like those of Italian, or Welsh, for instance), and the learner is hindered, not helped, if he tries to make a relation between the 'letter-sounds' in, for instance, *on* and *one*, *eat* and *great* and *threat*, *which* and *who*, and so on. Readers constructed on phonic lines – of the much quoted 'Pig in a wig did a jig' variety – often provide reading matter which has little interest or realism for the pupils and which usually involves them in the learning of fairly odd vocabulary items – a feature, of course, that is even more undesirable for immigrant pupils than it is for native British children. Phonic work is in fact necessary to some extent in reading – not at the introductory stage, however – if the pupil is to become independent of the teacher, and a good reader constructed on modern principles may include some 'concealed' phonic work.

However, there may be some groups of immigrant pupils for whom phonic work takes on a special significance. Greek or Greek-Cypriot immigrants who can already read their own language may be hampered in their reading of English by interference from the Greek alphabet, for they will attribute to apparently similar letters in English the sound values that they have in Greek. To remedy this, early phonic work is often found helpful if not necessary. Mature pupils of all nationalities who are learning to read for the first time, may also benefit from some early phonic work, though this should not be allowed to outweigh the basic 'look and say' approach outlined below which is ultimately best for these pupils too.[1]

But 'modern principles', as we have called them, insist first and foremost on *meaning* and *interest*, and on approaching reading in a way that has the maximum meaning and interest – as well as ease – for the pupils. This has been found to be best done by combining the 'look and say' and 'sentence' methods of teaching; words, or small groups of words, are shown as wholes to the pupils, and they are trained from the beginning to recognize these, again *as wholes* (not analysing them into 'letter-sounds'), which is in fact the way we read when we become proficient readers. As the items read are read for meaning, reading is purposeful from the very first stages and is never associated with mere mechanical drudgery.

Again, with immigrant pupils, as the whole method of teaching is structural, with the emphasis on words used meaningfully in complete utterances (i.e. from the very beginning not just *book* or *bag* but *This is a book*, *That's a bag*, etc.), the sentence method is most appropriate and can be easily adapted to the type of short utterance they have learnt to use and respond to all through their oral work.

The pre-reading activities which lead to reading in this way again follow the primary-school approach.

LABELS

When quite a small amount of oral work has been done, the teacher may begin to label some of the common classroom objects talked about in lessons, either simply with their names (clearly written in printscript) – *a chair*, *the cupboard*, etc. – or with the structural items that have been used in complete utterances in oral work: *This is a chair*, *This is the cupboard*, etc. But one must beware of the classroom sprouting too many labels: superfluity may well defeat the purpose. The purpose can in fact be simply defined as familiarizing pupils with the appearance of written forms: they are not being expected to 'read' them at this stage.

[1] Some interesting suggestions about an early introduction to carefully limited phonic work will be found in Allen and Cooke: *Living English for the Arab World*. Teacher's Book I (entry no. 12 in Bibliography).

G

Name labels on coat pegs, or even on desks, can also be introduced, and on pieces of classroom equipment such as tins of pencils and boxes of chalk. If the place where the duster is kept is clearly labelled *Duster*, then the association of written form, oral form and actual object in the pupils' memories will begin to be interfused. As time goes on, labels will be changed, and new, longer ones may be added such as *Put your straws here, Stand in line here*, etc.

FLASHCARDS

From here one moves rapidly on to the stage of presenting written items to be read and acted upon, especially at first through the use of flashcards. The more closely one can relate this work to reading matter in the textbook that is going to be used, the better, though there may obviously be an area of classroom language which is not in the text and which all the same the teacher finds it useful to introduce for reading purposes. Language used in imperative drills, for instance, as suggested in Step 1 of the Scheme of Work (p. 29 above) lends itself to this. The teacher can copy out some simple commands on flashcards, choosing if possible commands whose written forms show definite contrasts in the shapes of words and letters:

| Stand up. | Sit down. |

| Go to the window. |

| Come here. |

| Go to the cupboard. |

Flashcards are best made out of strips of cards, 3–4 inches wide and 15 inches long, or longer according to the length of the sentence. The card must be thick enough not to flop. The lettering used obviously needs care and should be in the style the pupils will be expected to use in written work, and should also relate to the print in the first readers the teacher intends to use, preferably with printscript a and g. Printscript, with letters $1\frac{1}{2}$ to 2 inches high, written with a felt-tipped pen or lettering pen, is often recommended, though some teachers prefer to use a stencil such as Econosign (brush stencil) or Uno (pen stencil). In printing flashcards the biggest problem is often in the spacing between letters and between words. Some published courses include flashcards, but teachers will often find these are inadequate and will want to make their own. It always helps to print the text in small letters on the reverse side of the cards so that the teacher can check on each one before showing it to the class; the usual method is to have the cards laid in readiness face downwards on the table or across the teacher's knee if, as often happens, he is sitting informally with a group of pupils.

There are many variations possible in flashcard work, but obviously those which involve activity are very popular at first. Thus flashing a set of commands may first be practised with the class as a whole, letting them respond with the appropriate actions. This can later be played as a team game or competition, to test individual responses and to see if in fact everyone is associating the required response with the words on the cards. Obviously not too many cards should be used at a time.

Cards with names of objects can also be used, again at first selecting items easily distinguishable in printed form; e.g. not

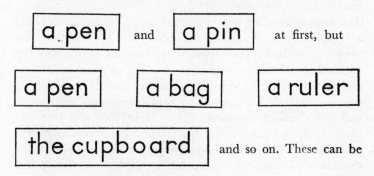

a pen and a pin at first, but

a pen a bag a ruler

the cupboard and so on. These can be

flashed and pupils respond by pointing or going to, or holding up the object in question. Individuals can begin to be asked to read cards as they see them. At a slightly later stage it may be considered appropriate for individual pupils to select the cards and show them to the rest of the class.

There are many possible variations on flashcard work. Cards may be distributed, and pupils have to go and place them on the appropriate objects; or, where duplicate cards are already displayed around the room (*This is the cupboard*, etc.), they may go and match their cards with those shown.

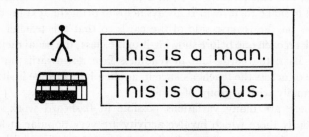

A pocket chart or flannelgraph can be used on which cards are at first placed opposite pictures: after sufficient practice the cards are removed and jumbled up, or displayed in random order elsewhere. Pupils have then to select a card and place it opposite the appropriate picture on the first chart or flannelgraph.

WORD RECOGNITION

The suggestions given so far mostly relate to the recognition of or a response to whole groups of words. This is implicit in the 'sentence method'. These procedures have to be intermingled with others whereby recognition of words alone is encouraged and tested. Much pre-reading apparatus can be used for this purpose, such as word-matching cards, snapcards, word lotto, and other sets of apparatus where identifying and matching single words is involved. But the teacher should also relate this procedure to the sentences his pupils now recognize. For instance, duplicates of flashcards in use can be made, and cut up into single words. Pupils are then given separate word cards and have to match them against the words on the whole flashcards:

| This is my desk. |

| This | | is | | my | | desk. |

Again, duplicate flashcards can be made with blanks on them instead of certain words. Pupils then have to select a separate card with the missing word on it to fit over the blank:

| This is a red lorry. |

| This is a   lorry. | | red |

'Extended' flashcards can also be used for the same purpose. Thus when the class can recognize certain cards such as

| This is a horse. |

| Put up your hands. |

new cards which extend the originals can be made, such as

| This is a black horse. |

| Put up your left hands. |

The pairs of cards can be contrasted and compared, and on other occasions individual pupils can be asked to come and frame the new words with their hands.

Slot-charts and notices displayed in the classroom for general purposes also help to encourage the habit of word recognition and should be so utilized by the teacher at odd moments with individual pupils. A good example of this is a 'birthday board'. This can consist of a permanent card with the words:

It is | | birthday today.

It is | Amahl's | birthday today.

The name of a pupil whose birthday it is can be slotted into the gap; if the board is to be in constant use, a slip with

| nobody's |

can be inserted on days when there is no birthday in the class. Similar charts for classroom jobs can be made with slots for interchangeable names, and, again for use when the appropriate language has been dealt with, a weather-board can be made along the same lines with slots to take the appropriate changes of date and weather:

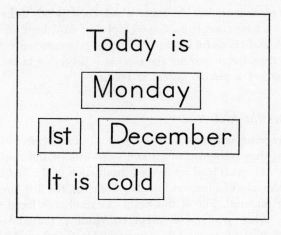

Today is

Monday

1st December

It is cold

PREPARATION FOR PHONIC WORK

Although at this early pre-reading stage no specific phonic work is recommended, it is possible to introduce activities which help to pave the way for it later. One simple exercise, to be based of course on vocabulary which the pupils are thoroughly familiar with orally, is listening to how pairs or groups of words begin and end, training pupils thus to identify sound correspondences (i.e. without showing the written forms). This can be done with the actual objects themselves, or with pictures (which can sometimes be found in pre-reading picture-books especially for this purpose): e.g.

initial sounds:	ball	bag	box
	shoe	shop	
	chin	chair	chain
word endings:	ball	wall	
	eye	tie	
	fish	dish	

Association of initial sounds with some letters can also be practised. Pictures of objects, with the initial letter printed clearly in the corner, can be used in the class; and games can be played in which a pupil has to select an object from a small collection (e.g. a box of plastic toys kept by the teacher for this purpose) and go and place it against the letter which corresponds to its initial sound. (A long concertina-shaped alphabet card kept on a shelf or window-sill is useful for this.) It cannot be too strongly stressed that in this kind of activity the teacher is *not* trying to teach the alphabet nor a phonic system of reading.

Reading the first reader

The foregoing activities, in which pupils in fact begin to read in so far as they recognize words and word-groups and respond to their meaning, all lead up to the introduction of the first reader, or, for the sake of a more comprehensive term, the first integrated reading material. For at this point the teacher is faced with a choice. What reader – or prepared reading material – is he going to give his pupils? It is conceivable that he will dismiss everything on the market to date as unsuitable; and if he is full of energy he may then go a long way on his own, producing reading material, flashcards, labelled pictures, individual reading cards, etc., for the class. Most teachers will find themselves without the time to do this, and will therefore look around to see what they can find to buy. They may realize that it can be a proud moment for a pupil when he gets his first book, and the motivation that this gives him may justify the use of one that contains a few inadequacies. For inadequacies there are bound to be in material that was not originally designed for this particular purpose.

The teacher has to select reading material to answer two needs: (1) to introduce reading as a skill to his pupils; (2) to introduce the reading of the limited area of English that the pupil can control orally. Unfortunately most of the books that constitute the reading schemes in use in our ordinary primary schools do not take this second factor into account; they are written for young children who already have a secure command of spoken English, who have a fairly extensive vocabulary, and are at home with a fairly wide range of tenses, etc. Thus a primer that starts off fairly simply, using plenty of illustrations and big clear print, may, linguistically speaking, be totally unsuitable for immigrant pupils. (Needless to say, the subject matter as well will usually mean that it is unsuitable for the older immigrant pupil who is beginning to learn to read.) On the other hand, very many of the books written for use in teaching English overseas, while at best they contain carefully graded language, with a lot of repetition and a limited vocabulary, make very little concession to the pupil who is tackling the skill of reading for the first time; the pages are often crowded with distracting detail, the print may be fairly small, and sometimes no allowance is made for the need for repetitive and easily recognizable units. In other words, these are pedagogically unsuitable in this particular case and will only be usable as first readers after a large amount of reading has already been practised beforehand. Obviously, this kind of textbook will be usable with pupils who can already read Roman script; though for them, as for the non-Roman-scripters, there is one other feature of these books that will often defeat the purpose in using them, namely their lack of interest. Many of them concentrate almost exclusively on bags and pencils, rubbers and rulers, the vocabulary used in most introductory oral work, and have little in the subject matter in their early pages to appeal to the imagination of the pupils.

However, the teacher will probably be better advised to turn to a linguistically sound book to start with than to one that he considers pedagogically sound. The details given in the select lists of courses in the Bibliography (pp. 237–244) should be of help. Teachers should obtain inspection copies of courses to see which they feel suit their individual needs best. If, on the other hand, a teacher feels inclined to use a primer printed for use with British children, he should carefully examine the linguistic content first, listing the structural patterns and vocabulary it uses and seeing how far these relate to the scheme of language work he has followed. If there is no correspondence, then obviously the book should not be used; if there is quite a good correspondence, then the teacher should prepare the way orally for any items in the book that the pupils do not yet know.

To sum up, in selecting first readers, teachers should bear in mind the following points:

Language

(1) The language of the book should relate to the language

practised orally in class. This is true of structure and vocabulary, though it is easier to pave the way for fresh vocabulary items than for totally unknown structural ones.

(2) There should be plenty of repetition of the items of language introduced in the book.

(3) The language items should be presented in situations which are appropriate to the pupils' age and interests and which are likely to appeal to them.

Reading-pedagogy

(1) The words in the book should be 'released' gradually, e.g. perhaps only a word or two – a character's name, for instance – on each page to start with, with clear pictures related to each item.

(2) Print should be large and clear. It should approximate to the script used by the teacher in pre-reading material. Print-script ɑ for **a** and ɡ for **g** should be used, and a sans-serif type print, as this makes for less distraction and easier identification.

(3) On later pages, more print can be introduced, but ideally this should still be accompanied by pictures. A few new words out of the stock known orally may be introduced per page.

A course which includes supplementary material such as printed flashcards will of course commend itself, but on the whole teachers will have to make these themselves, together with other apparatus to go with the reader such as matching cards and pictures, sentence cards, flannelgraph figures, etc.

If a teacher knows his class well, he will select the moment carefully when each child gets his first reader; individual progress should determine this. Reading from the book is best done individually or in small groups, the emphasis all the time being on accurate understanding of what is read, and on the whole business of reading for the pleasure of reading. This may seem an idealistic view, and in a large class it is all too tempting to concentrate on the mechanics of reading instead of on the reading itself. (Unfortunately a badly chosen book is unlikely to encourage children to read for pleasure.) And certainly teaching reading for meaning involves the teacher in considerable preparation of additional material, for flashcards, cards matching pictures copied from the text, etc., should all be used at this stage to provide different approaches to the reading of print.

Whether or not the teacher has the first pages of the reader read by the class as a whole, he must certainly find time to hear individuals read to him at intervals through the week. Those who progress quickly will need to be led on to supplementary readers. If supplementary readers are chosen from a different reading scheme, the teacher should check them carefully first to see if the language in them goes outside the range of that known by the pupils.

Consolidation of early steps in reading should be aided by the provision of extra material in the classroom. Wall pictures to match those in the book, with suitable captions printed by the teacher (dictated by the class from memory) can be put up in the classroom. This applies equally well to the 'story' type of reader as to the more structural type. Pictures of people or things in the reader can be drawn, and labelled by the teacher at the pupils' dictation (*This is Tom, This is his bicycle*, etc.); and individual picture-books, related to the contents of the reader, can also be made along these lines.

Books and reading

Immigrant pupils of any age, like British pupils who are at the start of reading, need to be given *incentive*. Incentive lies not only in the interest and pleasure to be gained from a particular text, but also in the whole idea of familiarity with books and reading. The immigrants' classroom should have plenty of books in it, preferably on an open display rack or in a book-corner, with picture-books and simple readers for them to turn to and choose from at set times. It may be that many of these will contain language outside the pupils' range, but for the present purpose this does not matter. Pupils have to be allowed to see – and feel – what it means to have access to the world of books.

Many of the picture-books and books of general interest for use in junior and secondary schools will be suitable. But teachers should also include books written within a limited vocabulary, many of which have been produced as supplementary readers especially for foreign learners of English. Several publishers specialize in this type of book, and their current lists should be consulted. 'Simplified readers', as these are called, can be found written within as narrow a vocabulary as 450 words and with a carefully edited structural content. They vary greatly in subject matter from folk tales, fairy stories and tales of modern adventure to re-tellings of the classics, and teachers should be able to find suitably easy reading books for elementary-stage pupils at all ages. Readers of the same type, but based on wider vocabulary, will of course be useful for slightly more advanced pupils.

First steps in writing

Broadly speaking, writing, like reading, should be seen as a skill linked essentially to meaningfulness and purpose and, therefore, to expression. As with reading, the mechanics should not be mistaken for the real thing. All the same, it is this mechanical aspect that has to be considered first, and again many teachers find themselves having to do something for which they have never been trained. They need to know something about the mechanical processes involved in learning to write.

These mechanical processes begin from the time a pupil learns to hold a crayon or pencil and to make controlled marks on paper with it. In the case of some immigrant children this early practice in learning to manipulate a writing tool has been missed and they may have to be given this rudimentary training. The teacher of infants will of course treat his immigrant pupils in the same way as British infants and for him there should be no real problem. The teacher of older immigrants who are also at this beginning stage can again learn from his colleague. It is, for instance, accepted practice for absolute beginners to learn to use thick crayons first and, as they gain in manipulative control, to move on to soft pencils.

There is, as with reading, a delicate balance to be maintained between writing 'properly' – i.e. writing words and sentences that have interest and meaning (although this may consist of nothing more than copying or tracing over what the teacher has written under a picture) – and learning to form letter shapes correctly. Obviously it is not ideal for a pupil to get into an early habit of making letters wrongly: one of the most important features of writing is the correct formation of letters and the order of the movements of the pencil or crayon, whether it goes up or down or round in a loop first, etc. The series of these movements has to be taught at some time, and techniques for learning them have to be introduced without, as implied, distracting the pupil too long from writing itself. (Teachers will probably find that in the course of developing their own individual style of handwriting they have acquired short-cuts to the formation of certain letters, and they may need to remind themselves of the basic series of movements needed to form the letters; the kind of guidance given in the illustration overleaf will also be found in handbooks on writing and in the copybooks designed for pupils' use referred to later in this chapter.)

It has been found with immigrants who cannot write a Roman script that the practice of writing patterns, as a preparation for writing and as continued training in rhythmic left-to-right movement with control and lightness of touch, is both a valuable and an enjoyed activity.[1] Many teachers of writing consider writing-pattern work as important in relation to real writing as prattle is in the infant's progress to real speech. Certainly teachers should examine for themselves the relation of the suggested patterns to actual writing, and also to general creative activity. It seems that in this form much work can be done towards establishing good handwriting later (correct letter formation *and* controlled muscular movements which are important for the development of writing style as a whole) in an enjoyable way which does not make 'penmanship' into unpleasant drudgery and which can be a useful compromise in the predicament suggested above. Younger children can be allowed to concentrate for quite a while on the actual patterns themselves, varying them and combining them, and also colouring them; older pupils can be put on to relating the patterns to individual letters fairly quickly,

[1] See Marion Richardson, *Writing and Writing Patterns*. The set of pupil's books (I–V) and the teacher's handbook are an indispensable introduction to the use of writing patterns (X).

A B C D E F G
H I J K L M N
O U P Q R S T
V W X Y Z
1 2 3 4 5 6 7 8 9 0 ! ? ; : . , " "
a b c d e f g
h i j k l m n
o p q r s t u
v w x y z

for instance, writing rows of letters between the patterns. They will not usually consider this kind of activity too childish, and it will be found of use even with pupils who can already write their mother tongue in Roman script but who need to make their writing conform more closely to the British style.

If writing patterns are introduced, letters will be taught in relation to the patterns (and not according to alphabetical order). A set of patterns suggested for use in the teaching of printscript is as follows:[1]

Pattern	Capitals	Small Letters
VVVV	A M V W	v w
≡ || ≡ || ≡	T F E H L I	l i
womuu	U G C O Q	u g q o a c t
mmm	P B D R	p b d r n m h e
\\\ X ///	X Y Z N K	x y z k
888888	S J	s j f

Most teachers prefer to teach capital letters first, mainly because many of these follow relatively simple patterns; but some prefer to teach small and capital letters together. It is not necessary, of course, to teach all the letters related to any one pattern at one

[1] Suggested in *The Peak Course. Course book for the teacher*, Standard I, Volume III, page 48 (I, 10).

and the same time; some letters which occur relatively infrequently (e.g. *x* and *z*) may be left till later.

In schools where there is a fixed policy as to which kind of handwriting should be taught, the style taught to immigrants should conform to the model unless it is considered totally unsuitable. At all events, the teacher should have a policy himself. He should be clear about what form of writing he is teaching, and he should be consistent in his use of it whenever he himself is writing on the board or elsewhere in class. If he teaches a printscript first, he should consider how and when he is going to teach his pupils to transfer to a more cursive style. The semi-cursive style of Marion Richardson is perhaps the best compromise solution to this whole question, and if this were to be taught from the beginning (i.e. not teaching printscript at all), then slightly different writing patterns would be introduced and probably in a different order from that suggested for the printscript patterns above;[1] e.g.

Writing Pattern   Small Letters

u l i t

n m h k p

v r w b

o e c

a d g q

s s f j x y 3

(Patterns for capital letters would be the same as those on the previous page.)

[1] For an excellent detailed treatment of a writing scheme based on the patterns that follow, see *The New Peak Course. Course book for the teacher*, Standard I, Volume III, page 46ff.

Whatever type of writing – printscript, semi-cursive or cursive – the teacher decides to teach, he should try to ensure that anyone else who teaches his class uses the same style as far as possible. He should also keep a constant check on the way pupils hold their pencils or crayons, the angle at which they place their paper or books, and their posture when writing. And he should not allow pen and ink to be used too soon: a soft pencil for early work on paper or in exercise books is probably the best. Allowing pupils to graduate to pens may be made a matter of prestige. When this step is taken, care should be paid to types of pen used: if pupils have their own fountain-pens, the matter may be out of the teacher's hands, though if a bad pen is the cause of bad writing he might forbid its use. Nibs provided for school penholders should preferably be rather thick. Ball-point pens are best avoided at first.

While discussing choice of equipment we might also touch on the problem of paper. There is a good deal of argument as to whether it is best to have lined paper or not, or to have double lines, or even upper and lower lines, which actually control the size of the letters. Many people object to the latter because of the way they force all writing to conform to the same size. While plain paper should be used for preliminary work on writing-patterns, most people seem to favour lined paper for actual writing, with the lines fairly widely spaced (e.g. at least $\frac{3}{4}$ inch apart). Language teachers who get their pupils to do quite a lot of drawing in the early stages often find it useful to supply exercise books in which blank pages alternate with lined ones.

Writing work

Early writing work will consist of copying, and while pupils are still mastering letter formation, they will begin to copy labels and flashcards, to write their own names, etc. The teacher will then prepare writing cards for them to copy, based on simple items already read in the reader or in other reading apparatus. Pupils can be encouraged to illustrate what they write, and to decorate their papers or books with writing patterns (for these should not be dropped too early once 'proper' writing is started).

Practices in written work should be short and frequent. Young children especially find the early stages of writing exhausting. Older pupils, if left too long unsupervised, may well take to copying matter which they cannot yet read. This should be avoided.

At this stage of writing particular attention needs to be paid to word-spacing, size and layout. It helps for the teacher to insist on a space between words the size of a capital 'O'. Letters with ascenders and descenders, 'above and below the line', need particular care.

Copybooks have not been mentioned in this discussion so far, and on the whole they seem to be disapproved of in British educational practice at the present time. They obviously can have a limiting effect if introduced in the junior school, but teachers of secondary-aged immigrant pupils may well find them a welcome and not too expensive aid. A set of copybooks designed for use overseas is available (see booklist at end of chapter) in which pupils are trained to use printscript and then to modify this by degrees to a cursive style. Teachers using these copybooks or basing copying material on them would of course have to see that the style of writing contained in them was used in other reading and writing apparatus designed for their pupils, and also in their own blackboard work. The books in question provide practice in letter formation, then proceed to the copying of words and sentences, thus including practice in word spacing, capitalization and punctuation. The teacher using them would also have to see that the vocabulary content had been adequately prepared for in oral and reading work beforehand.

Whether copybooks are used or not, the teacher will need to devise other simple but interesting forms of writing practice. In the junior school especially, the technique of the daily news bulletin can be very useful if worked at orally first. Pupils are encouraged to tell an item of 'news' to the class: 'Today is my birthday', 'We played ludo yesterday', 'Ali has measles'. This is often very popular and the teacher can draw a picture to illustrate the best item, and can himself write the news item under the picture for early reading practice. When pupils are at the writing stage they can then copy this under their own drawn versions of the event. In the same way, picture stories with short simple captions can be built up, the teacher writing the captions at the class's dictation and later the pupils copying these under their own drawings. In this way individual books can be built up, and it is encouraging for pupils if the teacher sews any loose sheets together to form such books.

Simple and extended copying work can be found in many of the workbooks published to accompany reading courses (see Section IV of the Bibliography). These workbooks can also provide a great deal of the material necessary for the next stage in writing, namely *controlled written work*, and teachers will find they can borrow many ideas from them. The aim of all this material at first is to give pupils the opportunity to write *correct* English. As they learn English, they are advancing by very small steps at a time, and in their written expression they must be given the chance to practise language that they know orally and to go on forming correct habits of usage. Written work should *not* therefore be devised to test their knowledge of English at this stage. The progression from copied to uncopied work should be as slow and as painless as possible, and this means that considerable time must be spent on controlled exercises. These need to be clearly devised and, if the pupils are expected to do them individually, should be as self-explanatory as possible, i.e. virtually mistake-proof. (For examples of different kinds of exercises see the illustrations facing p. 204 taken from different workbooks.)

Controlled exercises can take many forms. One of the easiest, and suitable therefore for use in the early stages, is sentence completion. This can be set out in different ways and need not become monotonous for the pupils. For instance, a series of short sentences containing blanks can be devised, accompanied by simple drawings which provide the cue for the word or words that are to be written in the blank spaces:

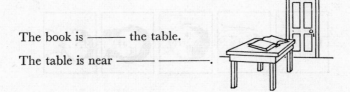

The book is ———— the table.

The table is near ———— ————.

Sample pages from pupil's workbooks

Read these five sentences:

This is Father.

This is Mother.

Here is Anil.

Here is Kanta.

Look at Mohinder!

Write them down.

Draw two of these pictures.

. Page 7 (seven)

1

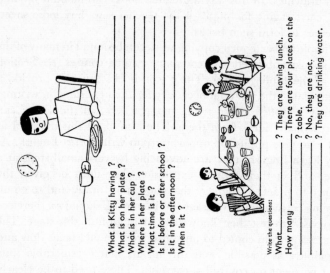

What is Kitty having?
What is on her plate?
What is in her cup?
Where is her plate?
What time is it?
Is it before or after school?
Is it in the afternoon?
When is it?

Write the questions:

What _____ ? They are having lunch.
How many _____ ? There are four plates on the table.
_____ ? No, they are not.
_____ ? They are drinking water.

2

1. Reproduced from *Reading through Doing* (O.U.P.), I, page 7.
2. Reproduced from A. W. Frisby, *The New Ship English Course*, Workbook 2, page 9 (entry no. 9 in Bibliography).

Or the blank can be filled with the appropriate word that has to be selected from a short list:

The boy ——— running after the ball.

| are |
| am |
| is |

(This is most valuable if the choice has to be from a list of structural words.)

Other sentence-completion exercises, in which there can be slightly more freedom of choice, can consist of 'half sentences' in which part or whole of the subject or predicate is missing and has to be filled in by the pupil:

The boy ————— his name on the blackboard.

————— is going to give me a pencil.

Simple substitution exercises can also form a basis for written work of this kind (see p. 145 above). A substitution table can be written on the blackboard and pupils asked to write down five or ten sentences from it. The simplest substitution table should leave room for choice in one column only; later, tables with two-column choices can be devised and an element of fun or nonsense introduced, though teachers should make sure in oral work beforehand that pupils understand what they are reading and also that they do not get into the habit of simply reading straight across the columns:

(i) *Simple substitution table*

	butter	
	milk	
I haven't any	potatoes	in my bag
	eggs	
	rice	

(ii) *Two-column choice substitution table*

	big	horse	
	red	policeman	
There isn't a	small	jug	in the classroom
	wooden	hat	
	tall	bicycle	

A type of controlled exercise found in many textbooks is one in which the pupil has to change a grammatical feature in a set series of sentences, e.g. change all the singular forms to plurals, or present tenses to past tenses. But on the whole, this is the least recommended of exercises. As well as being a dull, mechanical procedure, usually with very little apparent meaning for the pupil, it can often lead to the production of English sentences which would hardly ever occur in a meaningful context.

Controlled writing can include the combining of short sentences to form long ones (by the use of certain conjunctions, relative pronouns, etc.), and the extension of sentences by adding simple modifications to nouns or verbs in them (in the form of adjectives and adverbs, then later adjectival phrases, and clauses); these should all be provided in short lists from which pupils can choose the most appropriate item in each case.

Moving out slightly from this controlled work, pupils can gradually be asked to make their own substitutions or extensions to sentences, i.e. without having to select them from lists. They thus have a freer choice of items. They can also be asked to write out action chains that have been well practised in class, or to write simple descriptive sentences about a picture or model, again using language practised orally beforehand. This kind of exercise can be extended and elaborated on: for instance, an action chain can be written out and then rewritten so that it includes a list of time expressions such as *first, next, then, finally*, etc. Pupils can also be asked to unjumble and write out in correct order a series of sentences that should obviously follow a certain sequence (such as the description of a picture story or of a series of actions).

This kind of exercise obviously leads towards freer written work, and as pupils progress the teacher will aim at introducing them to the writing of stories, diaries, newspaper contributions, descriptions, poems, etc. But it would be good to see the kind of exercise described immediately above as a part of a definite transition towards this, and to devise other kinds of written work in which control is still exercised though more loosely. For instance, the teacher after telling a story to the class can ask a series of questions which the pupils then have to answer to produce a short paragraph of connected prose. Or a story or description can be written out with blanks left for pupils to fill in. (For help in devising this kind of work see especially entries 16 and 21 in the Bibliography, pp. 245 and 246.) And again, it should be stressed that all of this work should be thoroughly prepared orally before the pupils start writing it down. At this stage, too, written work can more easily be linked to activities outside the English-language lesson, to centres of interest and project work, and to visits paid outside school to the post office or park, so that interest and expression begin to interact.

Pupils will also begin to want to write words that they know orally but which they may well not have met in their reading. By this stage at the latest they will need to know the alphabet as a tool in looking up words in simple dictionaries (see Section IX of Bibliography, p. 252), and possibly for making their own individual picture dictionaries or notebooks. The teacher must encourage self-sufficiency in this respect, and train pupils to remember where a word can be found elsewhere in the classroom – for instance, on a wall chart or caption.

As the pupils gain more command of both oral and written English, the emphasis in their written work will be more and more in the direction of 'expression'. Enough is said of this in other sources, but the teacher of immigrants will often have to remind himself that this work depends for its success in some measure on his ability to understand what his pupils' interests in fact are. The more he brings in the outside world, the more he needs to take into account the fact that his pupils' school life, is no direct reflection of their deepest interests and attachments. Through reading and writing activities the teacher may well be helping immigrants in their adjustment to their environment, but it would be dangerous to think that this can easily be done or to force an artificial adjustment on pupils by insistence on forms of expression which are not really their own.

BOOKLIST TO CHAPTER 5

GAGG, *Beginning the Three R's* (X)
    A popular and very readable approach to modern primary school techniques in the teaching of basic subjects.

GRAY, *The Teaching of Reading and Writing* (X)

A survey of prevailing practices in the teaching of reading and writing throughout the world, and therefore of great interest to the teacher of immigrants who wishes to know more about his pupils' educational background. Also very useful for bibliographical purposes and for anyone wishing to know more about contemporary research in the field of literacy.

Reading

LEE and COPPEN, *Simple Audio-Visual Aids to Foreign-Language Teaching* (X)

Chapter 3 on 'Aids to Reading and Writing' very useful for practical details of pre-reading work and of construction of simple but essential apparatus.

SCHONELL, *The Psychology and the Teaching of Reading* (X)

A concise discussion of the psychological theory behind modern practice in the teaching of reading.

Writing

BELL, *Good Handwriting* (X)

A short work full of practical advice, originally written for overseas teachers. Contains a good discussion of the merits of different types of handwriting and hints on suitable equipment.

BILLOWS, *The Techniques of Language Teaching* (X)

Chapter 9 on 'The Teaching of Composition' is particularly useful for its account of different types of written work for use with foreign pupils.

INGLIS and GIBSON, *The Teaching of Handwriting*, Teacher's Book (Primary) (X)

Very clear instruction on basic principles and techniques to be employed in teaching writing to primary classes, with notes on writing materials and on the instruction of left-handed pupils.

RICHARDSON, *Writing and Writing Patterns*, Teacher's Handbook and Pupils' Books 1–5 (X)

The teacher's handbook explains Marion Richardson's system of teaching writing.

Copybooks

ALLEN and COOKE, *Living English for the Arab World* (II, 12)
Pupils' Books 1 and 2 contain simple copying exercises based on Marion Richardson script.

INGLIS and GIBSON, *The Teaching of Handwriting*, Pupils' Work Books 1-4 (X)
These are workbooks, not copybooks, designed for British pupils, and few immigrant pupils would be able to follow the instructions in them; however, the excellent practice material they contain could be drawn on by the teacher and the simple cursive style which they teach would be a most suitable one for immigrant pupils.

MILLER and HAKIM, *Progressive Writing-Books for Learners of English*, Books 1-4 (X)
Copybooks designed for use by overseas learners; they begin with copious guide lines and simple strokes, leading to exercises in letter formation in printscript, which modifies in Book 3 to a simple linked cursive hand.

6

'Remedial' language teaching – West Indian and other pupils

Most teachers feel that it is easier to teach English to pupils who know none to start with than it is to those who know some. Older immigrant pupils who enter the secondary school, and many adults, speak a 'fluent' but ungrammatical kind of English which we have loosely described as 'pidgin' in Chapter 1. It often seems that they have 'picked it up' without much instruction, and that for general purposes, in and out of school, it is fairly adequate. It is sometimes found that pupils who have had a good grounding in English in language classes also end up by speaking this broken kind of language. They, like those who have had very little or no instruction, find that when they really need to speak English, correct usage goes by the board: in the urgency of the moment meaning is conveyed by the main content words and with a reduced form of grammar – word-endings are left off, structural words omitted, etc. These 'bad' language habits sometimes seem to be too firmly set to be dislodged in the language class. Pupils, especially some of the older boys in secondary schools, often feel that the kind of English they speak is adequate for their purposes out of school and so they have little taste for the remedial work which the teacher may attempt with them.

Teachers who have West Indian pupils in their classes often find they have a problem which can be described in much the same terms as the above, although, as we shall try to show below, it is really of a different nature. The answer, though, may be the same in both cases.

In these language-teaching situations the principles underlying what has so far been said in this book hold good. While older pupils may want, and benefit from, a certain amount of grammatical explanation, their learning or re-learning of English must still take the form of *practice*. Language will only be used correctly by being used, not by being talked about. Progress is still made step by step, by learning or re-learning to use one structure correctly after another, revising and building on to the items that have gone before, practising newly presented ones with plenty of repetition. Mature pupils, who have already learnt to read and write, may have written as well as oral exercises to perform, the one reinforcing the other.

But in classes of older immigrant pupils, teachers often find an additional problem in a lack of homogeneity. The standard of English can vary considerably from pupil to pupil, sometimes according to their nationalities, sometimes because of the different lengths of time they have been in England, or, most commonly, simply because they have all learnt English in different ways and at different rates, with varying degrees of success. The teacher may well wonder where to start his remedial teaching, and it helps considerably if he tries first to make some kind of diagnosis.

He may test his pupils' English by getting them to talk to him, and to answer *carefully prepared* questions about a picture, or about a simple story or news event he has related to them; it is best to tape-record such answers if facilities are available and if the pupils are confident enough to do this with the teacher, as this allows him to play over their answers and to note features he might well have missed on the first occasion. If pupils can write, they should be given a very short simple dictation, and asked to write the answers to some simple questions. On a very small sample of such answers, oral and written, it should be possible to see, for instance, whether the pupils use the indefinite article correctly, similarly the definite article, the plural forms of nouns, the subject pronouns, the *-ing* ending of the present continuous tense, the agreement of singular verb with singular person and plural forms with plural persons, and so on (an itemization that can be made by reference to the scheme of work). A carefully devised test, oral and written, could cover these features so that from the pupils' answers the teacher gets specific knowledge about their grammatical weaknesses. (Weaknesses in pronunciation may of course be great and make some of the analysis of oral answers difficult for the teacher.)

Work in a variety of ways may then follow the diagnosis. Basically it must aim at eradicating faults, and the teacher should do this consistently, going over drills and exercises orally (and in writing where appropriate) and frequently revising those already covered. It may well be that pupils may find this corrective work tedious, as implied above, and a sense of plan and purpose in the teacher's conduct of it is absolutely vital. Drills and exercises should be dealt with as briskly and energetically as possible; some of the procedures suggested in Chapter 4 should be adopted, including the use of systematic oral drills, substitution tables, and the adaptation of dialogues and story material to practise chosen structural and lexical features. Many books of graded exercises are available (exercises which should not be confused with drills and which for oral work usually need some adaptation). Some titles are given in the relevant section of the Bibliography (Section III). From these, teachers should select and edit according to their need.

Pupils would obviously benefit from the sort of intensive repetitive practice provided by language laboratory work. At the present time, there is very little material available commercially that is suitable for this particular purpose, and any teachers who have already begun to write and record their own tapes will know how enormously time-consuming this whole process is. All the same, any teacher who has access to language laboratory facilities and has the necessary time and energy would be well advised to explore the possibilities. The utilization of recorded materials together with the sheer novelty of being in the language laboratory are ways of motivating pupils who otherwise often find it hard to knuckle down to this necessary repetitive work; the few experiments that have already been made with adolescent immigrant pupils in language laboratories are very encouraging. There is obvious need here for co-operation and interchange of materials between teachers faced with similar problems in different schools in an area.

Although it is suggested that it is only intense repetitive work that will effect an improvement in pupils' English, it should also be remembered that pupils of the age-group we are concerned with here are possibly needing to use English in very many everyday situations outside school. They therefore need practice in the conversational English of the shop, the post office, the launderette, etc., and the type of dialogue work suggested in Chapter 4 is of particular relevance. Dialogue work will also assist motivation, and teachers need to think of all possible ways of providing this. Project work involving the use of aids and apparatus (see next chapter) such as preparing a broadcast or TV programme or involving the class or group in the production of a wall newspaper should be considered. The fact that the teacher's main task is remedial teaching and that in language work this has to be based on constant repetition does not mean that the real purpose of language learning should be lost sight of in these lessons; wherever possible, the items of language to which main attention is being paid in drills and exercises should be built into and used within the framework of purposive interesting work.

West Indian pupils

The above discussion applies really to the older immigrant pupil from Asia, Africa or Europe who arrives at school or evening class already speaking a sub-standard or incorrect kind of English. It has been suggested that many teachers will have West Indian pupils who they feel fit into a similar category, i.e. they join classes, or, in particular, enter schools speaking a kind of sub-standard English. But a special word is demanded for this particular problem.

It has been found in practice that it is extremely difficult to say anything that is clearly helpful in terms of methods and materials for teaching English to West Indian pupils. What is perhaps more useful in the first place is to question *what* we should try to teach them rather than how, and what in fact is the nature of the language many of them speak when they enter our schools.

It has been called 'sub-standard' or 'incorrect' English, and it will be observed that not all speak it in the same way, and that indeed many seem to speak something very near to Standard English while some speak something very different. When it is obviously not Standard English, it would be better to call it 'non-standard' rather than 'sub-standard', and in so doing recognize it as something that does not claim to be Standard English in the first place. If this is understood, we can at least adopt a sensible attitude to the problem even if we cannot find an answer to it.

What then do so many West Indians speak if it is not Standard English? Depending on where they come from, i.e. which part of the Caribbean, they speak *a dialect of Creole English*, or *English-based Creole*, whichever we choose to call it. A Creole language is one that comes into being because of certain patterns of events, comings and goings of peoples, settlers, traders, migrants, slaves, in circumstances in which the native languages of the different groups are largely dropped in favour of another, but in the course of time leave their mark upon it. Languages, as we know, reflect the history of the people who speak them and in the case of the Caribbean this is a particularly colourful variegated history in which the main ingredients are to all intents and purposes the expulsion of the original Spanish colonists by the British in the middle of the seventeenth century and the subsequent massive importations of slaves from Africa, together with the arrivals of many smaller groups of peoples of different nationalities.

> Even today, with all the effects of standardized schooling, Englishmen (to say nothing of Welshmen, Irishmen, and Scots) speak their language in countless variations. Considering the history of the British Isles, this is in no way surprising. Nor should one be disturbed to find yet other variations where people of many kinds in a new colony have pooled their home differences, seasoned them with the tropical spices of Arawak and Carib Indians, Africans, Spaniards, Frenchmen, and assorted others, until a strong and tasty pepperpot of language is concocted. This, of course, is what has happened in Jamaica . . .[1]

and, we might add, in the other islands of the area.

The 'strong and tasty pepperpot of language' is in fact a language in its own right, for Creole languages are recognized as such by linguists. It helps us to understand the nature of a creole if we compare it with a pidgin. To the linguist, *pidgin* and *creole*

[1] F. G. Cassidy, *Jamaica Talk* (1961), p. 2.

are specific technical terms. A pidgin is a form of language used often by new settlers, or, on the other hand, by the newly conquered, who in the circumstances in which they find themselves learn to use a language other than their own but do so imperfectly, not getting all the grammar straight nor, for that matter, controlling a large vocabulary. A pidgin is thus not the speaker's native language, and is a reduced form of the original (often so reduced as not to consist of more than 700–1,500 words). Creole languages, and there are several of them, develop out of pidgins and become the native languages of subsequent generations; the resources of the original pidgin are developed from within and enlarged by borrowings. The form of the language becomes stabilized (in so far as a language is stable) and its grammar, phonology, etc., can be studied and described.

Much attention is in fact being paid at the present time to the Caribbean languages. The dialect of Jamaica, 'Jamaican Creole', has had most attention paid to it so that it is fairly easy now to read about it in linguistic sources. A study of this would help teachers understand why many West Indian immigrants have difficulty in being understood and in speaking and writing Standard English.

Some Jamaican Creole would in fact be intelligible to an English speaker; all the same, the differences are extensive enough for one to realize that it is not simply a variety of English but an independent language. We can for instance deduce several facts about its grammar – facts which show the wide divergence from English – by examining a few sentences such as the following:

1. *dem a mi fren dem* (they are my friends)
2. *mi a dem fren* (I am their friend)
3. *mi a go si dem* (I am going to see them)
4. *mi a go si mi fren* (I am going to see my friend)
5. *mi a go si mi fren dem* (I am going to see my friends)

We see, for instance, that Jamaican Creole does not indicate the plural of nouns when the number (i.e. whether it is singular or plural) is apparent from the context; when the context might leave room for some ambiguity, then the particle *dem* following the noun marks the plural as in (5). Pronoun usage is also very different from that in Standard English. The first person subject pronoun is seen to be *mi* (where Standard English has *I*), and the third person plural is *dem* (*them*). The verb *be* is mostly heard as *a* in all persons; *mi a go* for *I'm going* again shows a wide divergence from English usage.

The above points could be considerably expanded. For instance, nouns not only have no inflexion to mark the plural, but they have none to mark possession either. The pronoun system shows many other differences: subjective and objective personal pronouns are not differentiated and the full range of personal pronouns is simply:

	singular	*plural*
	mi	wi
	you	unu
	im, it	dem
(sometimes)	shi	

The verb system again differs from Standard English in many respects; tense, for instance, may be expressed solely by the context of the action or by some adverbial of time (e.g. *mi nyam pie til mi sik* = I ate pear till I was sick).

This very abridged account of how the grammar of Jamaican Creole differs from that of Standard English must suffice to substantiate our point.

The main implication for the teacher is surely that the pupil should not be treated as one who knows English already and is getting it wrong from carelessness or slovenliness. It also seems clear that such pupils would be better taught by second-language methods rather than first, and that many of the methods and materials suggested in this book will be of use in the teaching both of grammar and of pronunciation.

This is not to submit that this is the answer to the problem, for in this matter the pupil as much as the teacher is hard to convince; there would be no gain at all in *telling* a West Indian pupil that he did not speak English but another language. It would, however, perhaps be helpful to explain that 'his' English (i.e. Jamaican Creole, or some other dialect of the Caribbean) is one thing, and British English – which he must approximate to if he is to get on, make friends, pass examinations and interviews, etc. – is another, and while the use of the one is perfectly good and right and proper in some situations, the other is necessary in others. The West Indian pupil has in fact to be bilingual (as many are before they arrive at school, and as are many British pupils in their ability to switch from 'home' English to 'school' English) and the teaching he receives in school might take this into account. It is interesting to note that in Jamaica at the present time there is a change in the educational policy in some of the schools, so that English, instead of being taught to children as if it were their mother tongue, is being taught, and taught more effectively it is thought, as a second language.

While it is not suggested that segregated English-language classes for West Indians should be set up, it does seem as if many would benefit from having some teaching along the lines suggested here; teachers might try out some of the oral procedures suggested earlier in this book and also use some of the texts, readers, courses and books of language exercises suggested in the Bibliography.

SUGGESTED READING

CASSIDY, *Jamaica Talk* (X)
   There are many useful accounts of life in the West Indies and in West Indian communities in Britain, but *Jamaica Talk* is a highly readable account of Jamaican Creole itself.

Note. The examples of Jamaican Creole quoted on p. 215 are from W. A. Stewart, *Non-Standard Speech and the Teaching of English*, and R. B. Le Page, 'Creole English Dialects in the British Caribbean', in *Orbis VI*, both of which would be valuable further reading for those particularly concerned with West Indian language problems.

7

Aids and apparatus

It is unusual nowadays to find a classroom in a British school in which there are no visual aids and pieces of apparatus on view. Their general educational value is not questioned. In the primary school in particular one is impressed by the language content of much of the apparatus that can be seen, drawings labelled by teacher or pupils, charts, directions, individual and collective productions by the pupils, all geared to the activities and interests of life in and out of school. The teacher of English as a second language at whatever stage, could not do better than spend some time in an infant and junior school examining the visual aids and apparatus on view and seeing how it could be adapted to his purposes. The labelling of pictures and of pieces of work, for instance, with captions such as *John drew this, This is my house, Our Christmas tree, Mary wove this mat,* etc., the building up of models, the collecting of objects to form shops, houses, hospitals, are all closely linked to language learning, either in terms of stimulating language (*What are the boys doing in this picture? How many fish can you see in this bowl?*) or in terms of reinforcing by visual means what has been practised elsewhere.

The teacher of English to immigrants will find the use of aids and apparatus an essential element in his work. The ideas given here will be applicable to teaching at various levels. Some suggestions will obviously sound like ways of providing time-filling activity only, and it cannot be pretended that this is not necessary at first, especially for teachers who have to teach pre-reading classes for long periods at a time. But 'time-filling' activities can often be educational activity in the most basic sense, affording children the opportunity to experience the sight, sound and feel of things and to learn to manipulate objects and equipment which may be strange to them. Teachers will obviously take opportunities as they present themselves, with individuals,

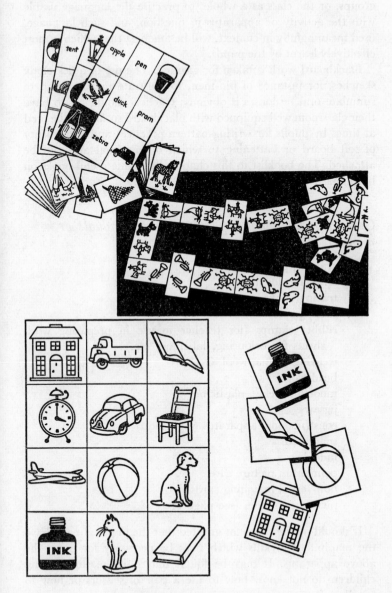

Simple pre-reading apparatus

groups, or the class as a whole, to practise the language usable with the activity or apparatus in question, and such language, used meaningfully in context, will be amongst that which is most effectively learnt by the pupils.

Blackboard work is taken for granted. The use of quick chalk sketches, for instance of pin-men, to illustrate meaning and to stimulate oral responses is obvious; teachers should try to have their classroom well equipped with blackboard surface (to be used at times by pupils for writing-pattern practice) and with plenty of soft board or battening to which other visual aids can be attached. The booklist to this chapter lists some useful books on blackboard drawing.

General occupational apparatus (for individuals or groups)

> crayons, paints, etc.
> templates for drawing
> tracing books
> sticky paper
> rubber stamps (for teacher to use in preparing work sheets for colouring, labelling, etc.)
> weaving (raffia, wool, etc.)
> bead work
> modelling (clay, plasticine)
> jigsaws
> constructional apparatus (e.g. Bildit)
> snap cards
> ludo
> pelmanism picture cards
> non-verbal matching cards
> picture dominoes (see page 219)

It should not be taken for granted that the pupils already have the manipulative skills which may be necessary for using the above apparatus. It may be found that quite mature-looking children do not know how to use a pair of scissors or how to handle paints or crayons.

With secondary-school pupils it should not be presumed that art and craft work should only be done in special art and craft lessons. If the teacher of immigrants has sufficient skill himself, he will do well to incorporate this kind of activity into his lesson time, paying particular attention to the language element that he can build into it.

Teacher's 'kit' for language work

> small plastic toys (animals, cars, soldiers, etc.)
> small bottles, boxes, tins of different shapes, sizes and colours
> coloured ribbons and pieces of other materials to illustrate such things as *thin/thick* (pieces of string and rope), *rough/smooth* (pieces of silk and sandpaper), etc.
> collection of cut-out pictures, mounted on card (illustrating actions, colours, prepositions, etc.)
> model of boy or girl (doll, or articulated cutout figure)
> puppets
> clockface
> cardboard money
> telephones
> doll's house

The teacher who is teaching English situationally may well be cramped by the classroom and from the very beginning should not rely solely on pens and pencils, books and desks, to provide the whole substance of his language work. Aids are needed to supply a larger context: pictures and other visuals are obviously used for this purpose, and especially 'to bring in the outside world', but the teacher should also consider what other objects and aids he can bring into the classroom to add interest to his work. Small toys like lorries or different kinds of animals will rouse more interest in the practice of simple structures than pens and pencils alone, and a collection of such objects (which can often be bought cheaply by the bagful) should be made. Several of the same object should be included to allow for the practice of plurals. Items to illustrate certain adjectives, and small amounts of 'uncountable' substances in polythene bags (rice, sugar, sand, etc.) are also useful. Obviously one does not want to introduce a lot of bizarre and relatively infrequent vocabulary just for the sake of novelty, and ingenuity must be tempered by common sense.

Colours, comparison of adjectives, etc., can also be practised by means of suitably chosen objects, for instance through collections of small cats or dogs or balls or boxes of different colours and sizes. The words for shapes themselves (*square, round,* etc.) can also be introduced and presented in various ways through similar collections. Some items may also have a special value for pronunciation practice, and objects and pictures might be collected to provide the situations for practising certain minimal pairs such as *pin/pen, frog/frock, ship/sheep, mouth/mouse.*

A small doll or articulated cutout figure or a puppet will be useful in many ways, not only for practising the vocabulary for parts of the body, clothes, right–left, some verbs of action, adjectives describing its appearance, etc., but even for practice of pronouns and possessive adjectives. (If the class consists entirely of boys then *she* and *her* can be introduced in this way.)

Puppets of course have many additional uses: they can be used as suggested in Chapter 4 to present short dialogues, or to give model answers to teacher's questions to show the class what is required of it, and in all sorts of entertaining ways in imperative drill, tense work, etc. If enthusiasm catches on, their use can be extended to include the acting of little dialogues and playlets by pupils. All teachers who have experimented with puppets in language teaching have found them a great source of motivation.

The clockface, cardboard money, and telephones (two at least) will obviously be used in the teaching of certain quite specific areas of language, but can also be put to good use in the presentation and practice of many different situations and centres of interest (e.g. travelling by rail or bus, inquiring about trains, shopping, emergencies involving the use of phone such as fires, accidents, and so on). The doll's house and its furniture also have many possibilities.

Pre-reading apparatus

plywood or plastic letters

felt letters for flannelgraph

alphabet cards and matching objects (e.g. small plastic toys for each letter such as *a*eroplane, *b*icycle, *c*ar, *d*og, etc.)

large pictures of single objects and matching initial letters

large pictures and matching flashcards

slot-charts (for weather, jobs, birthdays, etc.)

word lotto games

picture-and-word dominoes

small word-and-picture matching sets (see page 219)

flashcards, labels, etc. (made by teacher)

The value of the above kind of apparatus, some of it used by the teacher with the class as a whole, some of it by individual pupils, should be clear from the section on pre-reading activities (Chapter 5). The handling of letters and apparatus by the pupils has been recognized as a great help in teaching them letter recognition, and different variations on a tactile approach are therefore to be tried out.

There is a wealth of pre-reading apparatus on the market, but the teacher who manages to obtain this should always vet it first before handing it over to children to use on their own: he should ensure that it contains only language items already dealt with orally so that no strange pictures and words frustrate the pupil engaged in individual activity.

Even if the teacher is well supplied with commercially produced apparatus of this kind, he will probably need to make more for himself and to satisfy the quicker pupils. Pupils can also make their own individual picture-books from cutouts, labelling them themselves, and practising writing. Work cards for individual use can be produced on duplicating machines or by using rubber stamp pictures, for colouring and as a basis for writing. Ideas for work cards can be borrowed from workbooks provided with many courses, or when available and suitable, pupils can be provided with printed workbooks such as those suggested in the Bibliography (Section IV).

Visuals

> wall pictures and posters
> picture-story wall pictures
> composite wall pictures (made by pupils)
> flannelgraph and Cellograph kits
> film strips
> films

As suggested above, pictures and other visuals are used to provide a context for language work that goes beyond the walls of the classroom. (They also have other uses, of course, providing cheerful decoration and interest, stimulating pupils' desire for knowledge and their general enthusiasm. There is always the danger that pictures and posters can be left on display too long, so that they come to be taken for granted and ignored, and their value diminishes accordingly.)

Teachers should explore all the possibilities for providing interesting and *linguistically useful* visual materials. Many of the posters provided by the Post Office or by commercial firms are more than simply decorative, and the language teacher should try to develop an eye for what can be called the language content of these and other pictures. There are in fact several wall charts and picture-story picture sets especially printed for language teachers.

No picture should be thought of simply in terms of the vocabulary that it illustrates (though admittedly a picture provides a good situational way of introducing lexical items); rather the teacher should think in terms of the language his pupils have already learnt and particularly the kind of structural patterns which might be used in relation to it (e.g. in question-and-answer work: *What is this man going to do? What is the little girl going to do? What has the policeman just done? What has the boy bought in the shop?* etc.). The handbooks provided with some pictures give help in this direction and teachers should read them carefully to get ideas about this kind of work and to see how the pictures in question can be used at the level of English at which they are teaching.

Composite wall pictures, made by the pupils' all providing cutouts from magazines, or by their drawing, colouring and then cutting out certain items themselves, are also very useful. They can be chosen to illustrate a certain theme or a certain area of language (e.g. themes: *Winter*, *We saw these things in the park*, *Food we eat*; grammar – present continuous tense: *This man is running. This boy is jumping/riding a horse* . . . etc.).

Many teachers find the flannelgraph or flannelboard one of the most useful of all aids in language teaching. It can be used in an especially interesting way because with it the teacher can suddenly put up pictures (or words) and as quickly replace them with new ones or modify them with additions. Thus for story telling, or for presenting little scenes, or dialogues, or to drill prepositions or adjectives, it can be a very valuable device. (A flannelgraph or flannelboard is simply a piece of fleecy material such as Dorset drape or flannelette pinned to a wall or piece of soft board, or even hung over a blackboard. Cutouts, if backed with sandpaper or flockpaper, or with little pieces of similarly fleecy material, will adhere to the surface of it when placed against it. It usually has great novelty value, at least at first, and a stronger appeal than the blackboard. Plastigraph and Cellograph are more sophisticated forms of the flannelgraph, using plastic materials.)

Film-strips, like pictures, can be used for simple oral work, and several film-strips produced by the Educational Foundation for Visual Aids, originally for use in first-language teaching, are adaptable to the present purpose. There are some which show everyday objects or actions, one for telling the time, and so on. Where there are captions on the separate frames of the film-strip, the teacher should make sure that these do not interfere with oral work which he wants to base on the pictures.

Other film-strips are available that tell simple stories, which could be used for story-telling purposes and for stimulating oral work, though again, where there are printed captions on the strip, the teacher would have to exercise considerable discretion.

Films are on the whole not found to be as useful to the language teacher as film-strips and other visuals. However, they can sometimes be put to good use, especially if the teacher prepares his own commentary beforehand and then shows the film with the sound track switched off.

Aural aids

 radio
 gramophone
 tape-recorder
 language master
  etc.

Aural aids are listening devices such as the wireless, gramophone and tape-recorder, which in the first place enable language learners to listen to broadcast or recorded speech.

There is very little by way of direct broadcasting that is suitable for our present purpose. Recorded material available on discs includes simple children's songs, fairy stories, and some English-language teaching material such as dialogues, pronunciation drills, etc. Some of this might be usable in class where a gramophone was available, especially the stories and some of the dialogues, and it might be incorporated into lessons with immigrant pupils, though on the whole most of it is at too advanced a level and could only be used to give a fillip of interest to a class of older rather than younger pupils. Gramophone records moreover need careful handling. It is often difficult to select what is required from a side or band, although it is possible to buy a pick-up controlling device which enables the user to do so without damaging the grooves of the record.

But it is the tape-recorder that is likely to be of most use to the language teacher, both as a means of playing recorded material to a class (with the advantage over the gramophone of being used with more freedom, frequent stopping, starting and rewinding not affecting the quality of a recording on a tape), and sometimes too for the purpose of recording members of a class performing in English. A series of tape-recordings of pupils' speech at different stages in their progress through English classes is a valuable piece of linguistic material which would help teachers and others to evaluate their spoken English; and, as suggested in the previous chapter, recordings of pupils' responses are all but essential for teachers who wish to diagnose pupils' weaknesses before preparing special remedial language material.

USES OF TAPE-RECORDER

Tapes can be made of songs, rhymes, short dialogues and short stories, especially using voices other than the teacher's own. For dialogues and stories this is a specially useful form of presentation, or of re-presentation, of material already started in class. If realistic sound effects are added to establish the context (e.g. in a shop, at the railway station), the more attention will pupils pay to the recording. Material recorded for this purpose should be spoken at normal speed; repeat recordings, with gaps between utterances in which pupils can echo the voices on the tape, are also most useful.

Pupils who have learnt rhymes or poems by heart, or short dialogues or playlets, can be encouraged to record them and then to listen to themselves. It is generally found that immigrant pupils do not have a great faculty of self-criticism, and playback of recordings may not have any great language-teaching value; however, pupils usually find it very interesting to listen to their own voices, and it may encourage them to work harder to achieve better performance in all respects.

Tape-recorder projects such as those done with British children in school may also be tried out with immigrants who are a little more advanced; they may plan and record a 'broadcast' or TV programme, for instance, or prepare a special Christmas or New Year tape to exchange with another class or school.

With older pupils it may be possible to use tape-recorders for language practice in the way that language laboratories are now being used in modern-language teaching. This means, for instance, providing master tapes recorded with gaps between utterances in which the listeners can repeat whatever the master voice or voices say. Young and unsophisticated pupils will not usually be well enough motivated to do this kind of work or to try to repeat exactly what they hear, as it is difficult for them to see the purpose of it and they soon get bored with the repetition. However, it has been done with some success with older pupils. A responsible group can be left to sit around a tape-recorder for listening and repeating practice while the teacher occupies himself with another group of the class.

But this simple listening and repeating practice will be more effective again if each pupil can listen through headphones to the master tape, as in a language laboratory. Best of all, audio-active headsets should be used, i.e. headphones with a microphone attached which enables each pupil to hear his own responses, as well as the master recording, through the head-phones.

As suggested in the previous chapter, where there are full pupil-recording facilities in a well-equipped language laboratory, the teacher of immigrants will obviously consider using these too, so that his pupils can play back and listen to their own individual recordings. (But teachers should guard against time being too often wasted in playback.)

Apart from simple repetitive work, recorded material can also be used for getting pupils to practise structural drills. In this sort of recorded exercise, the teacher's voice on the master tape acts as a stimulus to which the pupil has to respond within the set framework of a grammatical pattern. This work has to be very carefully prepared beforehand, so that the pupil knows what is expected of him; and the taped exercises also have to be very carefully constructed and recorded so that there is no ambiguity in the response required from the pupil. (It is usual for this type of exercise to take the form of a stimulus given by the master voice, followed by a carefully timed pause in the tape during which the pupil has to record his reply, followed by the correct reply given by a second master voice.) Taped exercises need very carefully worded instructions and an introductory example or two, to show the pupil simply and exactly what is required of him. This sort of work, like the listening and repeating practice outlined above, should all be based on material presented live in class, so that pupils thoroughly understand what they are supposed to be doing. After practice with the tape-recorder or in a language laboratory, the material practised should be gone over live again and used in new situations.

In schools where audio-visual aids are being used for the teaching of modern languages, the teacher of English to immigrants should look to the possibilities of adapting similar methods and materials to his purpose. Before long, audio-visual courses for the teaching of English will be on the market, and some of this material will be of use in immigrant classes. The 8 mm. film loops which are being produced in America and here for use in language teaching will also offer possibilities to teachers in the near future. The Language Master (Rank Audio Visual) is a new transistorized machine into which can be fed visuals and reading matter on long cards; each card also carries a strip of magnetic tape, on to which the words on the card can be recorded, on one track by the teacher as a 'master voice', on another by pupils repeating or responding to what the master voice says. Blank cards can be prepared by the teacher, or a ready-prepared programmed course (designed for British slow readers) can be used. Several teachers of immigrants have already discovered the possibilities of this machine. All advances in language teaching have relevance to the teaching of English as a second language, whether it is abroad or at home in the teaching of English to immigrants.

APPARATUS AVAILABLE COMMERCIALLY

Advice and information about aids and apparatus can be sought from:

The Educational Foundation for Visual Aids, 33 Queen Anne Street, London, W.1

English-Teaching Information Centre, The British Council, State House, 63 High Holborn, London, W.C.1

National Audio-Visual Aids Centre, 33 Queen Anne Street, London, W.1

Overseas Visual Aids Centre, Tavistock House South, Tavistock Square, London, W.C.1

An indispensable source of information about aids and apparatus of all kinds – how it can be made, bought, borrowed (or even, in some cases, obtained free of charge) – is contained in the Appendixes to *Simple Audio-Visual Aids to Foreign-Language Teaching* by W. R. Lee and Helen Coppen (O.U.P.).

The main suppliers of the type of apparatus discussed in this chapter are listed below. Teachers should write for catalogues and should also consult those of local suppliers not listed here. In the following list, suppliers of recorded materials (tapes and/or discs) are marked '*Aud*'.

B.B.C., Bush House, Strand, London W.C.2 (*Aud.*)

Blackie & Son, 16 William IV Street, London W.C.2

Educational Supply Association, Pinnacles, Harlow, Essex

E.M.I. Records Ltd, 20 Manchester Square, London W.1 (*Aud.*)

Evans Brothers, Montague House, Russell Square, London W.C.1

Ginn & Co. Ltd, 18 Bedford Row, London W.C.1

Mary Glasgow & Baker Ltd, 140 Kensington Church Street, London W.8 (*Aud.*)

George Harrap & Co., 182 High Holborn, London W.C.1 (*Aud.*)

Linguaphone Institute Ltd., Linguaphone House, 207–209 Regent Street, London W.1 (*Aud.*)

Longmans, Green & Co. Ltd, 48 Grosvenor Street, London W.1 (*Aud.*)

Macmillan & Co., St Martin's Street, London W.C.2 (*Aud.*)

M.D.S. Visual Aids Centre, 78 High Holborn, London W.C.1

Thomas Nelson & Sons, 36 Park Street, London W.1

James Nisbet & Co., Ditswell Place, Welwyn Garden City, Herts

Oliver & Boyd, 39a Welbeck Street, London W.1

Oxford University Press, Ely House, Dover Street, London W.1 (*Aud.*)

Philip & Tacey Ltd, Fulham High Street, London S.W.6

Rank Audio Visual, Woodger Road, London W.12 (*Aud.*)

Tutor-Tape Company Ltd, 2 Replingham Road, London S.W.18 (*Aud.*)

University of London Press, Little Paul's House, Amen Square, London E.C.4 (*Aud.*)

Frederick Warne & Co., 1 Bedford Court, London W.C.1

The list of materials here is not intended to be in any way comprehensive, but all the items in it are recommended for use.

Apparatus, non-verbal

    Picture Dominoes (Arnold, Philip & Tacey)

    Picture Matching Sets (Arnold)

Hereward Observation Test Matching Cards (Philip & Tacey)

Pencil Control Tracing Cards (Philip & Tacey)

Janet and John Rubber Stamps (Philip & Tacey)

Dupress Pictorial Rubber Stamps – Common Objects (Philip & Tacey)

The Same and Not the Same Cards (E.S.A.)

Graded Pictures (E.S.A.)

Reading apparatus

Word and Picture Tombola (Arnold)

Picture and Word Matching Cards (Philip & Tacey)

Chelsea Individual Reading Apparatus (Philip & Tacey)

Motspur Singulars and Plurals Cards (Philip & Tacey)

Positional Word and Picture Matching Cards (Philip & Tacey)

Initial Missing Letter Flashcards (Philip & Tacey)

Wall-pictures, etc.

General Service English Wall Pictures (Longmans)
(8 large coloured pictures, especially designed for English-language teaching; accompanied by teacher's handbook. Pupils' workbooks are also published but would be suitable only for very advanced pupils.)

Wall Pictures for Guided Composition (University of London Press)
(16 black and white picture stories by Fougasse. Suitable for story telling at different levels, though several of the 'anecdotes' would be too sophisticated for many immigrant pupils. Includes some animal fables. Teacher's reference book provided.)

Happy Venture Wall Pictures (Oliver and Boyd)
(Coloured set; intended to accompany reading course for teaching reading to British children; useful for oral work, as are other sets of pictures of a similar nature which need not be used in conjunction with the readers with which they are published.)

New Chelsea Pictorial Alphabet Frieze (Philip & Tacey)
(9 sheets, coloured.)

Cellograph Set – Chameleon Street Scene (Philip & Tacey)
(Large colourful street scene with interchangeable houses, trees, etc. Very attractive.)

Flannelgraphs 1 to 8 (Arnold)
(8 stories, each with a set of illustrative flannelgraph figures; also matching toys to go with the stories if required.)

Film strips
Alphabet
What is it?
What shall we do?
Telling the time
An English Child at Home
Fat Pig
Jeremy's Day
Jeremy's Saturday
Green Engine
The Little Red Hen
The Three Wishes
(All available from the Educational Foundation for Visual Aids, 33 Queen Anne Street, London W.1)

Recorded material
The most helpful catalogues to refer to in selecting recorded material are the *Catalogue of Speech Records* issued by the Publications and Recorded Sound Department, Recorded Sound Section, The British Council (Albion House, 159 New Oxford Street, London W.C.1) and lists published by *English by Radio* (B.B.C., Bush House, Strand, London W.C.2) and the Linguaphone Institute (207–9 Regent Street, London W.1).

English by Radio B.B.C. records are not usually for sale in this country, but arrangements can sometimes be made to borrow them, for instance, through the British Council.

E.M.I. Records Ltd (E.M.I. House, 20 Manchester Square, London W.1) publishes two catalogues, *Children's Records* and *Records for the Primary School*, which contain sections on nursery rhymes and songs, dramatized stories, etc. This material was not originally intended for the second-language situation, but some of it is usable.

Note. Very little recorded material is directly suitable for use with immigrant pupils. Most of the titles suggested here would be usable with older school and adult pupils at a fairly advanced level of English; this is especially true of the pronunciation material. Those items considered to be of most use in the primary and lower secondary school are asterisked.

Pronunciation and Intonation

Records

Colloquial English Pronunciation. J. T. Pring – 2 7″ LP records. (Text and records from Longmans.)

English Intonation Practice. R. Kingdon – 4 7″ LP records. (Text and records from Longmans.)

English Intonation Reader. W. R. Lee – 6 78 r.p.m. records. (Text from Macmillan, records from Linguaphone.)

English Pronunciation. P. A. D. McCarthy – 3 78 r.p.m. records. (Text from Heffer, Cambridge, records from Linguaphone.)

Stress, Rhythm and Intonation. J. D. O'Connor – 2 10″ LP records. (B.B.C.)

Tapes

Better Spoken English. G. Barnard – 5 tapes. (Text from Macmillan, tapes from Tutor Tape.)

Living English Speech. W. S. Allen – 2 tapes. (Text and tapes from Longmans.)

Drills and Tests in English Sounds. L. A. Hill – 2 tapes. (Text and tapes from Longmans.)

Language Courses

Records

* *Hallo* – 18 7″ LP records, accompanied by pupils' worksheets and teacher's notes, for 1st-year course. (2nd and 3rd year courses in preparation.) (Records and printed material from Mary Glasgow & Baker Ltd.) (See entry no. 3 in Bibliography.)

Records

* *Joseph and Sarah* – 6 12″ LP records, each consisting of four lessons, for 1st-year (African) primary course; accompanied by wall-pictures and teacher's notes. (B.B.C.)

Tapes

Passport to English – 13 tapes, 16 filmstrips and teacher's manual. (Published by Didier, and available in this country through George Harrap & Co. Ltd.)

Grammatical Exercises
Tapes

Oxford Progressive Course for Adult Learners. A. S. Hornby – 2 tapes accompany each of the three books. (Text from Oxford University Press, tapes from Tutor Tape.) (See entry no. 13 in Bibliography.)

Oral Drills in Sentence Patterns. H. Monfries. (Text from Macmillan, tapes from Tutor Tape.) (See entry no. 19 in Bibliography.)

Dialogues
Tapes

Conuersation Exercises in Everyday English. Jerrom and Szkutnik – 4 tapes to accompany Books 1 and 2. (Text and tapes from Longmans.) (See entry no. 28 in Bibliography.)

English Conversation for Foreign Students. J. O'Judd – 1 tape. (Text from Harrap, tape from Tutor Tape.)

Songs and Nursery Rhymes
Records

* *Children's Singing Games* – 7″ LP record. (Talking Book Co. in association with Methuen.)

* *Nursery Rhymes* sung by Doris Gould – 7″ LP record. (HMV 7EG 8296.)

Time for a Song – 7″ LP record to accompany songbook edited by Lee & Dodderidge. (Text and record from Longmans.

BOOKLIST TO CHAPTER 7

ARNEIL, *Equip that Infant Room* (X)

BILLOWS, *The Techniques of Language Teaching* (X)

FRENCH, *Teaching English as an International Language* (X)

GATENBY and ECKERSLEY, *General Service English Wall Pictures* Teacher's Handbook (X)

LEE and COPPEN, *Simple Audio-Visual Aids to Foreign Language Teaching*

LEWIS, *The Use of Diagrams in the Teaching of English*

METHOLD, *Broadcasting with Children*

O.V.A.C., *Flannelgraph as an Aid to Teaching and Training*

RAMSHAW, *Blackboard Work*

STREVENS, *Aural Aids in Language Teaching*

TAYLOR, *Equipping the Classroom*

TURNER, *Introduction to the Language Laboratory*

WESTON, *The Tape Recorder in the Classroom*

Bibliography

Note. For further details of material listed here, teachers should obtain catalogues from the appropriate publishers. Those publishers principally concerned with the production of material in this field, are listed on page 230 above.

The Bibliography is divided into the following sections:

    I Courses – 1. Primary
   II Courses – 2. Secondary and adult
  III Language drill and exercises
  IV Workbooks
   V Plays, dialogues, etc.
  VI Readers – 1
 VII Readers – 2
VIII Periodicals (pupils)
  IX Dictionaries
   X Books for teachers (general bibliography)

Entries in Sections I to IX are briefly annotated to help teachers in their selection of material for use in class, and are listed alphabetically according to *title*. Items in Section X, which forms the general bibliography to this book as a whole and gives details of titles listed at the ends of chapters, are arranged under *authors*.

I Courses-1

This is a selection of courses originally designed for teaching English to overseas children in the primary school, which are found to be of use for teaching immigrants of primary school age. Few books designed for use with adults or in the secondary school overseas make sufficient allowance for the beginner reader and writer, and for older pupils who are learning to read and write for the first time the teacher has little choice but to turn to some of the books listed in this section (unless, of course, he makes his own materials). An indication is therefore given in the notes of those titles which are considered usable with older pupils as well.

A note is also given on whether a course is originally intended for use in any special region (e.g. West Africa, Malaya) or whether it is for general use and therefore free of regional colouring. Courses for special regions are included because they are very often designed on sound pedagogical and linguistic principles and are especially useful as first readers for pupils who are beginning to learn to read Roman script. Regional colouring by way of illustrations and occasional items of vocabulary may seem to make them unsuitable for use in some classes, but these features are often counterbalanced by the general attractiveness and serviceability of the books in question.

Teachers' handbooks are also noted; they are usually an indispensable adjunct to the language courses and in several cases provide a syllabus for the preliminary oral work to be covered before reading is begun. Some handbooks, as mentioned in Chapter 2 above, are valuable guides to language teaching in general.

1. ABSORBING ENGLISH (Hemming and Gatenby. Longmans)
   Non-regional

   Books 1, 2, 3
   Teacher's Book

This is a graded course for primary schools, based perhaps too firmly on the language of the classroom. Although it is designed for beginner readers and (in Book 3) helps pupils make the transition from printscript a and g to conventional print **a** and **g**, it is not suitable for use with really young immigrant children. It should be usable with European immigrant pupils and possibly with older Asian pupils.

The teacher's book contains suggestions for many procedures in oral work and is especially helpful on pre-reading activities, group work and language games.

2. GOOD ENGLISH (R. Okyne. University of London Press)
   Ghana

   Work in English 1 (pupil's workbook)

Teacher's Handbook 1
Work in English 2
Teacher's Handbook 2
Kofi's Hoop (reader 1)
Ali and the Cows (reader 2)

This course has a pronounced regional flavour, with illustrations depicting African children, etc. It is very slowly graded and every help is given to the beginner reader, both in the pre-reading exercises in the workbooks and in the design and content of the readers. The workbooks should be found to be particularly useful.

3. HALLO (Mary Glasgow and Baker, Ltd) Non-regional

A new type of course, designed for eight-year-old foreign learners, consisting of gramophone records, teacher's notes, and pupils' 'working scripts' which are work-sheets and meant to be expendable. Each lesson introduces simply graded everyday language about different topics (the family, the home, Christmas, etc.) and concludes with songs or activities for young pupils to engage in. This material should be a useful aid to teachers using more conventional reading and writing materials, but the grading of the language makes it unsuitable as a basic course.

4. LEARN AND ACT (Mary Baker. Longmans) Non-regional
Books 1, 2, 3

Very simple and slowly graded readers with a European background and with emphasis on pupil activity (through games, drawing, dialogues, etc.). Originally designed for use in the primary school, but suggested here as only suitable for use with European pupils who can already read and write but who are in need of extra practice. The careful phonological grading in Book 1 provides useful material for pronunciation teaching.

5. LIVING TOGETHER SERIES (D. Brazier, E. Cooke and E. Jones. Pergamon Press) Non-regional
Books 1–10

A set of readers especially designed for use with young immigrants. Each book is well illustrated with coloured photographs showing children of different nationalities in various situations at school and out of doors, all in an English (Birmingham) milieu. The text is short and clearly printed, and makes full allowance for the beginner reader, but the language is not always graded in the way most appropriate to the second-language learner (e.g. in its use of the simple present tense from a very early stage). The books should provide very attractive supplementary reading material for classes using a more carefully linguistically graded reading scheme.

6. MODERN ENGLISH FOR MALAYANS (John Parry. University of London Press) Malaysia

> Readers: *Kassim and Eng Hock*   *Come and Play*   *By the Sea*   } Teacher's Book 1
>
> *The Talking Clock*   *Looking for Adventure* } Teacher's Book 2

A brightly produced set of first readers with coloured pictures on every page, large clear print, and interesting material which includes stories and dialogues. Malayan regional colouring is prominent, but should not be at all unacceptable to Asian pupils, for whom this course is strongly recommended. It is one of the most obviously suitable courses for junior beginner immigrant pupils.

The work cards, picture-cards, wall pictures and flashcards which accompany the course, are also recommended. The teacher's books are useful, full of helpful advice, and with a very clear presentation of the language scheme behind the readers.

7. NEW NATION ENGLISH (Bruce Pattison and A. Taylor. Nelson) Africa

> Pre-reader, and Pupils' Books 1–6 (Book 4 divided into two parts, A and B)
>
> Key to New Nation English (teacher's guide to preliminary oral work)
>
> Teacher's Books to Pre-reader, 1, 2, 3, 4–6
>
> (Supplementary Story Books; see below, Section VI, no. 39)

A course designed for the African primary school and therefore with a strong cultural element (pictures of African children, references to mangoes, yams, rice, etc. in the text), some of which relates to the Asian as well as the African scene. The key gives detailed guidance on the oral presentation of language and on the introduction of reading and writing, and as suggested earlier teachers would find this very useful without necessarily using the complete course.

8. THE NEW OXFORD ENGLISH COURSE (FOR MALAYA) (G. J. Gurney and A. L. Jones. Oxford University Press) Malaysia

   Stages 1, 2, 3, 4 5
   Teacher's notes

This is a special adaptation for use in the primary school in Malaya of the *New Oxford English* course. Stages 1–5 consist of the work to be covered in the first two years, based on carefully graded structures and vocabulary. Stage 1 consists of a picture book on which controlled oral practice can be based. It is probably the later stages which will be found especially useful in immigrant classes, especially Stages 2, 3 and 4, which are reading books based strictly on the language intended to be covered in Stage 1. (Stage 5 goes on to introduce new material through reading.) Supplementary readers, and flashcards for use in the early stages are also provided, and wall-pictures for use at Stages 1 and 2.

These books are very well produced, beginning with large colourful pictures and small stretches of clear print on each page. The Malayan element is not really pronounced until the second reader (Stage 3), but this again would not make the course unacceptable to Indian and Pakistani pupils. Above all, the reading matter is of interest, dealing with children, simple adventures with animals, etc.

9. THE NEW SHIP ENGLISH COURSE (A. W. Frisby. Longmans) Non-regional

   Pupils' Books 1, 2, 3, 4
   Workbooks 1, 2, 3, 4

A four-volume course designed for the primary school, with careful control of structures and vocabulary. The books are clearly printed with the matter carefully spaced on the page, but would all the same be fairly difficult for pupils who could not yet read. Book 1 at least is suitable for use with European immigrant pupils in upper junior and secondary schools, but difficult for very young pupils. After Book 1 the pages become rather crowded.

Useful workbooks are co-ordinated with the readers to provide simple reading and writing practice, but again are probably only suitable for European pupils.

10. THE PEAK COURSE (Special Centre, Nairobi. Oxford University Press) Kenya (for use in Asian schools)

        Teacher's notes. Standard I, Vols 1, 2, 3
                       Standard II, Vols 1, 2, 3
                       Standard III, Vols 1, 2, 3

     Peak Reading Course: Picture Book
                             Link Reader
                             Peak Reader I
                             I live in East Africa (Supplementary Reader I)
                             Reading through doing (Workbook I), etc.

A course designed for use in English-medium primary schools for Asian (i.e. largely Indian) pupils in East Africa. It has therefore very much to recommend it, as the situation for which it was designed has many parallels with that of schools with Asian immigrants in this country. The teacher's handbooks contain very useful details of schemes of work in P.E., handwork, etc. (i.e. lessons which have to be conducted in English) and lists of indispensable structures and vocabulary. The pre-reader picture-book and link-reader (i.e. primer), the readers and workbooks are carefully co-ordinated with the language syllabus outlined in the handbooks and are designed especially for young beginner readers.

The illustrations are of an Indian family; some of the specific East African touches (e.g. references to zebras, giraffes, etc.) would need to be dealt with carefully in classes which included both Asian and European pupils.

II *Courses-2*

Courses for use in the secondary school and/or with adult immigrant pupils. (But see notes to I–1 above, and entries (1) and (9).)

None of these courses offers very much help to the beginner reader and writer except number (12). They are therefore mostly suitable for use with pupils who can already read Roman script, i.e. mainly European immigrants.

The general appearance of these courses (size, type of print, use of illustrations, etc.) and a more 'adult' approach in the choice of language they contain, make most of them appear very different from those in I–1 above; but the most important consideration for the teacher is the way the language in them is for the most part much more steeply graded, i.e. progressing fairly rapidly through English grammar and building up a large vocabulary in a fairly short space.

11. FOUNDATIONS OF ENGLISH (D. Hicks. Longmans)

> Books 1–3
>
> Teacher's Books 1–3

This course has a mainly adult approach. The first two books (each based on a vocabulary of 900 words) are especially useful and would be found suitable for European pupils.

12. LIVING ENGLISH FOR THE ARAB WORLD (W. S. Allen and R. Cooke. Longmans)

> Pupils' Books 1–3
>
> Teacher's Books 1–3
>
> A Practice Reader: Pupils' Book and Teacher's Book
>
> Flashcards
>
> Wall Pictures

This is a course for Arab learners in the secondary school overseas. It is included here particularly for the help it offers in the teaching of reading and writing to pupils of this age who already read and write a non-Roman script and who are therefore in the position of many Asian immigrant pupils in the secondary school. Teacher's Book 1 offers detailed instructions for the first 25 oral lessons which are meant to be covered before reading and writing proper are begun; but writing practice and 'alphabet practice' (simple phonic reading based on the flashcards provided with the course) are also meant to be introduced during the preliminary oral period and a detailed syllabus is given to help the pupils through the basic mechanics of these two skills. Simple writing exercises (based on Marion Richardson linked script) are included in Pupils' Books 1 and 2.

Much of the regional colouring of the text (Arab names, Eastern background, small but clear illustrations of Middle Eastern scenes) would not be puzzling to Asian pupils in general and the course as a whole can be recommended for use in secondary-school classes.

13. OXFORD PROGRESSIVE ENGLISH COURSE FOR ADULT LEARNERS
     (A. S. Hornby. Oxford University Press)
       Books 1–3
       Teacher's Books 1–3
This course, or the recently produced 'alternative version' *Oxford Progressive English Alternative Course* by A. S. Hornby and R. Mackin (Books A and B; C and D in preparation; all with teacher's notes), is especially suitable for classes of adult pupils of different European nationalities. The reading passages cover a variety of interesting topics and bring in the language of everyday situations. The language scheme is closely geared to that of Hornby's *Teaching of Structural Words and Sentence Patterns* (see booklist to Chapter 2 above). The alternative course covers the same ground as the original, but does so more slowly, with shorter reading texts and more exercise material. All the drills and exercises, and the specific pronunciation work, are especially useful. For intensive courses in the secondary school, these books would also be very suitable.

14. PRESENT DAY ENGLISH FOR FOREIGN STUDENTS (F. Candlin.
     University of London Press)
       Books 1, 2, 3
       Teacher's Books 1, 2 3
       (Readers and gramophone records also available; work-
         books and tapes in preparation.)
A popular course with adult learners, brightly produced with attractive illustrations and embodying useful dialogues in the

text. On the grammatical side it is rather steeply graded, but its attractive appearance often makes it more acceptable to pupils than other more linguistically sound courses.

15. SITUATIONAL ENGLISH (Longmans)

> Parts One, Two. Students' Book
> Parts One, Two. Teacher's Book
> Language Picture Series
> (Part Three in preparation)
> Records to accompany Part One in preparation

A course adapted from material especially prepared for teaching adult immigrants in Australia. The object of the course is to provide a firm grounding in oral English, consolidated soon afterwards by reading and writing. The language items are presented situationally, and are selected to meet the practical needs of the adult in his new society. This is a course therefore that seems particularly suited to the adult (and secondary-school) immigrant pupil in this country as it takes into account the way in which he finds himself having to use English outside the classroom.

The teacher's books are full of practical advice and make special allowance for the teacher's problems in dealing with multi-lingual classes, and also give valuable detailed lesson plans.

As an oral course it can be strongly recommended for adult pupils of all nationalities, but as it gives little help with the basic mechanics of reading and writing, it may not be found as useful with Asian as with European and other pupils.

III *Language drill and exercises*

Included here are books consisting solely of exercises, some intended for oral practice only, others which can be used for both oral and written practice. This material is arranged differently in each book though nearly all contain practice in elementary structures and could therefore be used by the teacher in the earliest stages of language teaching. This type of book will probably be found of most use to the teacher of secondary-school pupils, or adults, and also of West Indian pupils.

16. AN ELEMENTARY REFRESHER COURSE FOR OVERSEAS STUDENTS (L. A. Hill. Oxford University Press)
A book of simple exercises that revise and re-teach English grammar using well illustrated passages of continuous prose. Very good for remedial work.

17. INTERMEDIATE ENGLISH PRACTICE BOOK (S. P. Corder. Longmans) and KEY
Copious practice material, more suited to use with adult pupils than in schools, with grammatical explanations that teachers will find both useful and enlightening.

18. LIVING ENGLISH STRUCTURE FOR SCHOOLS (W. S. Allen. Longmans) and KEY
Grammatical practice in graded exercises for use at elementary, intermediate and advanced levels. Especially useful for remedial work at different levels.

19. ORAL DRILLS IN SENTENCE PATTERNS (Helen Monfries. Macmillan)
Simple repetitive drills based on the tags and responses of conversational English. Especially useful for brisk work with adult students. (Tapes are also now available to accompany the text, made by Tutor Tape Ltd.)

20. ORAL PRACTICE FOR FOREIGN STUDENTS (D. Byrne. Longmans)
Very useful teacher's book with plentiful suggestions for oral work from a very elementary level onwards. Many of the drills are of a simple repetitive nature and can be used for rapid-fire response work. Some of the procedures suggested would need careful planning and preparation on the part of the teacher, but would be well suited to the immigrant classroom.

IV Workbooks

Many language courses include workbooks, i.e. books in which the pupils write (and sometimes draw, colour, etc.). These are most copious at the primary level; many of the courses listed in Section I, for instance, include pupils' workbooks which are of course meant to be used in conjunction with the course books. They can, however, be used on their own if simple explanations are given and the work is prepared orally beforehand. The most useful and usable of these are listed here, together with particulars of some language courses which in fact take the form of workbooks (nos. 23 and 27).

As pupils write in their workbooks, these obviously have to be considered expendable and may therefore seem to be rather expensive items in a school budget. They are, however, found especially useful by teachers of immigrants who often have little time to prepare individual worksheets for their many pupils and who find that workbooks allow pupils to proceed at their own rate and also give them a healthy sense of achievement. Workbooks can of course be copied on to worksheets by teachers who wish to save expense and have time to do so.

Note. Workbooks do not usually offer much help with the actual mechanics of handwriting. For this, i.e. for training pupils to make letters correctly and to provide them with simple material for copying, teachers will probably make their own apparatus; there are, however, a few copybooks on the market designed for the foreign learner and some teachers may choose to have recourse to them. References are given at the end of Chapter 5; and see entry no. (12) above.

21. ABSORBING ENGLISH (Hemming and Gatenby. Longmans)
    See (1)
        Workbooks 1–3 in preparation
22. GOOD ENGLISH (Okyne. University of London Press) See (2)
    Work in English 1 and 2
23. INTERNATIONAL ENGLISH (Ridout. Macmillan)
        Books 1–5
    A course described as 'first steps in learning to read and write English as a foreign language', which is really a series of slowly graded workbooks with spaces for pupils to fill in from page one onwards. The print is fairly small, and all the books are copiously illustrated with pin-men drawings. Unsuitable for very young children in the primary school; useful for pupils in the secondary school and for adults who need simple basic writing practice.
24. NEW OXFORD ENGLISH COURSE (FOR NIGERIA) (French. Oxford University Press)
        Workbook 1. Parts 1 and 2

Workbooks 2 and 3

Workbook 1, Part 1, is non-verbal, providing excellent pre-reading exercises and practice in writing patterns. Workbook 1, Part 2, repeats oral work of the first year and begins simple copying writing work, with pictures to colour, etc. Later workbooks provide practice in simple writing, and include stories, puzzles, etc. The African colouring can be discounted fairly easily.

25. THE NEW SHIP ENGLISH COURSE (Frisby. Longmans) See (9)
    Workbooks 1–4

26. THE PEAK SERIES (Special Centre, Nairobi. Oxford University Press) See (10)
    Reading through Doing (Workbooks 1–3)

27. THE SHIP ENGLISH COURSE (Frisby and Cheeseman. Longmans)
    Books 1–4
An elementary course in which the pupils' books are workbooks. Carefully graded classroom language, and lively pinmen drawings. Very useful for secondary-school pupils.

V   *Plays, dialogues, etc.*

Publishers' catalogues will be found to list many books containing short plays and dialogue material for use in second-language teaching. The titles given here are specially selected for the sake of their simplicity, interest and general usability in the language lesson.

28. CONVERSATION EXERCISES IN EVERYDAY ENGLISH (M. F. Jerrom and L. L. Szkutnik. Longmans)
    Books 1 and 2
    Tapes A and B for Book 1
    Tapes C and D for Book 2
Graded exercises in the form of dialogues, with additional practice material. The dialogues are based on everyday situations. Suitable for use with adult pupils at an elementary and intermediate level.

29. EASY ENGLISH DIALOGUES (M. West. Longmans)
    Books 1 and 2
Short dialogues based on simple incidents in and out of doors,

some of them humorous, some whimsical. The dialogues are based on graded structures, beginning at the elementary level, and could be used (mainly with adults) as the basis of simple dramatic work.

30. THE FOUR FRIENDS (M. Lee and R. Mackin. Oxford University Press)

Six little animal plays, all very short and based on a limited vocabulary and simple structures, with plenty of amusing repetition. Suitable for young children, and entertaining as puppet plays.

31. LIFE IS LIKE THIS ('Pleasant Books in Easy English'. Longmans)

32. PLAYS AND STORIES ('Pleasant Books in Easy English'. Longmans)

The two preceding titles include simple plays suitable for use with adolescents and adults. They are selected from Stage 1 of the series, 'Pleasant Books in Easy English', which also includes plays at later Stages and of varying degrees of difficulty. (See no. 45 below.)

33. SEVEN LITTLE PLAYS. ('New Method Supplementary Readers'. Longmans)

For use at Stage 1, i.e. elementary level, and written within a vocabulary of 450 words. The plays are based on fairy stories, etc.

VI   *Readers-1*

Several publishers produce readers especially designed for learners of English as a second or foreign language, in which the vocabulary and grammar are 'controlled' (i.e. graded according to certain levels of difficulty and suited to pupils at different stages of learning English). Comparatively few are selected for mention here, and those that are, are chosen mainly to indicate the variety and kind of material readily available for use with immigrant pupils.

34. ENGLISH PICTURE READERS (Oxford University Press)

Grade I: *World's Great Stories*
Grade II: *Pictorial Classics*

Simplified editions of famous stories, with a picture on every page and comparatively little text. (King Arthur, Robin Hood, Aladdin, etc.)

35. GRADED ENGLISH READERS FOR HONG KONG (Longmans)
Graded readers for primary-school pupils, consisting of stories with a Hong Kong background. Very attractively produced.

36. THE LITTLE BOOKSHELF (Oxford University Press)
Stories and books of rhymes in very simple English, some with an African background. Well printed, with brightly coloured illustrations which make them generally attractive to pupils of all backgrounds.

37. LONGMANS' STRUCTURAL READERS (Longmans)
Graded readers which include stories specifically written for the series, and simplifications of existing works. Each grade includes titles suitable for use at primary and secondary levels and with adults.

38. MEN AND WOMEN AT WORK (Oxford University Press)
Simple readers about people's activities in different parts of the world engaged in different industries (e.g. rubber, oil, gold, cocoa, newspaper production, etc.), and very useful in connection with work on special projects.

39. NEW METHOD SUPPLEMENTARY READERS (Longmans)
Graded readers (from Stage 1 based on 450 words to Stage 7 based on 2,500), which include folk stories and fables, romances, adventure stories, and re-tellings of the classics and of modern novels.

40. NEW NATION STORY BOOKS (University of London Press) See (7)
Readers with an African background. Well produced, popular first readers.

41. NEW OXFORD SUPPLEMENTARY READERS (Oxford University Press) See (8)
Short stories in carefully graded English, especially for very young pupils. Mostly animal stories in Books 1–4 (Introductory grade), but with a wider variety of subject matter in later books (Grades 2–6). Large clear type and many illustrations.

I

42. THE OXFORD ENGLISH COURSE SUPPLEMENTARY READERS
(Oxford University Press)
Like the New Method Supplementary Readers, this series
includes many different types of story at each stage, including
fables, fairy stories and simplified classics.

43. THE OXFORD STORY READERS FOR AFRICA (Oxford University
Press)
Grades 1–4 include many simple versions of popular folk tales.

44. PATTERN READERS (Macmillan)
Readers based on graded structures and controlled vocabulary. Lavishly illustrated and especially suited to pupils in the
primary school.

45. THE PEAK SERIES READING COURSE (Special Centre, Nairobi.
Oxford University Press) See (10)
Read me a Story, I and II
In Praise of Famous Men
In Search of Living Things
International fairy stories, etc., very simply told, clearly
printed and well illustrated. Suitable for pupils in the first
year or so of reading English.

46. PLEASANT BOOKS IN EASY ENGLISH (Longmans)
Readers, simple in style and in vocabulary, but generally
adult in subject matter. They include very short stories,
playlets, and dialogues.

47. PRACTICAL READERS (Longmans)
Stories with quite a lot of action in them, dealing with everyday settings and familiar scenes. Controlled vocabulary and
structures, graded in stages from 1 to 4.

VII   *Readers-2*

It has been suggested earlier in this book that many of the readers
published for British children in the early stages of learning to
read are not suitable for use with immigrant pupils who do not have
the oral knowledge of the language (including control of structures and a fairly wide vocabulary) that most young British
pupils possess. Many of these readers, however, contain excellent
pictorial material – pictures of animals, of houses, scenes in town,

etc. – that the young immigrant can enjoy as much as the British child. In some cases the short captions that go with these picture-book readers can be treated as pre-reading material. In any case, these books, and many other attractively printed ones, are useful to have in order to provide picture material for immigrant pupils to talk about (especially pictures of their new surroundings, of British homes, etc.); as contents of a book corner or displayed on accessible shelves they can also serve to encourage the use of books as part of the pupils' educational experience.

Only a very few suggestions are given here of titles known to be especially popular with immigrant pupils; it is presumed that the average primary school will have supplies of or ready access to this kind of material.

48. BEFORE WE READ (Oliver and Boyd)
49. GAY COLOUR BOOKS (E. J. Arnold)
50. LADYBIRD BOOKS (Wills and Hepworth)
    Especially Key Words Reading Scheme, and People at Work series.
51. LET'S LEARN TO READ (Blackie)
    Especially Book I: *The House*
52. MY HOME SERIES (Longmans)
        My Home in India
        My Home in Italy, etc.
    Very difficult text, but useful for general interest and for pictures.
53. NEW COLOUR PHOTO BOOKS (E. J. Arnold)
54. PICTURE BOOKS (E. J. Arnold)
55. PILOT READING SCHEME (E. J. Arnold)
    Especially Pre-readers 1–4
56. RACING TO READ (E. J. Arnold)
    Books 1–4
57. READING WITH RHYTHM (Longmans)
    Especially Sets 1 and 2. Most useful for story-telling by the teacher.
58. ROUND AND ABOUT BOOKS (Oliver and Boyd)
59. TOWN BOOKS (Oliver and Boyd)

VIII *Magazines (for pupils)*

60. CATCH

A monthly magazine designed for 11 to 12 year-old learners of English. Written in simple language, with brightly produced short articles on a variety of topics, mostly about contemporary Britain. Includes cartoons, games and puzzles.

61. CLUB

A magazine for teenagers, with articles on current events, sport, music, etc. Contains quizzes and crossword puzzles, and would appeal to the older immigrant pupil whose English had reached a good level.

Note. CATCH and CLUB are published monthly, from October to June, by Mary Glasgow & Baker Ltd.

IX *Dictionaries*

In the early stages of language work, there is probably no need to supply pupils with dictionaries. Young pupils learning to read and write can be encouraged to make their own "picture dictionaries", and after a while may find some of the picture dictionaries printed for use in the English primary school are both attractive and useful. A few of these are suggested below, followed by a selection of dictionaries printed for more advanced learners of English as a foreign language. In this latter type of dictionary definitions are given in simple English and there are usually plenty of illustrations. Finally, reference is given to the standard pronunciation dictionary (no. 67), a book which mature pupils often find useful if, for instance, they meet new words in print for the first time and wish to discover for themselves how they should be pronounced.

62. EARLY WORD PICTURE DICTIONARY (Noel. Philip and Tacey)

A simple dictionary with about 250 illustrated nouns and verbs each printed with a corresponding sentence. In full colour.

63. A FIRST LADYBIRD KEY WORDS PICTURE DICTIONARY (McNally. Wills and Hepworth)

A well-illustrated picture dictionary, including about 90 words in frequent use.

64. PILOT READING SCHEME DICTIONARIES 1–3 (Devenport. E. J. Arnold)
    A set of simple picture dictionaries, attractively produced and usable with or without the accompanying reading scheme.

65. STORY MAKER'S PICTURE DICTIONARY (Noel. Philip and Tacey)
    Illustrates and groups 360 words dealing with everyday scenes (e.g. at the station). Like (60) above, very attractively produced and made of strong material to resist wear and tear.

66. LONGMANS' JUNIOR ENGLISH DICTIONARY (Frisby. Longmans)
    A dictionary for elementary or post elementary students, for example those who have completed about 4 years of learning English. Contains 5,500 head words, all defined within a vocabulary of 1,500 words. 800 illustrations.

67. THE PROGRESSIVE ENGLISH DICTIONARY (Hornby and Parnwell. O.U.P.)
    A slightly more advanced dictionary again, with 8,500 head words all simply defined.

68. THE ADVANCED LEARNER'S DICTIONARY OF CURRENT ENGLISH (Hornby, Gatenby and Wakefield. O.U.P.)
    Standard work of reference for advanced overseas students, and suitable for inclusion in school or college library. Contains *c.* 20,000 entries and gives phonetic transcriptions of head words.

69. AN ENGLISH PRONOUNCING DICTIONARY (Jones. Dent)
    A dictionary which gives pronunciations, not definitions, of English words (including proper names) and which, like (66), is a standard work of reference for foreign learners.

X *Books for teachers (general bibliography)*

This section includes full bibliographical details of titles referred to in the text or in the booklists to the separate chapters. It concludes with a note on periodicals.

Textbooks, and handbooks to courses, already listed in earlier sections of this bibliography, are not repeated in the present section.

ABERCROMBIE, D., *Problems and Principles in Language Study*. Longmans, 1963

AICKMAN, D. J., *Rhymes for Speech and Action.* University of London Press, 1960

ALLEN, W. S., *Living English Speech.* Longmans, New Edition 1965

ARNEIL, ISABEL, *Equip that Infant Room.* Nelson, 1960

BARNARD, G., *Better Spoken English.* Macmillan, 1959

BELL, C. R. V., *Good Handwriting.* Longmans, 1961

BILLOWS, F. L., *The Techniques of Language Teaching.* Longmans, 1962

CASSIDY, F. G., *Jamaica Talk.* Macmillan, 1961

DANIEL, M. V., *Activity in the Primary School.* Blackwell, Oxford, 1947

FINOCCHIARO, MARY, *Teaching English as a Second Language.* Harper, New York, 1958

FRENCH, F. G., *English in Tables.* Oxford University Press, 1960

FRENCH, F. G., *Teaching English as an International Language.* Oxford University Press, 1963

GAGG, J. G., *Beginning the Three R's.* Evans, 1959

GAGG, J. G., *Common Sense in the Primary School.* Evans, 1951

GATENBY, E. V. and ECKERSLEY, C. E., *General Service English Wall Pictures.* Teacher's Handbook. Longmans, 1955

GRAY, W. S., *The Teaching of Reading and Writing.* Unesco and Evans, 1950

HALL, R. A., *Linguistics and Your Language.* Anchor Books, 1960

HALLIDAY, M. A. K., MCINTOSH, A. and STREVENS, P., *The Linguistic Sciences and Language Teaching.* Longmans, 1964

HILL, L. A., *Drills and Tests in English Sounds.* Longmans, 1962

HORNBY, A. S., *The Teaching of Structural Words and Sentence Patterns. Stages 1–3.* Oxford University Press, 1959–62

HUME, E. G., *Learning and Teaching in the Infant School.* Longmans, 1952

INGLIS, A., and GIBSON, H. E., *The Teaching of Handwriting.* Nelson

JONES, D., *The Pronunciation of English.* Dent, 1958

KELLERMANN, MARCELLE, *Two Experiments on Language Teaching in Primary Schools in Leeds.* The Nuffield Foundation, 1964

KINGDON-WARD, W., *A Book of Rhymes and Jingles.* A. & C. Black, 1954

LEE, W. R., *An English Intonation Reader.* Macmillan, 1960

LEE, W. R., *Language Teaching Games and Contests.* Oxford University Press, 1964

LEE, W. R. and COPPEN, HELEN, *Simple Audio-Visual Aids to Foreign Language Teaching*. Oxford University Press, 1964

LEE, W. R. and DODDERIDGE, M., *Time for a Song*. Longmans, 1963

LEWIS, M. M., *The Use of Diagrams in the Teaching of English*. Ginn, 1959

MCCALLIEN, C. and STREVENS, P., *English Speech*. Books 1, 2, 3. Teacher's Books 1, 2, 3. Longmans, 1960.

MCALLISTER, ANNE H., *The Primary Teacher's Guide to Speech Training*. University of London Press, 1963

METHOLD, K., *Broadcasting with Children*. University of London Press, 1959

MILLER, D.C. and HAKIM, S., *Progressive Writing Books for Learners of English*. Oxford University Press, 1963

MINISTRY OF EDUCATION, Pamphlet No. 43. *English for Immigrants*. H.M.S.O., 1963

O'CONNOR, J. D., *A Course of English Pronunciation*. B.B.C., 1955

OVERSEAS VISUAL AIDS CENTRE, *Flannelgraph as an Aid to Teaching and Training*. O.V.A.C., 1961

LE PAGE, R. B., 'Creole English Dialects in the British Caribbean' in *Orbis* VI, Louvain, 1957

PALMER, H. E., *The Principles of Language Study*. Oxford University Press, 1964

PALMER, H. E., *The Teaching of Oral English*. Longmans, 1954

PALMER, H. E. and PALMER, D., *English through Actions*. Longmans, 1959

QUIRK, R. and SMITH, A. H. (Eds.), *The Teaching of English*. Oxford University Press, 1964

RAMSHAW, H. G., *Blackboard Work*. Oxford University Press, 1957

RICHARDSON, MARION, *Writing and Writing Patterns*. Books I–V, and Teacher's Book. University of London Press, 1949

ROBERTS, P., *Patterns of English*. Harcourt, Brace and World, Inc., New York, 1956

SANSOM, C., *Acting Rhymes*. A. & C. Black

SANSOM, C., *Speech Rhymes*. Introductory Book, and Books 1 and 2. A. & C. Black

SCHONELL, F. J., *The Psychology and Teaching of Reading*. Oliver and Boyd, 1961

SMITH, D. A., *Rhymes for Rhythm*. Macmillan, 1964

STEWART, W. A., *Non-Standard Speech and the Teaching of English. Language Information Series, 2.* Center for Applied Linguistics of the Modern Language Association of America, 1964

STREVENS, P., *Aural Aids in Language Teaching.* Longmans, 1956

STREVENS, P., *Spoken Language.* Longmans, 1956

SWANN, MONA, *Trippingly on the Tongue.* Macmillan, 1955

TAYLOR, A., *Equipping the Classroom.* Nelson, 1960

TURNER, J. D., *Introduction to the Language Laboratory.* University of London Press, 1965

WARD, IDA C., *The Phonetics of English.* Heffer, Cambridge, 1958

WEST, M., *Improve Your English.* Longmans, 1948

WESTON, J., *The Tape-Recorder in the Classroom.* National Committee for Audio-Visual Aids in Education, 1963

Periodicals

ENGLISH LANGUAGE TEACHING

A journal of articles, correspondence, reviews, etc., all concerned with English as a foreign or second language. While many of the articles deal with problems that only face overseas teachers of English, there is much useful information about methods, new textbooks, audio-visual materials, etc., that would be of interest to teachers of immigrants. (It is published three times a year, October, January and May, by the Oxford University Press in association with the British Council. Subscriptions should be sent to the O.U.P. Warehouse, Press Road, Neasden, London W.10; 5*s* single issue, 12*s* 6*d* annually post free.)

O.V.A.C. BULLETIN

Published twice yearly, and containing useful articles and reviews of new publications for use overseas, and with especially valuable information about aids and apparatus for use in language teaching. (Annual subscription of 10*s* to O.V.A.C. Publications Service covers both bulletins and other publications; single issues cost 5*s* to non-subscribers. The address of the Overseas Visual Aids Centre is given on p. 229 above.)